PUBLICATIONS ON ASIA
OF THE SCHOOL OF
INTERNATIONAL STUDIES

Number 33

This book is sponsored by the South Asian Program of the School of International Studies (formerly the Institute for Comparative and Foreign Area Studies) of the University of Washington, Seattle.

Vedda Villages
of Anuradhapura

THE HISTORICAL ANTHROPOLOGY OF A
COMMUNITY IN SRI LANKA

JAMES BROW

UNIVERSITY OF WASHINGTON PRESS
SEATTLE AND LONDON

Library of Congress Cataloging in Publication Data
Brow, James.
　　Vedda villages of Anuradhapura.

　　(Publications on Asia of the School of International Studies ; no. 33)
　　Bibliography: p.
　　Includes index.
　　1. Veddahs. 2. Kinship—Sri Lanka—North-Central Province. 3. North-Central Province, Sri Lanka—Social conditions. I. Title.
II. Series: Washington (State). University. School of International Studies. Publications on Asia ; no. 33.
DS489.25.V4B76　　301.45'09549'3　　77-16663
ISBN 0-295-95585-6

Publications on Asia of the School of International Studies is a continuation of the series formerly entitled Publications on Asia of the Institute for Comparative and Foreign Area Studies.

To my father and mother
Keith and Molly Brow
with love and gratitude

Contents

Illustrations

Preface

This monograph has several aspects. First, it is an account of the social institutions of a caste group (*variga*), located in Anuradhapura District in the North Central Province of Sri Lanka, that is barely mentioned in the existing literature. As such, it is offered as a basic contribution to the descriptive ethnography of the island. Second, it is an historical study that examines the operation of a kinship system during a period of considerable upheaval and change. Particular attention is paid to the impact of a very rapid rate of population growth, and the work should be of interest to scholars, outside the narrow ranks of Sri Lanka specialists, who are concerned with exploring the relationship between population growth and social change. Third, although very little has previously been written about the people described here, they bear a famous name; for they call themselves Veddas (*Veddi minissu*), and are so called by their neighbors. Thus, while there is today no direct contact between the subjects of this study and the better known Veddas of the eastern part of the island, the present work is a further addition to the already prolific literature on the supposed descendants of Sri Lanka's aboriginal inhabitants, and it addresses some of the complex problems of Vedda history and sociology. Fourth, the study has implications for the theoretical understanding both of the Dravidian kinship systems of South India and Sri Lanka and of bilateral systems elsewhere that lack enduring kin groups. These four aspects are closely related to one another. The first two pervade the whole monograph, while the third is the particular subject matter of the first chapter. The theoretical significance of the study is discussed in the final chapter.

The study is based on two years of field research, from June 1968 to June 1970, during which time my wife and I lived and worked in Kukulewa, the largest of the Vedda villages in Anuradhapura District. By means of formal and informal interviews, direct observation, questionnaires, surveys, casual conversation, the study of official and unofficial records and other documents, and so forth, we compiled an extensive corpus of data relevant to the analysis of the village's history and social structure. The present work, however, is more than the study of a single village community. It is an attempt to comprehend the whole network of kinship and marriage within an endogamous caste group that is dispersed among forty-five other villages besides Kukulewa. Since the unique quality of anthropological findings is held to stem in large measure from what can be accomplished by prolonged and intensive study of the particular local community in which the researcher lives, it will be useful to indicate the scope of the research that was conducted in those Vedda villages in which we did not reside, but whose analysis is crucial to the work at hand.

Our formal investigations in the villages other than Kukulewa were restricted to matters of kinship and economic organization. They were conducted at various times during the second year of the project with the assistance of a number of students from the Department of Sociology at the University of Sri Lanka at Peradeniya. However, the total number of man-days spent in villages other than Kukulewa was no more than two hundred, an average of about five per village. Obviously we do not have the detailed familiarity with these villages that we have with Kukulewa, but I believe that the data that we did obtain are adequate for our purposes here.

In these other villages we used questionnaires designed to elicit genealogical and basic biographical data, and also some economic information, particularly concerning occupations and property. With very few exceptions these questions were asked of at least one member of every household in every village, and each household was visited by the interviewer. Clearly the data thus obtained are not all equally reliable. In general I am persuaded that the aggregated genealogical and demographic information is relatively firm, if incomplete in some particulars. Genealogies intersect and can be compared with one another, while the availability of census reports, which sometimes contain the number of houses and the age distribution of the population in each village as well as the total population, provide an historical base for the analysis of the contemporary situation. For the specific purposes of the present work, it is this genealogical, biographical, and demographic information that is most crucial, and despite the shortness of our stay in most of the Vedda villages I believe it to be sufficiently reliable and complete.

Property is another matter. Readers of *Pul Eliya* (Leach 1961a) will be aware of the complexity of land tenure in this part of the world, and I cannot pretend that I am able to undertake an exhaustive analysis of it in all the Vedda villages. Although we were unable to inspect official records for all the villages, or even accurately to measure the extent of paddy lands within them, the individual interviews, combined with brief physical inspection, afford a crude measure of the total extent of land in each village, its distribution, and an outline of the history of its use and tenure.

With regard to cultural norms, our informal questioning suggests that there is very general agreement among the various villages concerning inheritance, marriage, and the definition of correct behavior between specified categories of kinsmen. At least there appears to be as much agreement between Kukulewa and any other Vedda village as there is within Kukulewa itself. Thus, although its size alone debars Kukulewa from being considered entirely typical of the Anuradhapura Vedda villages, a common culture as well as similar ecological conditions impose a certain uniformity on all the villages, and justify the disproportionate use of the richer data from Kukulewa to illustrate social processes that appear to be common to all the Anuradhapura Veddas.

Research was carried out under a grant from the Foreign Currency Program of the Smithsonian Institution, Washington, D. C. Supplementary funds were provided by a Dissertation Improvement Grant from the National Science Foundation. Preparation of the manuscript in its original form as a doctoral dissertation was begun while I was being supported by a Kent Fellowship, administered by the Danforth Foundation, and was completed with assistance from the Faculty Research Fund of Swarthmore College. The manuscript was revised during a sabbatical leave from Swarthmore.

I was taught anthropology at the University of Washington, principally by Professors Edward B. Harper, Charles F. Keyes, Gananath Obeyesekere, Simon Ottenberg, and E. V. Winans, to all of whom I am deeply grateful. I have also benefited from discussions with my colleagues in the Department of Sociology and Anthropology at Swarthmore College, especially Steven Piker and Hans Mueller. The critical comments of Professor Nur Yalman, who read the manuscript in its dissertation form, have been especially stimulating in effecting revisions. I owe a further debt of thanks to Professor James Gair, of Cornell University, who introduced me to the study of the Sinhalese language.

A special acknowledgment must be made to Gananath Obeyesekere, who guided me into the anthropology of Sri Lanka and who was Professor of Sociology at the University of Ceylon, Peradeniya (now the University of Sri Lanka at Peradeniya), during the period of my research. He and his wife Ranjini were an unfailing source of encouragement, support, inspiration, and hospitality.

Many other people in Sri Lanka were extraordinarily kind and helpful. I think especially of Mr. and Mrs. D. B. Ellepola, G. P. Elangasinhe, H. A. I. Goonetileke, Sarath Amunugama, Peter Burleigh, Nilhan de Silva, and Jock and Judy Stirrat, whose period of field research overlapped my own. Thanks are also due to the management and staff of Tissawewa and Nuwarawewa Resthouses in Anuradhapura.

Tissa Wijeratne made a most valuable contribution to the work as my principal field assistant. George Gomez preceded him in that position. The students in the Department of Sociology at the University of Sri Lanka at Peradeniya who participated in the research were Percy Liyanage, Sena Bulankulame, Gunasena Hapugoda, Conrad Ranawake, T. T. Gamage, Daya Jayasekere, T. Abeyrama, L. Weerasinghe, and A. M. Samarasinghe. I thank all of them.

Margery Lang, at the Institute for Comparative and Foreign Area Studies at the University of Washington, has been a most patient editor. Annabel Bitterman, in the office of the Department of Anthropology at the University of Washington, and Pauline Feldman, secretary of the Department of Sociology and Anthropology at Swarthmore College, have been generous and helpful in innumerable ways. I am also grateful to Barbara Smith, who drew the maps and helped with the figures, and to Sarah Stapleton, for bibliographical assistance.

Above all, I here acknowledge the loving help of my wife Judy, herself an anthropologist of forceful insight, who did much of the research on which this work is based, and who sustained me in every way while I did the rest. She also took the photographs.

Finally, I thank the warm-hearted and hospitable people who are the subject of this book.

With the exception of kinship terms, Sinhalese words appear here with diacritical marks omitted. When such words occur in English as it is spoken in Sri Lanka their plural forms are often adapted to conform to common English practice, and they are so written here. Thus the plural of *kapurala* (priest) appears as *kapuralas* rather than as the Sinhalese *kapuralayo*. The names of villages are spelled as they appear on the Survey Department's maps. Caste names are capitalized, both in Sinhalese and in English translation, so that a cultivator, for example, is an agriculturalist but a Cultivator is a member of the Goyigama (Cultivator) caste.

TABLE OF SYMBOLS

△ man (living)
○ woman (living)

▲ man (deceased)
● woman (deceased)

marriage

divorce

siblingship

classificatory siblingship

Kukulewa △ man originally from Kukulewa

✕ △ man of non-Vedda origin

⟶〰⟶△ immigrant man

△⟶〰⟶Kukulewa man who has emigrated to Kukulewa

△⟶〰⟶✕ man who has emigrated outside the Vedda community

◇ man or woman

VEDDA VILLAGES OF ANURADHAPURA

The Historical Anthropology
of a Community in Sri Lanka

1

The Ethnological Context

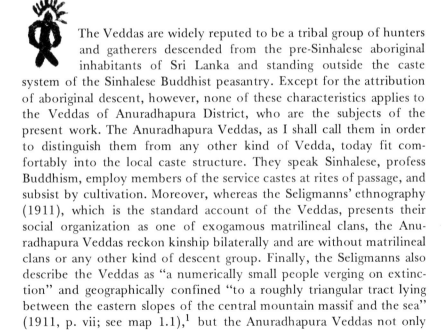The Veddas are widely reputed to be a tribal group of hunters and gatherers descended from the pre-Sinhalese aboriginal inhabitants of Sri Lanka and standing outside the caste system of the Sinhalese Buddhist peasantry. Except for the attribution of aboriginal descent, however, none of these characteristics applies to the Veddas of Anuradhapura District, who are the subjects of the present work. The Anuradhapura Veddas, as I shall call them in order to distinguish them from any other kind of Vedda, today fit comfortably into the local caste structure. They speak Sinhalese, profess Buddhism, employ members of the service castes at rites of passage, and subsist by cultivation. Moreover, whereas the Seligmanns' ethnography (1911), which is the standard account of the Veddas, presents their social organization as one of exogamous matrilineal clans, the Anuradhapura Veddas reckon kinship bilaterally and are without matrilineal clans or any other kind of descent group. Finally, the Seligmanns also describe the Veddas as "a numerically small people verging on extinction" and geographically confined "to a roughly triangular tract lying between the eastern slopes of the central mountain massif and the sea" (1911, p. vii; see map 1.1),[1] but the Anuradhapura Veddas not only

1. The Seligmanns define the Veddaratta, or Vedda country, more precisely as "an area of about 2400 square miles . . . bounded on the west by the Mahaweli Ganga, from the point where, abandoning its eastern course through the mountains of the Central Province, the river sweeps northwards to the sea. A line from this great bend passing eastwards through Bibile village (on the Badulla-Batticaloa road) to the coast will define the southern limits of the Vedda country with sufficient

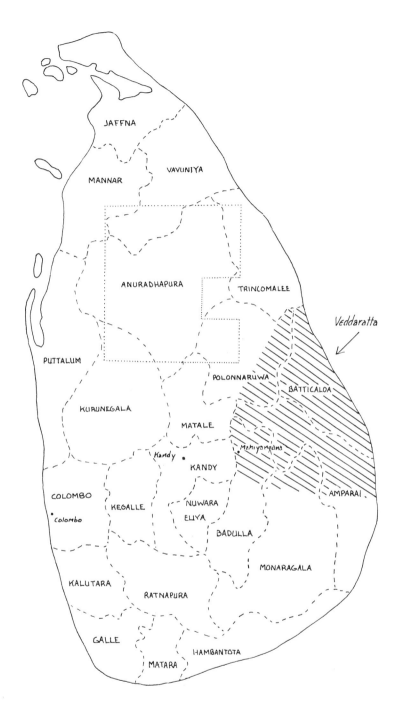

Map 1.1. Sri Lanka, showing the Vedda country (Veddaratta), the administrative districts, and, in dotted outline, the Anuradhapura Vedda area shown in detail in Map 2.1, page 41.

live outside this area but have also been experiencing a rapid rate of population growth since before the time of the Seligmanns' researches.

These discrepancies already raise more problems than can be resolved within the compass of this book, the restricted focus of which precludes any attempt to produce a comprehensive account of all the Veddas. What is possible, however, and indeed necessary, is to locate the present work with reference to the existing corpus of writings on the Veddas. A critical examination of the Seligmanns' interpretation of Vedda social organization will then lead to a discussion of the various criteria that have been employed to categorize the Veddas and will reveal, in this respect, a marked contrast between what has become conventional among anthropologists and the usage of ordinary Sinhalese villagers. Comparison of these contrasting usages will in turn not only clarify what relationship exists between the Anuradhapura Veddas and their more famous namesakes who inhabit the Veddaratta, or Vedda country, in the eastern jungles, but will also provide an ethnological context for the subsequent analysis of Anuradhapura Vedda social organization.

EARLY EUROPEAN ACCOUNTS OF THE VEDDAS

The Veddas are one of the most famous and one of the least known peoples in the literature of anthropology. As a "savage race" of "primitive" hunters and gatherers living close to the civilized Sinhalese but remaining distinct from them, they have excited the interest of the ethnologically curious through two millenia.[2] But the Veddas have always loomed larger in myth than in history. Many of the authors who have written about them never actually encountered them, and more or less fabulous representations of them have often been used to buttress an ideology, a world view, or a theory of social evolution. Accounts of the *yakkhas,* or demons, in the *Mahavamsa* and in other ancient texts have commonly been taken to describe the ancestors of the Veddas, and the myth of their royal and demonic descent given in the *Mahavamsa* still serves to validate their position in the caste hierarchy. Early travelers in South Asia who described the native demons of Sri Lanka have also been interpreted as referring to the Veddas, while among more recent writers the few valuable reports are swamped by numerous and often secondhand statements of superstition and prejudice, the

accuracy, while its eastern limit is the coast" (1911, p. vii). This area contains the whole of the present Batticaloa District, and parts of Polonnaruwa, Amparai, Badulla, and Monaragola districts (map 1.1).

2. See Goonetileke (1960; 1970, pp. 379-87) for an invaluable and comprehensive bibliography of the Veddas.

uncritical acceptance of which has facilitated their employment in
laying the "factual" foundations of more or less preposterous theories
of social evolution (e.g., Spencer 1897-1906, passim).

Any new account or reassessment of Vedda social organization
must centrally engage itself with the Seligmanns' classic ethnography.
As Leach has observed, "there is no source which in any way compares
in authority, scope or detail" with their book (1963, p. 68). It is
immensely superior to anything that preceded it, and it has continued
to dominate everything written since. There has in fact been very little
original research into Vedda society since 1911. Some physical anthropology has been done, but on the sociological side recent accounts (e.g.,
Spittel 1951; 1957; Wijesekera 1964) have been theoretically unsophisticated and largely anecdotal. In particular, the Seligmanns' presentation of the Veddas as being organized in exogamous matrilineal clans
does not appear to have been critically scrutinized by those who have
had subsequent firsthand experience of the Veddas. But the Seligmanns' version of Vedda social organization has not gone unchallenged.
In 1963 Edmund Leach, basing his argument "almost entirely upon
the Seligmanns' own published record" (1963, p. 68), produced a
devastating critique that has, at the very least, made the acceptance of
Vedda matrilineality problematic.

In the history of social anthropology, the Seligmanns' work occu-
pies a transitional position. Based on one of the earliest pieces of field
work to be conducted by professional anthropologists, it can be presented as a pioneering contribution to the development of modern
theory and methods, but it can also be seen to be imbued with concerns
that were more characteristic of the nineteenth than of the twentieth
century. As representatives of the newly professional discipline of
anthropology, the Seligmanns certainly introduced unprecedented
standards into Vedda ethnography, but their interpretation was still
conditioned by certain theoretical presuppositions and a general intellectual orientation that they shared with a number of their predecessors. An assessment of their representation of Vedda social organization is therefore facilitated by examining their monograph as the
culminating work in a tradition of writings about the Veddas that was
gradually developed throughout the colonial period of Sri Lanka's
history.

The Portuguese were the first colonial power in Sri Lanka, but
Portuguese accounts of the Veddas are rare. Pedro Teixeira saw people
who may have been Veddas (Teixeira 1902), but other Portuguese
accounts date only from the time when the Dutch had replaced them as
the colonial power in Sri Lanka. The earliest useful report is that of
Rycloff Van Goens, commissary and later governor of the Dutch

colony in Sri Lanka from 1658 to 1675, whose memoirs to his successors (Van Goens 1932) contain detailed and precise recommendations for the political and economic improvement of the colony. Van Goens's interests were pragmatic, and when he wrote of the Veddas it was not, as later writers were to do, in order to speculate about their ancestry or to moralize about their spiritual and material condition, but rather to emphasize their potential usefulness to the Dutch as a labor force of unusual flexibility. Their unique position in the caste system renders them "not subject to the whims and prejudices" of other groups. They are admittedly "fairly savage," but they are "brave fellows in the hunt and expert bowmen besides" (1932, p. 44). And he goes on to recommend that their services and allegiance be secured and their labor employed.

Van Goens's account was written a few years before that of Robert Knox (1911; originally 1681), who is justly the most famous of all early European writers on Sri Lanka, being a reliable and perceptive ethnographer of many aspects, besides the condition of the Veddas, of traditional Sinhalese society. Knox was captured on the coast of Sri Lanka and spent eighteen years as the prisoner of the king of Kandy before he escaped and returned to England, where he wrote his comprehensive *Historical Relation of the Island of Ceylon*, based largely on his own experiences. During his captivity, Knox was able to visit several parts of the island and to investigate and participate in many aspects of Kandyan culture. He was a scrupulous and thorough reporter, observant and skeptical, whose account of the Veddas introduced a number of the themes that were to occupy the attention of later writers. Indeed he also provided them with much of their material. In measured tones he describes such Vedda customs as their technique of preserving meat by storing it in a hollow tree stopped up with honey and clay, their practice of giving hunting dogs as marriage portions, their distinctive arrowheads, their scant clothing and peculiar hair style, and their practice of "silent trade" with the neighboring Sinhalese. His dry, matter-of-fact reporting is convincing; he was obviously a man not easily fooled. For example, he faithfully recounts the story he was usually told, that the Veddas catch elephants by driving an axe into the soles of their feet while they are asleep, but his reason rebels at it. Elephants are too wakeful to allow the necessary approach, and the soles of their feet are too hard.

From Knox we also learn that there are two kinds of Veddas, a "tamer sort [who] are in some kind of subjection to the king," and "who occasionally performed military service on his behalf," and a "wilder sort" who "never shew themselves" (ibid., pp. 61-62).

Another facet of Knox's sober reporting is his reluctance to attempt any profound explanations of the customs he records. For this reason his account remains descriptive, a miscellaneous collection of exotic practices. It is notable that he makes no reference to the origins of the Veddas, nor to their physical appearance beneath their long hair and loin cloths. These were interests that came to occupy a central place in writings on the Veddas only in the nineteenth century. In Knox's time the exotic varieties of nature, such as the savages of Sri Lanka, were still largely mysterious curiosities. Only later did they become elements to be fitted into a dynamic theory of social development, a scheme to which the key was increasingly felt to reside in history.

The origins of the Veddas were nevertheless touched upon in another seventeenth-century account, that of Father Queyroz (1930), whose *Temporal and Spiritual Conquest of Ceylon* was published in Lisbon in 1686. The treatment, however, is cursory. Queyroz reports that the Veddas are descendants of the common people of Anuradhapura, the ancient capital of the Sinhalese, who were unable to follow the court when the city was abandoned in the face of foreign invasion. The people of Anuradhapura, we are told, "betook themselves to the forests in those mountains; and being deprived for a long time of the urbanity of the Court and communication with men, in those mountain ranges, they became altogether wild barbarians, and they are the Bedas, which means brutes." Queyroz does not tell us the source of this curious story, but goes on to announce the Veddas' lack of law, religion, home, and clothing. He also describes the practices of "silent trade" and meat preservation, mentioned by Knox, and tells us further that "the natives understand only a few rough and badly uttered words" (ibid., pp. 16-17).

Knox had simply reported that the Vedda speak Sinhalese (1911, p. 122). Queyroz's denigration of the Veddas' ability to speak marks the initial appearance of an idea that was to fascinate many nineteenth-century writers, particularly the less responsible ones who relied on secondhand information. Nineteenth-century accounts abound with references to the "broken" dialect spoken by the Veddas and its poor vocabulary; some even doubted that the Veddas could speak at all (see Percival 1805, p. 283; Selkirk 1844, p. 80; Pridham 1849, pp. 451-52; Tennent 1859, 2: 440; Bailey 1863, pp. 297-98; Hartshorne 1876, p. 417; Deschamps 1892, pp. 376-77).

Perhaps the most valuable parts of Queyroz's short account are his references to the Veddas' social relations, both internal and external. He tells us that ". . . there gather together for . . . hunts a hundred and more men every three months in four different places to kill and feast. . ." (1930, p. 17). No later writer reports Vedda gatherings on such a scale. Queyroz also tells us something of the relations obtaining between the Veddas and the Kandyan king. The latter apparently had great confidence in the Veddas and at times of crisis in his wars with the Portuguese committed both his treasure and his wives to their safekeeping (ibid., p. 17). Although Queyroz's account does not merit the same degree of confidence as Knox's, this report is particularly intriguing because little is known of the relations between the Sinhalese kingdom and the Veddas, while the topic is one of some moment to the physical as well as the cultural anthropologist. It is, moreover, a topic that writers from the nineteenth century onwards were unable to investigate directly.

In general, seventeenth-century writers on the Veddas were neither systematic nor analytical in their reporting. For the most part they were not tempted to indulge in hypothetical speculations, but were content simply to record what they saw and what they were told. Their accounts are essentially unelaborated lists of the stranger customs of the savages. They are mainly taken up with the visible facts of technology and economics, and this presumably reflects not only their practical interests but also that this was the kind of information that was most readily available to men who scarcely made direct contact with the people they described. Probably for the same reason there is little mention of the physical features of the Veddas from this period. An interest in cultural history is also no more than embryonic. In the nineteenth century, while the customary practices of Vedda technology continued to excite the imagination, there was a broadening of interest to include these previously neglected topics, as at least the more ambitious authors attempted to ease the facts of Vedda culture into some bolder framework of historical or evolutionary development.

The eighteenth-century literature on the Veddas appears to be extremely thin, but in the following century, and especially after British rule was established, the number of accounts steadily increased. These writings are the work of many hands. Administrators, soldiers, adventurers, missionaries, doctors, sportsmen, and, toward the end of the century, professional scientists, are all represented. Their writings appear in periodicals as various as the *Gentlemen's Magazine* and the *Transactions of the Ethnological Society*, or in books whose concern may be *An Account of the Island of Ceylon* (Percival 1805), but may just as well be *The Rifle and the Hound in Ceylon* (Baker 1898). Within this diverse literature one can discern a pattern of uncertain steps whereby questions of nature and of culture, of race and language, gradually came to be distinguished. And in this process, because the orientation of nineteenth-century writers was increasingly historical, issues became those of the origin of the Veddas and of the physical and cultural similarities and differences that have existed both among the Veddas themselves and between the Veddas and the Sinhalese.

As Kennedy has observed, "by the close of the 18th century it was an accepted fact among European geographers and historians that Ceylon possessed a population of 'wild men' who were physically and culturally distinct from their more civilized neighbors and who were identified by the term 'Vedda'" (1974, p. 97). Nineteenth-century authors faced the problem of accounting for these differences. Did the Veddas and the Sinhalese share a common ancestry, and, if so, at what time in history? For several reasons investigators were mostly inclined to answer this question in the negative. In the first place during most of the century it was by no means generally accepted that different races of man shared a common ancestry even in the most remote antiquity. On the contrary, it was still quite widely believed that the several races had been the subjects of different acts of creation. Moreover, there was little or no idea of racial change through time. "Mixed marriages" might produce hybrids and racial "impurity," but the sophisticated concepts of population genetics were still well in the future. Besides, it was generally held throughout the century that most Veddas had no contact with the Sinhalese. Even the more settled Veddas, although "they have long associated . . . have not yet intermarried with the neighbouring Sinhalese" (Bailey 1863, p. 282).

Most writers, then, found little to persuade them that the Veddas and the Sinhalese shared a common origin. On the other hand the two peoples did speak the same language, and for those who recognized this fact it represented a tempting basis for asserting a genetic connection. Those who succumbed to the temptation seem also to have entertained romantic notions of the free and noble savage. Percival cautiously suggests the possibility that ". . . the Bedans are merely a part of the native Candians, who chose to retain their ancient savage freedom, when their brethren of the plains and vallies submitted to the cultivation of earth and the restraints of society" (1805, pp. 282-83). Forty years later Selkirk was still asserting a similar argument that

some of them [i.e., the Veddas] speak a broken dialect of the Sinhalese, which would lead to the supposition either of their having been banished into the jungles, and compelled to live separate from the rest of the inhabitants, or that when the rest of the people were cultivating fields and sowing and planting for their support, and subject to the control of government, they still, to retain their liberty chose rather to retire into the fastnesses of the country. . . . [1844, pp. 80-81]

By the middle of the century this was distinctly a minority, and, one might say, an ill-informed opinion. Selkirk appears not to have encountered the *Mahavamsa*, the early Sinhalese chronicle, whose authority supplied the decisive argument for assigning different origins to the Sinhalese and the Veddas. But even before Tournour's translation appeared in 1837 the opinion was being advanced that the Veddas were descended from the pre-Sinhalese aboriginals of Sri Lanka. Percival (1805, p. 282) allows this possibility and Fellowes (1817, pp. 245-46) apparently accepts it. After the *Mahavamsa* was made available, the Veddas were quickly identified as the descendants of the *yakkhas,* the aboriginal demons whom Prince Vijaya, the legendary founder of the Sinhalese nation, encountered when he arrived on the island. Most of Forbes's chapter on the Veddas (1841, pp. 75-84) is devoted to the tale of Prince Vijaya and the *yakkhas,* and both Bennett (1843, p. 252) and Pridham (1849, pp. 451-52) also favor the identification of the *yakkhas* and the Veddas. Even Lieutenant De Butts, for whom the Veddas' "early history is buried in obscurity, and recorded only in absurd and Oriental tales," feels that "there can be, however, no doubt as to their being the descendants of the aborigines of the island" (1841, p. 145). A few years later this opinion received the full support of Sir James Emerson Tennent's erudition, the ancestral identity of the Veddas and *yakkhas* being asserted with copious references to Pliny, Hiouen Thsang, Albyrouni, and the author of *De Moribus Brachmanorum* (1859, 1: 331, 372, 539-40, 569; 2: 438). Evidently this battery of authorities was irresistible, for by 1863 Bailey was able to write: "*It has always been assumed*, that the Veddahs of Ceylon are the descendants of the race which originally peopled the island, or at any rate, of that which inhabited it prior to its conquest by Vijaya and his followers" (1863, p. 306; emphasis added).

It is important to note, however, that agreement on this issue was only achieved by the influence of textual authority. There was no possibility of consensus emerging from arguments based on the distribution of cultural traits. The language question in particular had only confused the issue. Nor were the techniques of physical anthropology available at mid-century able to illuminate the problem. In the previous century Valentyn (1726, p. 49) had noted the small stature of the Veddas, but their biological study only effectively began with the work of John Davy (1821), "a physician who formulated a scientific description of these people on the basis of autopsy examinations" (Kennedy 1972, p. 30).[3] Moreover, while most writers of the early nineteenth

3. Kennedy's paper should be consulted for an authoritative and critical review of the history of physical anthropological studies of the Veddas.

century acknowledged that the Veddas were of no more than moderate height, they could not agree even on such an eminently visible characteristic as their skin color. Joinville describes them as ". . . black, like all the Sinhalese" (1803, p. 435), but writing only two years later, Percival asserts that ". . . they seemed to be a race entirely different from the other Ceylonese: their complexions were fairer, and inclining to a copper colour" (1805, p. 283). This disagreement persisted. To Bennett (1843, p. 253) they were reported to resemble the Sinhalese, while Selkirk's informant told him they were ". . . fairer than the other inhabitants of the island" (1844, p. 81). Differing from both, Bailey describes them as ". . . rather darker, or more properly, more dusky in complexion" (1863, p. 282). In this situation the contribution physical anthropology might make towards clarifying the biological relationship between Veddas and Sinhalese had to wait upon the development of more precise observations and more refined techniques of analysis.

A few of the more ambitious authors were not satisfied merely to separate the Veddas from the Sinhalese, but sought also to relate the former to other and more distant peoples. According to Bailey it was Tennent who first argued "that the aborigines of Ceylon were probably a branch of the same stock which colonized the Dekkan" (Bailey 1863, p. 307). Bailey himself was of the same opinion, asserting that ". . . the results of my own careful and personal inquiries into the customs and superstitions of the Veddahs . . . establish . . . their identity with those of many of the hill tribes of India, and fully justify the assumption of the common origin of the people" (ibid.). Here the claim of racial affinity rests solely on the alleged discovery of common cultural traits. But it came to be supported by the physical anthropologists who considered the question toward the end of the century (Virchow 1888; Sarasin and Sarasin 1892-93; see also Parker 1909; Seligmann and Seligmann 1911).

Most investigators, however, were content to restrict their inquiries to the relationship between the Veddas and the Sinhalese, and although by the middle of the nineteenth century it was generally agreed that the two peoples were two distinct races, each endowed with its own way of life, important problems remained. In particular, it was necessary to explain the persistence of Vedda primitiveness, since it was now recognized that the Veddas had lived in proximity to their civilized neighbors for at least a thousand years. It was known that the Veddas spoke the Sinhalese language, and there was considerable evidence of their former participation in the Kandyan kingdom, most notably as soldiers, so why had they failed to become civilized? Why were they without law or religion or even matrimony, as many asserted? Why did they speak only "broken" Sinhalese, limited to a few words? Not all writers faced these questions directly, and those who did produced various answers.

For some there was no problem. The Veddas were simply savages and that was that. What else could be expected of people whose "intellectual capacity . . . is as low as it can possibly be in any persons endowed with reason . . . [who] are wholly unable to count or to comprehend the significance of number . . . [and who are unable] . . . to form any but the most simple mental synthesis . . ." (Hartshorne 1876, p. 413). But most writers did better than this. Some, as we have seen, dwelt on the Veddas' distaste for the constrictions of civilization, pointing out ". . . the fascination of that high degree of freedom which belongs to the savage state" (De Butts 1841, p. 152). More commonly, among the responsible authors, it was argued that despite their proximity the Veddas enjoyed little real contact with the Sinhalese. It is often unclear here whether this was felt to be only a recent development, for the same authors often refer to the quite intimate interaction that existed between the Veddas and the Sinhalese during the Kandyan period. But certainly in describing the current situation their tendency was to emphasize that the "wilder" Veddas at least have virtually no contact with the Sinhalese.

Here they made use of the distinction introduced by Knox when he divided the Veddas into a wilder and tamer sort. Nineteenth-century writers commonly asserted that while there was some modest communication between the tame (village) Veddas and the Sinhalese, there was none at all between the latter and the wild (forest, rock, or jungle) Veddas. Thus Percival, writing at a time before the British obtained control of the whole island, when the Veddas appear to have been more widely distributed than they afterwards became, says that the Veddas in the "province of Bintan" in the east of the island "are completely savage . . . and have never entered into any intercourse with the other natives, or scarcely ever been seen by them" (Percival 1805, p. 284). On the other hand, "those bordering on the district of Jafnapatam, and the tribes who inhabit the west and southwest quarters of the island, between Adam's Peak and the Raygam and Pasdan cories, are the only Bedahs who have been seen by Europeans, and are much less wild and ferocious than those who live in the forests of Bintan" (ibid.).

Forbes tells us that the village Veddas "communicate, although they do not mix, with the other natives of the island" (1841, p. 76) and that the forest Veddas make contact with the Sinhalese only through the intervention of their "brethren of the villages" (ibid.). Selkirk (1844, p. 81), Pridham (1849, p. 454), Bailey (1863, p. 282), a Tamil

(1865, p. 70), Deschamps (1892, p. 392), Baker (1898, p. 11), and Furness and Hiller (1901) also allow only very minimal communication between at least a section of the Veddas and the Sinhalese. Some writers do not even allow the village Veddas their role as intermediaries between the wild Veddas and the Sinhalese. Pridham, who follows Bennett (1843, p. 256) accurately but without acknowledgment, informs us that the ". . . domesticated Veddahs hold their wilder brethren in great fear and abhorrence, and seldom meet without coming to blows" (Pridham 1849, p. 454). De Butts (1841, p. 149) and Tennent (1859, 2: 443) also deny any friendly interaction between the two classes.

TABLE 1.1

CLASSES OF VEDDAS

"Wild" Veddas	"Tame" or "domesticated" Veddas
Rock, jungle, or forest Veddas	Village Veddas
Food collectors	Food producers

There can be no doubt that Vedda groups displayed significant differences in their ways of life and in the degree of their association with Sinhalese civilization. The distinction between hunting and cultivation is obvious and important, and almost every writer after Knox made it. But the association of hunting with wildness, and hence with isolation, is too neat. After all some wild Veddas undertook a little cultivation, and even at the end of the century some village Veddas were still subsisting by food collection (Furness and Hiller 1901). What is beyond dispute is that the division of the Veddas into two strictly separated categories,[4] although certainly a reflection of real cultural variation, enabled the European writers to accommodate the fact of interaction between the Veddas and the Sinhalese with the thesis that at least some of the Veddas were totally isolated. But a suspicion that this division may have been forced is aroused by Forbes's observation that the Vedda headmen (Kandyans of the neighboring districts who could have exerted no more than nominal authority if the

4. Some writers, including the Seligmanns, also make use of a third category, that of the "coast Veddas." These are Tamil-speaking Veddas who live on the east coast of Sri Lanka near Batticaloa, where they subsist more from fishing than from hunting. For the sake of convenience I shall concentrate here on those Veddas whose association has been with the Sinhalese rather than the Tamils, but will deal briefly with the Tamil-speaking Veddas subsequently.

other accounts are to be believed), "in talking to Europeans generally exaggerated the wild nature of the Veddas" (1841, p. 76).

It is also notable in this connection that the Seligmanns' informants were unwilling or unable to maintain the distinction between the two classes of Veddas on which the Europeans insisted (Seligmann and Seligmann 1911, p. 32). A further indication of the latter's tendency to exaggerate the isolation of the wild Veddas is provided by the continued propagation by at least some of them of the story that the wild Veddas engaged only in "silent trade," avoiding direct contact with the Sinhalese. This was still being presented as current practice by Selkirk (1844, p. 81) and Tennent (1859, 2: 440), although Bailey who, unlike some of the other writers, did have considerable firsthand experience of the people he was describing, reports that ". . . they are not now, nor have they been for very long, so shy as to be prevented from bartering freely enough with the Sinhalese" (Bailey 1863, pp. 285-86).

It is hard to resist the inference that many Europeans were disposed to overemphasize the isolation of at least some of the Veddas from the influence of the Sinhalese. This could be achieved by enforcing a rigid division between the two classes of Veddas, and by permitting access to the Sinhalese to only one class. The wild Veddas could then be presented not simply as the descendants of the aboriginal inhabitants of the island but as their living representatives, as the unalloyed representatives of a pure and primitive race, and as the bearers of an equally pure and primitive way of life. I am not suggesting that these nineteenth-century authors intentionally misrepresented the facts, but it is clear that the search for racial and cultural purity became an increasingly dominant theme in their inquiries, and that their ability to discover it was greatly enhanced by the division of the Veddas into two kinds. Even the Seligmanns, whose ethnography ushers in the period of modern anthropology as applied to the Veddas, were still under the spell of these concerns. The first sentence of their monograph reads: "The Veddas have been regarded as one of the most primitive of existing races" (1911, p. vii), and their whole account is permeated with the desire to separate the customs of the "pure-blooded" Veddas from those of "half-breed" combinations of Sinhalese and Vedda strain. They feel that just as the pure Veddas can be distinguished from the half-breeds, so the "authentic," "original," and "ancestral" customs of the Veddas can be discovered, customs that are quite distinct from those of the Sinhalese and of those village Veddas who have mixed with the Sinhalese (see Leach 1963, p. 69, for a criticism of these assumptions).

As a result of all this the poor village Veddas came to be somewhat disparaged. De Butts finds them "less interesting" (1841, p. 146). Bailey asserts that they "have not maintained so complete an isolation from other races as those I am about to describe, and consequently are not worthy of the same attention" (1863, p. 281). Hartshorne (1876, p. 406) likewise directs the ethnologist's exclusive attention to the wild Veddas. And while the Seligmanns allow some respectability to those village Veddas who have retained a degree of isolation and the more important of their traditional customs, those who have mixed with the Sinhalese are described as "degenerate" (1911, p. 48).

This partiality, and the associated failure thoroughly to disentangle questions of race from those of culture continued to hamper analysis and to bias interpretation. Thus Virchow, one of the leading physical anthropologists of his day, concludes his analysis of the Veddas by allowing

at best the possibility of placing the Veddahs on a level with the Andamanese and the Australians, whilst, according to present facts, they must be placed decidedly lower. A people who do not even possess clay vessels, who have no knowledge of domestic animals beyond the dog, who are unacquainted with the simplest forms of gardening and agriculture, who lack almost every kind of social institution, who are not even counted among the outcasts by their civilized neighbours, cannot possibly ever have had the means which make a higher culture of any kind possible. [1888, p. 108]

Likewise the Seligmanns' relentless pursuit of a pure Vedda culture among pure-blooded Veddas leads them into a great deal of trouble. Their difficulties are suggested on the very first page of their monograph: ". . . with all my efforts I was able to meet only four families, and hear of two more, who I believe had never practised cultivation. *Pure-blooded Veddas are not quite so rare as the statement implies.* The Danigala community, the best known 'wild' Veddas of Ceylon, are still reasonably pure-blooded, though they have adopted many Sinhalese habits, including cultivation . . ." (1911, p. vii; emphasis added).

Beyond the simply descriptive parts of their monograph, the Seligmanns were concerned to establish two related hypotheses, neither of which, as will be seen, was original to them. They sought to show, firstly, that the pure Veddas of the present day "represent the aboriginal [i.e., the pre-Sinhalese] inhabitants of Ceylon" (ibid., p. 415); and, secondly, that the Veddas share a common origin with the hunting tribes of South India (ibid., p. 422). In this endeavor their procedures, like their objectives, were strictly within the traditions established by their predecessors. What was novel and distinctive, besides the unprecedented thoroughness of their field research, was the priority they gave to questions of social organization and, specifically, to the importance they attached to their account of Vedda matrilineality. These were matters of quite recent interest.

During most of the nineteenth century the emphasis in ethnographic reporting was on technology, subsistence, and the more startling aspects of Vedda culture and biology. Much effort was expended, for example, in debating such esoteric questions as whether or not the Veddas could laugh (Hartshorne 1876, p. 409; Deschamps 1892, p. 379; Walker 1898, p. 13). It was only in the second half of the century that a concern with matters of social organization and religion emerged. Pridham, for example, had found it sufficient to observe that the Veddas "exhibit no traces of remotest civilization nor any knowledge of social rites" (1849, p. 454). They are, moreover, "without any regular religion" (ibid.). The long struggle to supplant such disdainful ignorance was undertaken by the more thorough and responsible investigators in the later nineteenth century (Tennent 1859; Bailey 1863; Nevill 1886-87; Parker 1909), and reached a climax with the Seligmanns.

The matrilineal interpretation of Vedda social organization was an historical but not explicitly an evolutionary hypothesis in the sense of earlier theories of unilinear social evolution. The Seligmanns make no reference to McLennan or Morgan or any other of their anthropological predecessors who had argued that matrilineal organization represented an early stage in a universal process of social evolution. Its more restricted significance was twofold. First, it served to distinguish Vedda customs from those of the Sinhalese: "There is as far as we can ascertain no evidence of there having been an organization into exogamous [matrilineal] clans among the Sinhalese, but there is not the least doubt that this exists among the Veddas . . ." (1911, p. 416). Vedda matrilineality thus provided empirical evidence for the thesis that Vedda customs could be discovered that had not been contaminated by contact with the Sinhalese; these customs could then be taken to represent the pristine social organization of the aboriginal inhabitants of Sri Lanka. Second, while it is unknown among the Sinhalese, "an organization into exogamous clans . . . is a characteristic of many of the more primitive Jungle (Dravidian) peoples of India" (ibid.). Slipping as comfortably as Bailey had from the discovery of cultural commonalities to the assertion of racial identity, the Seligmanns could then conclude that the Veddas are "part of the same race as the so-called Dravidian jungle tribes of Southern India" (ibid., p. 422). Sociology had thus arrived, but as a crutch for conjectural history.

The case for a pure Vedda culture, however, was only made at tremendous cost, and by means of assumptions and procedures that cannot be accepted today. The Seligmanns set out to describe the last remnants of an authentic Vedda culture that was radically different from that of the Sinhalese. On the one hand were the pagan Veddas, hunters and gatherers organized into matrilineal clans. On the other were the Buddhist Sinhalese, peasant cultivators organized in endogamous castes. The difficulties involved in establishing this fundamental opposition were immense, but they were often quite casually dismissed by the Seligmanns. Thus, the speaking of Sinhalese by the Veddas would seem to present a serious problem, but the Seligmanns simply assert that "it is generally admitted that a people may adopt a foreign language while retaining its old customs and without greatly altering its old method of life" (ibid., p. 417).

Again, they admit that many Vedda religious practices are similar to those to be found among the Sinhalese, but since similar practices are also to be found among the Dravidian jungle people of India, it follows for them that it is the Sinhalese who have adopted these practices from the Veddas, and not vice versa. Even more serious, perhaps, was that many people who called themselves Veddas were almost entirely ignorant of what the Seligmanns determined to be the authentic, traditional Vedda culture. Their approach to this problem was to adopt a variant of the distinction already made by Knox when he divided the Veddas into a wilder and a tamer sort. In the nineteenth century, as I have shown, it had become conventional to differentiate the village Veddas, who undertook some cultivation, from the wild Veddas, who were exclusively food collectors.

The Seligmanns, again confounding race and culture, chose to add their distinction between the pure and the degenerate Veddas. But the exclusive concern with the pure Veddas that their ethnological interests and historical hypotheses dictated persuaded them that there were only "three Vedda communities which still retain enough of the old Vedda mode of life to make a study of their organization valuable" (ibid., p. 59). Thus, their lengthy account of Vedda culture is a representation of a way of life to which only a small minority of Veddas actually subscribed. The majority was simply dismissed by the arbitrary branding of its culture as "degenerate."

CASTE AND CLAN

A suspicion that the Seligmanns may have been predisposed to discover matrilineal clans among the Veddas does not, of course, prove that none of the Veddas were so organized, any more than the subsequent discovery of matrilineal organization among some of the Sinhalese disproves any connection between the Veddas and the jungle tribes of South India. The interpretation of Vedda social institutions must ultimately rest upon more direct evidence, and as regards the classic wild Veddas of the Veddarata this means an almost exclusive dependence on the Seligmanns' report.

Further field research would certainly encounter fascinating problems but would be unlikely, in my opinion, definitively to resolve all the questions concerning the former social organization of the wild Veddas, whose lives have been severely disrupted by events of the last sixty years. Many of their communities have been relocated, often under government auspices in connection with the attempt to develop the agricultural potential of the region, and there have been a number of other efforts made, both officially and unofficially, to mitigate and ameliorate their conditions of life. During the same period the professional primitivism of which the Seligmanns had already complained (1911, p. vii) has grown to meet the demands and exploit the credibility of increasing numbers of Sinhalese as well as foreign tourists. The descriptions of their kinship organization that were offered me by self-styled Vedda chiefs during my own brief excursion into the Veddarata suggested less a personal experience of ongoing social institutions than an indirect acquaintance and distorted understanding of the works of Spittel and the Seligmanns.

Unfortunately anthropologists, as well as Vedda chiefs, are likely to find the Seligmanns' account largely intractable. Like many subsequent ethnographers the Seligmanns give us their interpretation of Vedda society while providing very few of the observations on which that interpretation is based. Thus they indicate that they were often confused by Vedda statements about their kinship organization, but only once or twice do they report what their informants actually said. Moreover, the data they do report are often difficult to interpret. They provide genealogical diagrams of three of the communities they studied (ibid., pp. 60-61), but their textual discussion is too sketchy to enable the reader to make the diagrams fully intelligible. They note that the same names are often shared by several Veddas, but there is no way of telling, for example, whether the man named Badena who is represented as the son of Poromala Walaha is the same man as the Badena who is shown elsewhere as the husband of Kandi. Typographical errors aggravate the problem. Thus Kaira appears to have enjoyed a successful marriage with his brother Randu Wanniya that produced two children! Equally important is that while the Seligmanns investigated a number of Vedda communities, they did not remain in any one of them long enough to observe the significant social groups in action. Their account contains firsthand descriptions of a number of Vedda ceremonies, but for social organization they had to depend entirely on informants.

Given these difficulties and deficiencies, it is not possible to provide a definitive solution to all the problems of Vedda social organization. What is possible, however, is to offer an interpretation of the available data that is more plausible and consistent than those that have previously been put forward. This demands a direct confrontation not only with the Seligmanns' account but equally with Leach's radical reinterpretation.

The Seligmanns describe the Veddas as being organized into exogamous matrilineal clans. Leach's critical review (1963) compares the data reported by the Seligmanns with that contained in recent studies of neighboring Sinhalese peasants (Tambiah 1958; Leach 1960; 1961a; Yalman 1960; 1962), and argues that "the kinship organization of the Veddas, as exhibited by the Seligmanns, is almost identical to that of the Kandyan Sinhalese as recently described by Tambiah, Yalman and myself" (Leach 1963, p. 68). He points out that the social groups the Seligmanns interpreted as "exogamous clans" were described by the Veddas as *waruges*, which is the Sinhalese term *variga*. Among the Sinhalese this term denotes a social group of bilateral type that may be described as an endogamous kindred or "subcaste." Leach proceeds to reinterpret the Seligmanns' material with this in mind and concludes that "their account is quite consistent with the hypothesis that the organization of the Veddas into distinct *waruge* corresponds to an awareness of caste distinctions. The behaviour of the Veddas with respect to their *waruge* is seen to be strictly analogous to the behaviour of Kandyan Sinhalese with respect to their *variga*" (ibid., p. 77).

This radical reinterpretation is possible because both the Seligmanns and Leach acknowledge that there are considerable variations in Vedda social practice. Their disagreement is over the principles, or ideal rules, of Vedda kinship rather than who actually married whom, or what his *waruge* affiliation was. The Seligmanns and Leach offer contrasting explanations of the practical variations, but they agree that the *waruge* is to be defined in terms of marriage and descent rules. The Seligmanns argue that the Vedda *waruge* was originally an exogamous matrilineal clan, but that some Veddas, through contact with the Sinhalese, have become degenerate and have ceased to practice many of their customs, including that of clan exogamy. Leach argues that the Veddas are aware of caste distinctions and that the *waruge* is ideally an endogamous unit, but that demographic factors often prevent caste principles from being translated into action. His argument is ingenious, but it does not resolve all the problems presented by the Seligmanns' materials, and it is not the only possible alternative interpretation.

Leach reports that among the Kandyan Sinhalese of the North Central Province the word *variga* means "variety" or "kind" and is used to "denote categories of human being of all kinds. Thus the Tamils—a linguistic category—form a *variga*, but so do the Moslems (*marakkal*)—a religious category. The castes of Washermen and Drummers, which are social categories, are *variga*, but so are the Väddā, and that is a cultural-racial category" (1961a, p. 23). He goes on to describe the basic sociological features of the Kandyan Sinhalese *variga*: "No matter what the type of *variga* may be, the ordinary expectation is that in any one village the regular inhabitants will be members of one *variga* only" (ibid.). And a few lines later he writes: "In the Sinhalese conception the essential characteristic of a *variga* is its endogamy. Members of one *variga* should intermarry with one another, but are strictly forbidden from marrying with the members of any other *variga*" (ibid.).

Now whether or not the Vedda *waruge* is to be classified as a sub-caste, it is quite evident from the Seligmanns' account that what are for the Sinhalese "ordinary expectations" and "essential characteristics" are extremely rare occurrences among the Veddas. The Seligmanns visited more than a dozen communities and also reported at second-hand on several others, but all except three of these certainly contained members of more than one *waruge*. Moreover only one of these three villages can confidently be shown to have been inhabited by members of no more than a single *waruge*.

Dambani was the only one of the three that the Seligmanns visited personally. They describe it as a thriving settlement of village Veddas, but they were able to obtain only very meager information from its inhabitants. The latter were the notorious "show Veddas" who had been utterly spoilt by presents from "distinguished visitors" (1911, p. 50), and who frustrated the Seligmanns' inquiries with their insistent demands for presents. The anthropologists were quickly persuaded that "it was impossible to do any good work among such spoilt people" (ibid., p. 51). The villagers professed not to know to which *waruge* they belonged, but relations between them and the Seligmanns were evidently so bad that it would be presumptuous to accept their igno-rance as genuine. One outside informant thought they really did not know their *waruge* affiliation, but another told the Seligmanns that both Uru and the Namadewa *waruges* were represented there, while a Vedda from another village said that his mother came from Dambani and that she was a Namadewa woman (ibid., p. 52). The Seligmanns

themselves seem to have been afflicted by this confusion. At one point
they conclude that the Uru *waruge* was represented at Dambani (ibid.,
pp. 52, 72), but elsewhere they claim that the Dambani Vedda "probably belong to Namadewa *waruge* and descent is probably matrilineal"
(ibid., p. 78).

A second possible exception to the finding that more than one
waruge was represented in each community is provided by the village
of Bingoda. The Seligmanns did not visit this village, but they met
several of its inhabitants, all of whom told them that they belonged to
the Unapane *waruge*. It seems imprudent on such scanty evidence to
assume that no other *waruge* was represented at Bingoda, and the
Seligmanns themselves later inferred that "the Morane clan probably
also exists at Bingoda" (ibid., p. 72), though they fail to substantiate
this claim with any firm evidence.

The final exception was the village of Rotawewa, "the inhabitants
of which say they are descendants from Veddas—although all accounts
show that they are indistinguishable from their Sinhalese neighbours"
(ibid., p. 74). These people, who were not visited personally by the
Seligmanns, all said that they belonged to the Morane *waruge*, and
indeed, they apparently did not know of any other. They provide the
only clear instance to support Leach's thesis that the Vedda *waruge*
corresponds to the Sinhalese *variga*, in so far at least as "the ordinary
expectation is that in any one village the regular inhabitants will be
members of one *variga* only" (Leach 1963, p. 23). It is true that some
Sinhalese villages are inhabited by members of more than one *variga*,
but almost without exception these are large villages (Yalman 1962,
p. 549; Leach 1960, pp. 118-19). All the Vedda villages described are
small; yet with only one or two exceptions they contain representatives
of more than one *waruge*.

The second characteristic of the *variga*, which according to Leach is
"essential," is its endogamy. This characteristic is evidently not essential among the Veddas. The Seligmanns write: "Every Vedda belongs to
a *waruge* or clan, as the term may be translated, and among a large
number of the Vedda communities still existing, exogamy is the absolute rule" (1911, p. 30). The problem here is to determine how many is
a "large number" of Vedda communities. Later it appears that ". . .
exogamy prevails among the Veddas of Bintenne and Tamankaduwa
and clan descent is matrilineal. These conditions prevail at Godatalawa
and therefore must be assumed to have existed at Galmede whence the
Godatalawa family had come, but strangely this and the nearly related
Sitala Wanniya Veddas were the only communities to the east of the
Badulla-Batticaloa road in which exogamy prevailed" (ibid., pp. 74-75).

Leach seizes upon these exceptions to assert that clan exogamy "was treated with complete indifference by half or more of the Veddas whom the Seligmanns encountered" (1963, p. 73). This seems to be an exaggeration. In fact the Seligmanns identify seven communities in which *waruge* exogamy was consistently practiced, and only three wherein there was evidence of marriage within the clan.

Leach acknowledges that a rule of *variga* endogamy is not well observed by the Veddas, but he is not persuaded that the rule does not stand, at least as an ideal. His argument is that *waruge* exogamy is an accident rather than a custom. In the first place he criticizes the size of the Seligmanns' sample. The latter report that in all eight marriages recorded in Yakure, a community of village Veddas, *waruge* exogamy was observed. For Leach "this hardly seems an adequate sample" (ibid., p. 74). In fact, however, the Seligmanns recorded forty-two marriages among the village Veddas, and *waruge* exogamy was observed in each case.

Leach's second argument is more powerful. He points out that these are quite small communities and that several *waruges* are often represented in each. Each *waruge* will be represented by relatively few persons, and members of the same *waruge* are likely to be classificatory siblings rather than eligible spouses. Leach argues then

> that a Vedda will very frequently be faced with a choice of evils. So few marriageable females will be available that he will be compelled either to marry a girl of the wrong *waruge* or else a girl of an "incestuous" kinship category. And in such situations, it seems he ordinarily prefers to marry into the wrong *waruge*, so much so that, in the very small groups, it has become standard ethic to marry a girl of another *waruge*. [Ibid., p. 77]

It may be pointed out, firstly, that it is not only the "very small groups" that practice *waruge* exogamy. Secondly, the argument rests upon the assumption not only that *waruge* endogamy is the ideal, but also that local endogamy is both the ideal and the practice. Now *variga* endogamy and local endogamy may be closely associated among the Sinhalese, but there is little or no evidence, at least in the Seligmanns' account, to support a similar claim for the Veddas. Leach's explanation of the failure of the Veddas to observe *waruge* endogamy simply assumes the practice of local endogamy. Yet although the Seligmanns acknowledge themselves unable to substantiate their hypothesis that Vedda clans were once localized (which, combined with their account of exogamous clan organization, would imply also local exogamy), they do present incidental and scattered evidence of affinal ties between different Vedda communities.

It is unfortunate, however, that they offer no assessment of the extent to which the various Vedda settlements they studied were in direct communication with one another. The affinal connections they do mention link settlements that are within a few miles of one another, yet the area of their study includes Vedda communities that are up to seventy miles apart, and the inhabitants of such distant settlements were almost certainly quite unknown to one another, as their descendants are today. It seems highly probable that the Veddas did not form a single network of kinship and marriage, but were divided into a number of discrete groupings, each of which was more or less completely isolated from the others. In such circumstances, the possibilities and implications of which will be further discussed, Leach's demographic point would regain some force, but at the same time the presuppositions of his more general argument would appear more vulnerable, for if the Veddas were composed of several unconnected social groupings there would be little reason to assume that the term *waruge* was necessarily defined identically by all of them.

Moreover we are left wondering quite what is left of the *waruge* when Leach has finished with it. On the one hand we are told that the Veddas are aware of caste distinctions and that the *waruge* is ideally endogamous. On the other hand we are told that it has become "standard ethic" to marry out of the *waruge*. Such contradictions are not unprecedented, but this one seems to be peculiarly pointless, for Leach also argues that it is only in the context of a potential marriage that the Veddas become aware of differences of *waruges* (1963, p. 77). Are we to believe then that the Veddas remember and maintain their *waruge* organization solely so as to be able to present themselves with insoluble ethical problems when they want to get married?

At any rate it is clear that the *waruge* organization of the Veddas differs significantly from the Sinhalese *variga* organization. In particular the Vedda *waruge* is neither an exclusive residential group nor is it endogamous. Yet the Veddas and the Sinhalese do both use the same term to describe social divisions within their respective communities.

In the light of his own writings, both on Sri Lanka and on more general issues in social anthropology, Leach's treatment of this problem is somewhat unexpected. Throughout his article on the Veddas he implicitly assumes that a single understanding of how the *waruge* is to be defined, at least as an ideal scheme, is common to all the Vedda communities, and he does not doubt that exogamous clans and endogamous subcastes are structures of radically different type. Yet in his *Political Systems of Highland Burma* (1954) he had already demonstrated that common use of a system of symbols does not imply that the symbols are uniformly interpreted by all those who use them, while in his

Malinowski lecture (1961b) he had strongly warned anthropologists not to become trapped by their own conceptual schemes, suggesting, for example, that it might be profitable to consider patrilineal and matrilineal modes of organization as being less radically opposed than it had become conventional to assume. Nevertheless, in the Vedda article, having noted that among the Sinhalese the term *variga* "denotes a social group of a bilateral type such as Rivers would have described as an endogamous kindred or 'sub-caste,'" he goes on to pose the following questions:

> If the Seligmanns were right in saying that the Vedda *waruge* is an exogamous descent group, how should it have come about that the Veddas should use such an utterly inappropriate Sinhalese term? Alternatively if the Vedda social unit is of a kind which does *not* occur in Sinhalese society, surely one might expect that the Veddas would have devised their own terminology rather than borrow a Sinhalese term *meaning something precisely the opposite?* [1963, pp. 69-70; emphasis added]

But might not this "opposition" be experienced more by the anthropologist than by the Veddas? Or if there is some commonality between Vedda and Sinhalese usage, might this not be at a more abstract level than that given by marriage and descent rules? And might not the evident variations in Vedda social practice at least partly reflect ideological differences among the Veddas themselves? Somewhat similar questions have previously been raised by Marguerite Robinson in her article on the Kandyan kinship system, where she reports that even among the Kandyans themselves there are "wide variations in both the employment and the ideology of *variga*" (1968, p. 420). In order to tackle them it may be useful to return to Leach's original discussion of the Sinhalese *variga* in his book on *Pul Eliya*, where he translates the word as "kind" or "variety," and notes that it is used to denote categories of human beings of all kinds (1961a, p. 23; see also 1963, p. 22).

It does not follow from this that the "kinds" of persons thus categorized need necessarily form endogamous groups. Leach notes that various criteria—linguistic, religious, social, cultural, and racial—are at times employed by the Sinhalese in their categorization of different *varigas*. It is true that from the Sinhalese point of view these *variga* groups do also form endogamous social units, but this is a consequence of the caste principle that one should marry someone of one's own kind (*variga*). Caste principles and the rule of endogamy are only one way among many of identifying a kind of person. Where the principles of caste are in lesser vogue, quite different criteria may be employed to isolate and distinguish kinds of persons, and elsewhere Leach acknowledges that "caste differences among the Vedda are very much less pronounced than among the Sinhalese" (1963, p. 77). It may be thought that the members of a clan might equally constitute a kind of person, one fundamental difference between a caste and a clan deriving from their opposite answers to the question: Should one marry a person of the same or of a different kind (cf. Lévi-Strauss 1963; 1966, especially chapter 4).

In other words, the Sinhalese *variga* and the Vedda *waruge* may be equivalent terms employed to categorize human beings, but it is unnecessary to assume that the criteria used in these categorizations are everywhere constant; that is, the groups identified as *varigas* or *waruges* may be ordered by various social principles and may be in differing kinds of relationship with one another. We know there is considerable variation among the kinship systems of Sri Lanka. Both patrilineal and matrilineal, as well as bilateral, forms of organization have been described (Yalman 1967). More specifically, while the term *variga* is used to describe a bilateral and endogamous grouping among the Sinhalese of Anuradhapura District, among certain other Kandyan Sinhalese the same term describes a group that is matrilineal and exogamous (Robinson 1968).

One is tempted to inquire whether comparably structured variation may not also obtain, not only as between the Sinhalese and the Veddas, but also among the latter themselves. Both Leach and the Seligmanns, as I have pointed out, recognize that there is considerable variation in Vedda social practice, and they also agree that these variations are to be explained as deviations from a uniform ideal, although they differ in their interpretations of that ideal. For the Seligmanns, the ideal is the "pure" culture of Vedda matrilineality, deviation from which is a symptom of degeneracy, whereas for Leach it is principally demographic constraints that prevent the Veddas from practicing their common ideal of *waruge* endogamy. But what are the grounds for assuming a uniform Vedda ideal in this regard? Might not some groups of Veddas have institutionalized caste principles and bilateral kinship while others have adopted and maintained matrilineal organization? In what sense, in short, is Vedda society a single society that manifests a unitary culture?

These questions rest on a prior one that can no longer be evaded: who is to be considered a Vedda?

"VEDDA" AS A SOCIAL CATEGORY

When I was in Sri Lanka to do research on the Veddas, I was frequently told by middle-class, urban Sinhalese what the Seligmanns were already being told in 1907, namely that "there are no real Veddas left" (Seligmann and Seligmann 1911, p. 13). Yet in Anuradhapura District

alone there are today at least six thousand people who call themselves
Veddas and who are so called by their neighbors. Clearly there are
different definitions of who is a Vedda.

The middle-class opinion seems to derive from the line of thought
that informed the Seligmanns' own work and that, since 1911, has been
amplified, popularized, and more widely disseminated in the writings of
Spittel (1951; 1957) and others, as well as by means of newspapers,
magazines, and films. The Veddas are here thought of as a remnant
group of primitive hunters, racially distinct from the Sinhalese and
formerly speaking a separate language, who until recently preserved
their ancient way of life in the eastern jungles of the Veddaratta. I have
already shown how this reduction of the Veddas to "a numerically
small population verging on extinction" (Seligmann and Seligmann
1911, p. vii) stemmed from the inability of nineteenth-century investigators to separate matters of race and culture, and from their insistent
attempts to isolate pure types of both race and culture among the
Veddas, who could than be represented as the island's aboriginals.

My own approach is quite different. Questions of race are not
wholly irrelevant to the sociological concerns of the present work, but
I am prepared to consider as *Veddas* all those who identify themselves
as such and who are so described by their neighbors, regardless of their
actual racial origin. In other words, my usage of the term *Vedda* corresponds to that of the villagers themselves, and it is a usage that is quite
distinct from the one that has become conventional among anthropologists and, through them, among the urban Sinhalese. The difference is
neatly illuminated in a passage from one of the most sophisticated of
recent anthropological studies of Sri Lanka, a passage in which Nur
Yalman describes a type of chena (swidden, or shifting, cultivation)
settlement to be found in Uva Province that is distinguished from other
types of Sinhalese village settlement by the total absence of irrigated
rice agriculture.

These communities are usually extremely poor, and lacking rice fields, eke out their
existence by the cultivation of finger millet and vegetables. Often, also, they resort
to hunting like the ancient Veddas who are known to have inhabited parts of the
Uva Province until recently (Seligmann and Seligmann 1911). It is notable that the
Sinhalese who live in established paddy-cultivating villages consider these people to
be wild, backward and dangerous. They will often refer to them simply as Veddas,
even though there are now no linguistic or other racial differences between them. It
is quite possible that some of these settlements on chena lands may really be of
Vedda origin, but even half a century ago the Seligmanns noted that it was extremely difficult to find true Veddas. [1967, p. 23]

Besides the identification of "true" Veddas by means of racial and linguistic differences, note how in this passage even recent Veddas are described as "ancient," as well as how linguistic differences are taken to be a kind of racial difference. By contrast the Sinhalese villagers who are Yalman's informants appear to be using the term *Vedda* to describe a more general condition of "backwardness" that is here associated with differences in subsistence activity.

A broad usage that employs both cultural ("wild, backward, dangerous") and socioeconomic (hunting, chena cultivation) criteria also obtains among the villagers of Anuradhapura District although there even the practice of some irrigated rice cultivation does not, at least in the short run, necessarily disqualify a community from being considered Vedda.

Nevertheless the occupational criterion is important. It has long been pointed out that the term *Vedda* is derived from the Sanskritic *vyadha*, which means someone who wounds or pierces, that is, a hunter (see, e.g., Bailey 1863, p. 280), and in every instance with which I am familiar the Veddas are associated with hunting. But nowadays this association is often tenuous. Game supplies have been severely depleted throughout Sri Lanka, and in the Vedda villages of Anuradhapura District hunting contributes very little to subsistence. But game is prized, the few successful hunters are respected, and everyone asserts that his grandparents lived principally from the chase.

Occupational distinctions are also emphasized by a group of people living near Dambulla who acknowledge their Vedda descent but claim also to belong to the Goyigama (Cultivator) caste. They simply told me that while their ancestry (*paramparawa*) was Vedda they had long ago given up hunting to become paddy cultivators and were therefore to be considered Goyigama (see chapter 6, note 1).

The association of hunting and chena cultivation with wildness and backwardness is not, of course, fortuitous. Hunting is most feasible in the least populated parts of the country and chena cultivation, by its very nature, cannot support as dense a population as can irrigated rice agriculture. These occupations are therefore most prominent in the sparsely populated parts of the country that are remote from the centers of Sinhalese civilization. Moreover those villagers who subsist from chena cultivation, supplemented perhaps by some hunting or even by a little paddy cultivation, generally make a poorer living than those whose access to irrigable land and an adequate water supply allows a primary dependence on paddy cultivation. Economics, as well as isolation, preclude their full participation in Sinhalese culture.

To put it another way, one might say that the Sinhalese describe as Veddas those among them whose poverty, isolation, and means of livelihood prevent them from meeting certain standards of the general culture.

Diet provides an illustration. The image of himself as a rice cultivator and consumer is fundamental to the Sinhalese villager, whether or not he is a member of the Goyigama, or Cultivator, caste, and its expressions are quite conventional and taken for granted. The polite inquiry as to whether someone has eaten is "*bat kawwa de?* " which translates literally as "have you eaten rice?" rice here being equated with food in much the same way as the Biblical daily bread. This form of inquiry is entirely conventional even among the Veddas of Anuradhapura District, who undertake wet rice as well as chena cultivation, but whose meals less often contain rice than *kurakkan*, or finger millet, the main chena crop. Moreover there is sometimes lively discussion among these Veddas over the respective merits of the two foods, the virtues of rice being challenged by the claim that *kurakkan* is more nourishing and gives greater strength. These arguments run parallel to, and indeed express, further disagreements among these Veddas as to whether they should be considered a variety of Sinhalese or whether they should be recognized as a people quite distinct.

The marginality of the Veddas is also expressed in more elaborate rituals. At the Vedda *perahera*, or "Procession of the Veddas," held annually at Mahiyangana in Badulla District, all the various groups of Sinhalese who participate form a single moral community that is ritually distinguished from that of the Veddas. In the course of the ceremony the latter are dramatically denied access to the sacred places of Buddhism, demonstrating, as Obeyesekere's penetrating analysis makes clear, the exclusion of the Veddas from "the Sinhalese Buddhist moral community" (1966, p. 20). Nevertheless, as Obeyesekere also points out, the Veddas "are not total strangers, for both Sinhalese and Veddha are united in worship of the guardian deities, Saman and Skandha, protectors of the secular and supernatural order of both Veddha and Sinhalese" (ibid.).

Elsewhere there is no insistence either that the Veddas be excluded from the Sinhalese Buddhist community or that those who espouse Buddhism cease to be Veddas. The Anuradhapura Veddas, for example, although their knowledge of the Buddhist scriptures is meager and their practice of Buddhist rites rare, all describe themselves as Buddhists without their status as Veddas being in any way impaired.

Somewhat similarly, the conventional wisdom that the Veddas stand outside the Sinhalese caste system does not hold true for the Anuradhapura Veddas, who regularly employ members of the service castes at rites of passage. Likewise Sinhalese villagers do not insist that

those they call Veddas speak a separate language from themselves.
Awareness of racial differences also seems to play a quite subordinate
part in the folk attribution of Vedda status. The idea that those they
call Veddas are a quite different people from themselves is hardly likely
to be questioned by Sinhalese villagers, for they inhabit a cultural
milieu in which the ideology of caste is ubiquitous. A fundamental
feature of the caste regime, of course, is the principle of endogamy
that, however poorly practiced, at least sustains the idea that different
kinds of people do not, or should not, interbreed. Moreover each group
typically enjoys its own myths of origin, which define its separate
identity. Certainly in Anuradhapura District, comments about the
physical separateness of the Veddas refer more to these kinds of mytho-
logical and ideological considerations than to observed physical differences.

Thus although to be a Vedda is in some sense to differ from the
Sinhalese norm, there are Veddas who have to some degree adopted all
the characteristic attributes of Sinhalese peasants. There are Veddas
who grow paddy under irrigation, Veddas who practice Buddhism,
Veddas who participate in the caste system, Veddas who look just like
Sinhalese peasants, and so on. One may suspect here the operation of a
cultural lag, such that the assimilation of distinctively Sinhalese characteristics does not immediately entail the loss of Vedda identity, but one
may also observe that the categorical distinction between Vedda and
Sinhalese has to describe a range of continuous cultural variation. As
Leach remarks, while noting that the point had already been fully
demonstrated by the Seligmanns, "the culture of the 'Village Veddas'
merges quite readily with that of the ordinary Kandyan (Sinhalese)
peasant" (1963, p. 68). If in one aspect, then, the term *Vedda* denotes
a kind of popular ideal type in polar opposition to that of the paddy-
cultivating Sinhalese Buddhist peasant, in practical life many people are
described as Veddas whose culture displays few of the features of the
ideal type.

It was doubtless in order to discriminate within this range of
continuous cultural variation that there developed the distinction
between the wilder and the tamer sort of Vedda that Knox adopted. A
similar function is performed by the distinction between the jungle
Veddas (*kala Veddho*) or rock Veddas (*gal Veddho*) and the village
Veddas (*gam Veddho*). All Veddas are wild in relation to the Sinhalese,
but some are wilder than others. And it is peculiarly the anthropologists,
and those influenced by them, who have consistently striven to strip
away the contaminating accretions of Sinhalese influence in order to
discover the concrete embodiments of the ideal type of the pure and

true wild Vedda. Sinhalese villagers, by contrast, are content to describe as Veddas those whose culture is *relatively* wild or uncivilized, those whose distinctive traits, and whose mode of subsistence in particular, express their remoteness from the mainstream of Sinhalese culture.

The attributes of wildness and backwardness, which describe their isolation and marginality, serve also to disparage the relatively poor and unsophisticated Veddas. But there is an ambivalence here, for the Veddas also enjoy high status among the Sinhalese. The myths that validate this status provide a further expression of the intricate relationship between the two peoples.

The central myth is that of Prince Vijaya, the legendary founder of the Sinhalese nation, whose story is thoroughly familiar to the Veddas of Anuradhapura District as well as to the Sinhalese, although it was apparently unknown to the Veddas the Seligmanns described (1911, pp. 28, 165). The relevant part of the myth tells how Vijaya, on his first arrival in Sri Lanka and before he sent back to India for a bride of comparable status to his own, cohabited with a demon princess named Kuweni, who gave birth to two children, a boy and a girl. As the reputed descendants of the incestuous union of these siblings, the Veddas lay claim to royal ancestry and the high status appropriate to it.

The myth neatly defines the flexible and ambiguous relationship between the Sinhalese and the Veddas. By stressing descent from Vijaya, the common origins of the two people can be brought to the forefront, while descriptions of the Veddas as "the children of Kuweni" accentuate their separateness. In this connection it is worth pointing out that it is precisely the wild Veddas who are reputed to have been organized matrilineally and for whom descent from Kuweni, had they been aware of the myth, would have been given structural priority. The Veddas of Anuradhapura District, on the other hand, who reckon kinship bilaterally, can lay equal claim to both Vijaya and Kuweni, and do in fact vary among themselves in the relative weight they give to the two ancestors. These internal differences provide a further expression of their disagreements as to whether they should be considered a variety of the Sinhalese or as a separate people.

Besides supporting the Veddas' assertion of royal descent, the myth of Vijaya and Kuweni also allows them to claim both to be the autochthonous possessors of the land and to be in intimate contact with the supernatural world. These claims are reinforced by other myths, at least in Anuradhapura District.

The Anuradhapura Veddas refer to themselves not only as *Veddi minissu* (Vedda people) but also as *Wanni minissu* (Wanni people). The latter term is also sometimes applied indiscriminately to all natives of the Wanni, the extensive dry jungle that includes Anuradhapura District, but it is not adopted as a caste name by any other group. Use of the term *Wanni* also links the Veddas to the Vanniyar aristocrats, with whom a common ancestry is sometimes claimed (cf. Leach 1961a, p. 75).

The Vanniyars, who are the hereditary guardians of the Sacred Bo Tree in Anuradhapura, are also considered to be ancient inhabitants of the area, and may be grouped by the Veddas with themselves in opposition to all the other Sinhalese, who are seen in this context as relative newcomers. The Veddas explain that all the local Sinhalese (sometimes including the Vanniyars, sometimes excluding them) are the descendants of Indian captives settled in the region by King Gaja-bahu (cf. Obeyesekere 1970). This myth, which is challenged by neighboring Sinhalese of different castes, enhances the Veddas' claim to high status, which is already established by their descent from King Vijaya and the putative kinship connection with the Vanniyars. At the same time the Gajabahu myth also supports the claim to original possession of the land, which otherwise derives from descent from Kuweni.

Descent from Kuweni also provides the basis for the Veddas' reputation for mediumistic talents, for Kuweni, it will be recalled, was a demon (*yakkhini*), and it is this association, I suspect, that underlies Yalman's informants' description of the Veddas as "dangerous" (1967, p. 23), since in Sinhalese belief the demons are not only powerful but characteristically malevolent.

Demons rank low in the heriarchical structure of the Sinhalese pantheon (Obeyesekere 1966), but the quality of the Veddas' supernatural connections is enhanced by their further association with the powerful god (*deyo*) Kataragama (Skandha, Kandoswami), whose second wife, Valli Amma, was raised by Veddas. Vedda *kapuralas* (priests) are particularly attentive to Kataragama *deyo* and are called upon to intercede with him by Sinhalese clients as well as by their own people.

Myth, then, serves to place the Veddas in relation to the Sinhalese as well as to the supernatural. In general it can be said that besides being looked down upon for their backwardness, the Veddas are feared and respected for their mediumistic faculties and are at the same time allowed high status on account of their putatively royal descent. But it must also be recognized that the mythic idiom is dynamic and flexible enough to tolerate varied and even conflicting interpretations, which can in turn be brought into at least partial correspondence with variations in the actual life situations of different groups of Veddas. For example, in the course of an hypothetical process of "Sinhalization," whereby a community of Veddas takes up wet rice agriculture, engages more actively in Buddhist rites, begins to participate in the reciprocal services of the caste system, and so, in the course of time, becomes recognized as Sinhalese rather than Vedda, it can readily be imagined which different aspects of the myth of Vijaya and Kuweni are emphasized by those who are concerned to hasten or retard the process. This may, indeed, be the appropriate context in which to view the disagreements about status among the Anuradhapura Veddas that I have already described.

An exhaustive account of the wide variation that the folk category *Vedda* embraces would go far beyond the scope of the present work, even were the materials available. On the basis of available ethnographic research, which has been limited to a few communities, it has been possible only to suggest the range of that variation. To describe the historical background of Vedda variability would be an even more daunting task, for the archeological record is slight, historical documentation sparse, and ethnological investigations few. The biological character and cultural attributes of different Vedda groups are, in each case, the result of a unique historical experience that is as yet largely unknown and that may indeed remain, in important respects, inaccessible. Nevertheless it may be useful briefly and quite speculatively to suggest some of the sources of variation, both racial and cultural, that is to be found among those who are called Veddas.

To take racial variation first, while myth sustains the notion that all the Veddas are descended from Vijaya and Kuweni, it is evident that Vedda populations may, in fact, have quite varied genetic histories. Physical anthropologists have established a biological affinity between certain groups of recent Veddas and an aboriginal population known as the Balangodese (Kennedy 1965; 1974). The Balangodese specimens display a polytypic pattern that is not characteristic of Sinhalese, Tamil, or any other major population living in Sri Lanka today, but the frequency of phenotypic characters that they share with the Vedda specimens that were studied is significantly high. It seems probable, however, that other groups of people who are known as Veddas share few of these distinctive features and that some, indeed, have no greater admixture of aboriginal genes than is normal within the Sinhalese population as a whole. It is useful to distinguish two ways in which this may have come about.

First, there has been individual migration into Vedda communities that at one time may have been biologically representative of the aboriginal population. The Seligmanns' account, for example, abounds with references to Vedda communities into which Sinhalese or Tamils have at some time been admitted, while among the Anuradhapura Veddas approximately 15 percent of present-day marriages are with non-Veddas. There is no reason to suppose that this is only a recent phenomenon. It is not at all unlikely that for many centuries the remoteness of Vedda settlements has made them attractive to those who, for whatever reason, may have wished to escape the constrictions of Sinhalese society. The Veddas seem to have welcomed such refugees. Knox reports that "some of the Chingulays [i.e., Sinhalese] in discontent will leave their houses and friends, and go and live among them, where they are civilly entertained" (1911, p. 101).

Second, in the course of time whole communities that were once Sinhalese may have become Vedda. This is most likely to have occurred during periods of chronic economic decline, especially when accompanied by political dislocation. For example, the collapse of the Polonnaruwa civilization and the associated population movements towards the southwest of the island between the thirteenth and fifteenth centuries transformed what had been the very center of a magnificent civilization into a remote and backward region (Indrapala 1971). And as the massive irrigation system upon which the civilization had rested fell into decline, the importance of chena cultivation relative to wet rice must surely have risen in the economy of those who remained in the area. If one can assume that the popular Sinhalese usage of the term *Vedda*, then as now, gave priority to sociocultural over racial features, then it does not seem extravagant to hazard the guess that some of the Sinhalese communities that remained behind may have become Vedda. And if a further unverifiable speculation be permitted, it seems equally possible that, on a smaller scale, this kind of ethnic transformation, associated with a change in economic circumstances, has been going on in both directions throughout Sinhalese history. In brief, it may be anticipated that different Vedda communities are quite varied in their biological make-up, with some being indistinguishable from the Kandyan Sinhalese while others are almost as distinct as the aboriginal Balangodese.

Cultural variability is hardly likely to be less. Even in recent historic times the Veddas are known to have been still widely distributed throughout the island. On the basis of a study of place names, Bailey inferred the former presence of Veddas in Sabaragamuwa Province (1863). Later studies have identified Vedda place names also in the Western Province and in the Kandyan area (de Zoysa 1881; Wijesekera 1949; Raghavan 1953). Nevill discovered Sinhalese manuscripts that describe Veddas inhabiting Puttalam in the fifteenth century and Matale in the seventeenth century (Seligmann and Seligmann 1911, p. 11).

Reviewing this and other evidence that also suggests the presence of Veddas near Hurulla and Trincomalee, as well as in the Wanni region near the Jaffna peninsula, Kennedy has concluded that "as late as the seventeenth century the Veddas were probably ubiquitous" (1967, p. 14).

There is no evidence, however, that the Veddas at this time constituted what could be called a single society, or that their culture was everywhere uniform. Even today, when those who are called Veddas seem to have become largely confined to the eastern and north central parts of the island, they are divided up into a number of groups that have no direct communication with one another. For example, the Anuradhapura Veddas have no direct contact with any of the Vedda communities in Polonnaruwa District, let alone any of those in Badulla or Batticaloa districts, with the sole exception of the village of Rota-wewa, which is located near Minneriya in Polonnaruwa District. And the people of Rotawewa, while fully integrated by ties of kinship and marriage into the community of Anuradhapura Veddas, are not themselves in touch with any other groups of Veddas in Polonnaruwa District.

The Veddas have always lived on the periphery of Sinhalese civilization, either in the more inaccessible and least populated parts of the interior, or externally at the limits of the civilization's geographical reach. In any particular region the Vedda communities may have been closely linked to one another, but different regions have less commonly been in direct contact with one another around the periphery than they have been indirectly related through the intermediacy of the Sinhalese.

That Vedda groups have often been more closely connected with the Sinhalese than with one another illuminates the question of Vedda variability in two ways. Not only does it help make comprehensible the considerable differences in the degree to which the Veddas manifest the general attributes of Sinhalese culture, but it also suggests another source of variation, for Sinhalese culture and social organization are themselves internally and regionally variable. Local variants of Vedda culture are, in part, the product of interaction with local variants of Sinhalese culture, and to that extent differences among the Veddas may be expected to reflect differences among the Sinhalese.

This point has some significance for the problem of Vedda kinship organization. It will be recalled that Leach's critique of the Seligmanns' analysis of Vedda kinship focuses on their interpretation of the term *waruge* as "exogamous [matrilineal] clan," and that Leach himself asserts that "*among the Sinhalese* this term denotes a social group of a bilateral type such as Rivers would have described as an endogamous kindred or 'sub-caste'" (1963, p. 69; emphasis in the original). I have already noted that his statement is not entirely correct. Leach's interpretation of the term *waruge* or *variga* certainly holds good for the Sinhalese villagers of Anuradhapura District, where his own field work was conducted, but there are indeed Kandyan Sinhalese elsewhere who do use the term to describe groups that are matrilineal and exogamous (Robinson 1968). Moreover, matrilineal organization is especially common along the east coast of Sri Lanka (Yalman 1967, pp. 282-331), and it is precisely the Veddas inhabiting the eastern parts of the island whose kinship system has been described as matrilineal.

But if the discovery of widespread matrilineality in areas contiguous to those inhabited by the Veddas whom the Seligmanns studied seems to give some support to their interpretation of Vedda kinship, it is evidence that must be handled with great caution. It is certainly suggestive, but the processes of diffusion, acculturation, and cultural change are extremely complex, and the historical record of such processes among the Veddas is sparse. The safest course is to suggest that interaction and change may have taken several forms. Some groups of Veddas may have adopted the forms of kinship organization employed by their Sinhalese neighbors. Others, as I have suggested, may be the descendants of Sinhalese who were cut off from the mainstream of the national culture to become, in the course of time, Veddas, and these may have simply retained their former kinship structures. Others again may have adopted forms of kinship that were distinct from those around them. As Yalman has argued, differences in kinship organization between adjacent peoples may be seen as "diacritical indices which set off one community from the other" (ibid., p. 305).

Up to this point, for the sake of simplicity and because the data are more plentiful, I have discussed Vedda relations with their neighbors as though all those neighbors were Sinhalese. This, however, is not the case, for there are a considerable number of Veddas whose affinities are with the Tamils, the dominant ethnic group in the north and on the east coast of Sri Lanka, rather than with the Sinhalese. Unfortunately, little has been written about the Tamil-speaking Veddas, and my own field research was unable to encompass them, so my treatment of them must be both brief and tentative. It seems likely, however, that in many ways the structure of relations between the Tamils and the Tamil Veddas parallels that between the Sinhalese and the Sinhalese-speaking Veddas, and in particular that the Tamil Veddas are a marginal people, both culturally and geographically, who are thought to be backward and impoverished.

But two important differences demand notice. First, given the more complex structure of castes among the Tamils, and the different series of myths that support it, the status afforded to the Tamil Veddas and their articulation into the caste system almost certainly differ from the Sinhalese pattern. Second, there are occupational differences. The best known Tamil Veddas are those the Seligmanns describe as coast Veddas, who inhabit the east coast north of Batticaloa, where they make their living from fishing rather than from hunting, as well as from shifting cultivation.

Not all Tamil-speaking Veddas, however, are fishermen. In the interior of the island, around the border between Anuradhapura and Vavuniya districts, which roughly marks the boundary between the Tamils to the north and the Sinhalese to the south, the circle of endogamy that contains the kinship and marriage relations of the Sinhalese-speaking Anuradhapura Veddas is not completely closed, and a few connections are maintained with Tamil-speaking villages further north. The Anuradhapura Veddas identify these Tamil speakers as being, like themselves, Veddas; however, I cannot say that they are not also known by some other name among the Tamils because I was unable to pursue these connections into their Tamil cultural context. Be that as it may, these Tamil-speaking Veddas in Vavuniya District are cultivators rather than fishermen. It appears, then, that there are cultural differences among the Tamil Veddas just as there are among the Sinhalese Veddas.

Emphasis on the range of variation in Vedda culture should not be allowed to obscure the similarity of structural position that is shared by all the Veddas. Whatever the cultural differences among them, all the Veddas stand in much the same relationship to the Sinhalese. But a certain ambiguity persists, because this relationship appears different from different perspectives. From the vantage point of Sinhalese civilization, the Veddas are peripheral; they are a marginal people whose remoteness deprives them of full participation in the national culture. But from a more detached perspective, the relationship appears as one of distinctive opposition, the Veddas being defined by the characteristics they do not share with the Sinhalese. They are hunters rather than paddy cultivators, pagans rather than Buddhists, and so on. This opposition, of course, contributes equally to the definition of what is distinctive about the Sinhalese. From this point of view, Vedda culture might even be described as an anti-(Sinhalese) culture. I would also suggest, although this is almost entirely speculative, that relations between the Tamil Veddas and the Tamils may prove to approximate closely to the Sinhalese pattern.

But there is also a third, and grander, perspective available, one in which the position of the Tamil Veddas and the Sinhalese Veddas moves from homology towards identity. The primary division of the Veddas into Tamil- and Sinhalese-speakers reflects what has been the major ethnic opposition in Sri Lanka for hundreds of years, and relations both between the Sinhalese Veddas and the Sinhalese and between the Tamil Veddas and the Tamils demand to be looked at in a perspective that can encompass this fundamental polarity. In this larger context, the position of both the Sinhalese Veddas and the Tamil Veddas now appears to be equivalently interstitial. Certainly within the last two hundred years the Veddas have come to be largely confined within the broad arc that separates the Sinhalese from the Tamil part of the country, a kind of cultural no man's land within which it is perhaps structurally appropriate to find a group of people who can present themselves as neither Sinhalese nor Tamil.[5]

In summary, I have been trying in the present section to elucidate the ordinary folk usage of the term *Vedda*. In contrast to the conventional anthropological pursuit of the pure Veddas, ordinary Sinhalese employ the term *Vedda* in a way that is more structural than historical, and is inherently comparative. Very few, if any, cultural characteristics are common to all those who are known as Veddas that are not also shared by at least some of the Sinhalese. One should not, therefore, expect to find, let alone assume, that all the different groups of Veddas share exactly the same type of social organization or that their social organization is radically different from the forms displayed by the Sinhalese. I regret that I have been unable to determine whether the wild Veddas the Seligmanns studied were ever organized into matrilineal clans, but I shall be content if I have at least restored that possibility. More generally, I have been concerned to establish that some groups of Veddas may have been unilineally organized while others, such as the Anuradhapura Veddas, have adopted forms of bilateral organization that are strictly similar to those of their Sinhalese neighbors. Doubtless some will still object that the Anuradhapura Veddas are not real Veddas, but such prejudice is unbecoming to the social anthropologist, who must at least begin his work by aligning himself with his subjects in an attempt to comprehend the particular social reality that *they* have constructed. Finally, I have also tried to show that despite the extensive variability of Vedda culture, the position of the Veddas relative to the Sinhalese is everywhere homologous, and that it is only

5. My thoughts on this have been stimulated by an unpublished paper by R. L. Stirrat, in which he argues that "between the two dominant cultures there is a 'shatter-belt,' a zone of minority groupings which have attempted to escape from the wider problems and their frontier position by turning to alternate social identities" (Stirrat n.d.: 29).

when examined within a structural context that includes the Sinhalese as well as the Veddas (or, even more grandly, that includes both the Sinhalese and the Tamils as well as the Veddas) that what is both common and distinctive to all the Veddas is revealed.

2

The Village and the State

The Anuradhapura Veddas[1] form a single caste group (*variga*), which is widely dispersed but mainly contained within the boundaries of Anuradhapura District in the North Central Province of Sri Lanka (map 2.1). As is customary in the island's Dry Zone, the Veddas inhabit their own separate villages, which are scattered among those of other *varigas*. The present Vedda population is about 6,600, which is approximately 3 percent of the total population of the district.[2] In 1891 the Vedda population was about 1,150, which was 1½ percent of the total for Nuvarakalaviya, as the present Anuradhapura District was then still commonly called.

The general pattern of settlement in Anuradhapura District is one of small agricultural communities concentrated around their independent village tanks, or reservoirs, and separated from one another by a mile or two of scrub jungle. There are a number of small centers of trade and administration in the district, such as Medawachchiya, Horuwopotana, and Kekirawa, but Anuradhapura itself is the only

1. Hereafter, I shall refer to the people now identified as Anuradhapura Veddas simply as Veddas. It is not to be inferred from this that what I have to say about them applies to Veddas in other parts of Sri Lanka.

2. The population of Anuradhapura District at the 1953 census was 229,282. This includes 58,014 people in the former Kandyan province of Tamankaduwa, which has since been separated to form Polonnaruwa District. From its inception in 1873 until the establishment of Polonnaruwa District, the North Central Province formed a single administrative district, composed of the two former Kandyan provinces, Nuvarakalaviya and Tamankaduwa. In 1891 its population was 75,333, of which Nuvarakalaviya contributed 69,302 and Tamankaduwa 6,031.

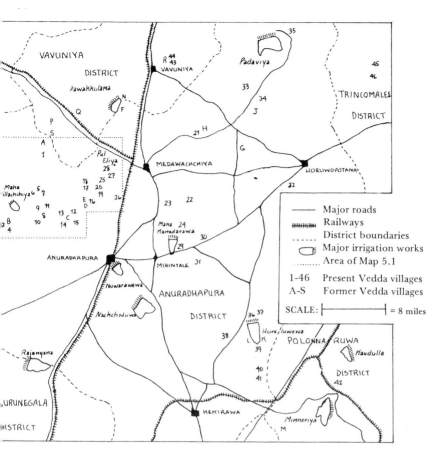

Map 2.1. Anuradhapura Vedda Villages

KEY:

Present Vedda Villages

1. Tantrimalai
2. Kuda Tammanawa
3. Heratgama
4. Katukeliyawa
5. Tambiyawewa
6. Pathiyapothana
7. Gonewewa
8. Wanniya Helambewa
9. Maha Helambewa
10. Kuda Nikawewa
11. Nawakkulama
12. Maha Ehetuwewa
13. Ihala Oyamaduwa
14. Ihalawewa
15. Andarawewa
16. Siyambalagaswewa (B)
17. Irigehewa
18. Peenigale
19. Wanniya Palugollewa
20. Kokkatiyawa
21. Pandiggama
22. Welewa

23. Diviyaubendewewa
24. Elapatgama
25. Magurahitiyawa
26. Medagama
27. Tulaveliya
28. Kalavelpotana
29. Siyambalagaswewa (A)
30. Kukulewa
31. Kirimetiyawa
32. Elapatwewa
33. Kanugahewa
34. Rambekapuwewa
35. Bogahawewa
36. Migahapattiya
37. Dambagahaulpota
38. Moragoda
39. Halmillewa
40. Maha Migaswewa
41. Pusdiwulwewa
42. Rotawewa
43. Malayaparantikulama
44. Katamankulama

45. Adampane
46. Bakmikada

Former Vedda Villages
A. Nochchikulama (A)
B. Suriyadamana
C. Kuda Ehetuwewa
D. Pahiwalayagama
E. Hunupolayagama
F. Kohombagaswewa
G. Ihala Tammenawa
H. Gallewa
J. Manakande
K. Migahapattiya
L. Dambagahaulpota
M. Gallinda
N. Nochchikulama (B)
P. Mucalkutti
Q. Mayailmuttalyittakulam
R. Kurundankulam
S. Kongarayankulam

town of any size or substance. Otherwise the general pattern is disturbed only by the major colonization projects (Padaviya, Huruluwewa, etc.; see map 2.1), which the government has established in recent years in its attempt to restore the great irrigation works of ancient Sri Lanka and to extend the area under permanent paddy cultivation (Farmer 1957). These large colonies, in which land has been granted to natives of Anuradhapura District as well as to those from other parts of the country, have certainly had an impact throughout the district, but the great majority of the population continues to inhabit the small, traditional, agricultural villages.

The district's population contains minority communities of Tamils and Moslems but the Veddas, who speak Sinhalese and profess Buddhism, are more closely integrated into the dominant Sinhalese culture. The most immediately evident sign of Vedda distinctiveness is their relative poverty. Their villages conform to the general pattern, but with few exceptions their tanks are smaller and less reliable than those of other castes. When discussing this state of affairs the Veddas draw on the myths that I have mentioned previously. They claim that, as the original inhabitants of the area, all the land formerly belonged to them. Then people of other *varigas* came to settle in the area and the Veddas were asked to give them tanks and land to cultivate. Their royal descent entailed the regal obligation to be generous in providing the means of livelihood, and they could not refuse. They gave the new settlers the best tanks and were eventually left with only the smallest and least desirable for themselves.

The relative poverty of the Veddas does not stem from their pursuit of a mode of subsistence that is fundamentally different from that of their neighbors. The way they apportion their energies among the various occupations that are available may be unique, but despite their traditional reputation as hunters the occupations they follow are those that are common throughout the district. These occupations are overwhelmingly concerned with agriculture of two radically different types. There is wet-rice cultivation carried on in permanent, privately owned fields that are irrigated from the village tanks. These tanks are constructed by damming a natural watercourse by means of a long earth wall, or bund, behind which the monsoon rains that feed the stream are caught and stored for subsequent distribution to the fields. Second, there is chena cultivation (Sinhalese: *hena*), chena being the Sinhalese English term for what is generally known as swidden, slash-and-burn, or shifting cultivation. In this agricultural regime, a portion of the scrub jungle that surrounds each village and that is equally accessible to all is cultivated for one or two years without benefit of artificial irrigation before being abandoned for a much longer period to allow for its regeneration. The sociology of these two modes of agriculture is examined in detail in chapter 4.

We do not know how long the Veddas in this area have been settled agriculturalists. Members of the present generation say that their grandparents lived mainly from hunting, and there is no doubt that game of all kinds was more plentiful in an age when a single British army officer could claim to have shot more than twelve hundred wild elephants (Tennent 1859, 2: 323; cf. Gooneratne 1970, where Sri Lanka's present elephant population is estimated at a thousand). But nineteenth-century reports refer to the Anuradhapura Veddas as "domesticated Veddas" (Brodie 1856-58; government agent quoted in Leach 1961a, p. 75), which in the normal usage implies chena if not also paddy cultivation. The relative importance of these occupations a hundred years ago remains uncertain. An assistant government agent in Vavuniya wrote that the Veddas "are entirely dependent on hunting and occasional chena cultivation" (quoted in Lewis 1895), while according to Parker, "a few only cultivate paddy, the rest live by chena cultivation, hunting and honey-collection, especially the latter" (1887, p. 15). On the other hand, official grain tax registers indicate that in the 1870s at least some Veddas were growing substantial amounts of paddy (see, e.g., Sri Lanka National Archives file 20, vol. 27, which includes figures for the Vedda village of Kukulewa). Thus although at one time hunting was undoubtedly more central to the Vedda economy than it now is, paddy cultivation has also been important for at least a hundred years. There is no need therefore to exempt the Veddas from the implications of Leach's assertion that in this part of Sri Lanka "the basic valuable is scarce water rather than scarce land" (1961a, p. 17). This requires that any analysis of the local social structure take adequate account of the arrangements by which the water needed to irrigate the paddy fields is stored and distributed.

In the following sketch of the history of Anuradhapura District I therefore pay particular attention to the forms of control exercised over the village irrigation works, especially as they have changed over the last 150 years. This is not intended to demean hunting, chena cultivation, or any other occupations that may at some time have been more important than paddy cultivation in the Vedda economy. It simply recognizes that, in contrast to the undeveloped resources of the jungle, to which all have equal access, irrigation works and their associated paddy fields represent a substantial capital investment, comprise the village's major fixed assets, and are subject to individual ownership. They thus provide a central focus for political action within the individual villages. At the same time they are also subject to some measure of external control by the administrative apparatus of the state, analysis of which will indicate, in at least one important respect, the degree of autonomy that the village community has enjoyed. The administrative relations that connect the village to the state impose constraints on the forms that political action can take within the village, and must therefore be included in the analysis of the structure of social relations within a group of villages that appear never to have composed an entirely autonomous and independent society.

Nuvarakalaviya (as I shall refer to Anuradhapura District when discussing the more remote past) was the center of the ancient Sinhalese civilization that flourished there between the third century B.C. and the twelfth century A.D. The present inhabitants still live in the shadow of that extravagant period in Sinhalese history. They refer to the area as the *Raja rata* (land of the kings), and the ancient tanks and temples continue to create a more pervasive ambience than do the more recent roads and railways, schools and hospitals.

Nuvarakalaviya has suffered extreme vicissitudes of political fortune, but the inexorable facts of geography have ensured a measure of continuity with the past. The district is situated in Sri Lanka's Dry Zone and receives an average annual rainfall of no more than seventy-five inches. Most of this falls between October and December in the period of the northeast monsoon, although in some years there is also valuable precipitation in April and May when the southwest monsoon brings rain more generously to other parts of the island. But the rains of neither monsoon are entirely reliable, the runoff is rapid, and the soil poor. Irrigation is therefore necessary if paddy is to be cultivated in permanent fields. But the construction of irrigation works is an expensive investment and their location is largely determined by topography. In the course of history many tanks have been abandoned, but they have scarcely less often been later restored. Present-day villages are commonly on the sites of ancient settlements (see, e.g., Leach 1961a, p. 101), and the present irrigation system is a restored version of the one that was slowly constructed during the period of the Anuradhapura kings.

The elaboration of massive irrigation works that were made to support a prosperous and expansive kingdom in an area of poor natural fertility suggests an instance of Wittfogel's "hydraulic civilization" (Wittfogel 1957). But Leach (1959) has denied the application of Wittfogel's model to the case of Dry Zone Sri Lanka on the grounds that whatever the despotic inclinations of individual monarchs the regime itself was closer to feudalism than to "oriental despotism." Part of Leach's argument emphasizes that there were (and still are) two distinct categories of irrigation works, "the small reservoirs (tanks) associated with individual villages and the very much larger central reservoirs and feeder canals which now, as formerly, are under the control of the central government" (1961a, p. 17; cf. Gunawardana 1971). It was this traditional autonomy of the village irrigation system, not merely the collapse of the massive state system, that enabled Dickson, in 1873, to describe the province as "composed of a number of small agricultural republics, each of which has its tank with the field below it" (1873, p. 9), a characterization that is repeated by Pieris (1956, p. 236).

In the thirteenth century the capital of the Sinhalese kingdom, which had earlier been moved from Anuradhapura to Polonnaruwa, was shifted out of the Dry Zone altogether. The Jaffna Peninsula was in Tamil hands and Nuvarakalaviya, formerly the very center of the kingdom, had become a border province. Drought and disease may have abetted the political disturbances of the times in introducing the long decline the region now underwent (Murphey 1957; Indrapala 1971). Irrigation works fell into disrepair, the population declined, and many tanks were abandoned. When Robert Knox escaped from his long captivity in Kandy in the seventeenth century, he chose to flee through Nuvarakalaviya because that was the most sparsely inhabited part of the country (Knox 1911, p. 246).

Separated from the capital by dense jungle, Nuvarakalaviya became increasingly independent of royal authority. The local aristocrats, the Vanniyars, were able to play off their nominal superiors in Kandy against the Tamils in Jaffna, and later the Dutch. When the British annexed the Kandyan provinces in 1815 Sir John D'Oyly, the first British Resident, wrote that "the government of the province of Nuvarakalaviya is hereditary in the family of Kumarasinhe Vanniya and his brother" (D'Oyly quoted in Ievers 1899, p. 60; see also Lewis 1895; Nagel 1948; Pieris 1956, pp. 249-51; Leach 1961a, pp. 19-20). A few years before this the Vanniyar chief, the Vanni Unnehe, had been in revolt against the Kandyan king and had received British aid. In 1817, however, he joined the rebellion of dissident Kandyan chiefs against the British and was arrested and imprisoned in Galle.

His family suffered no lasting disadvantage from this miscalculation. The British were at first no more able to administer the province directly than the Kandyan kings had been. Even in 1832 it was admitted that governmental control was little more than nominal in Nuvarakalaviya (Ievers 1899). In 1834 the British released the Vanni Unnehe and restored him to full honors. Although he died two years later, other members of his family, enjoying the title and office of Ratemahatmaya, succeeded him as the senior native agents of indirect British rule.

In the middle years of the nineteenth century the affairs of Nuvarakalaviya were of minor concern to the colonial government. Between 1833 and 1873 the region was administered as part of the Northern Province in which it formed a backward Sinhalese division of a predominantly Tamil province. In 1873, however, a sense of obligation to improve the material condition of the remote villages and the prospect of the resulting increased revenue prompted the British to bring together Nuvarakalaviya and Tamankaduwa, which had been administered as part of the Tamil Eastern Province, in the formation of a new province, the North Central Province, to be administered under a government agent at Anuradhapura.

The Vanniyar family survived this change just as it had survived the earlier transition from the Kandyan kingdom to the British colonial regime. Its members continued to fill the office of Ratemahatmaya until 1938 when the administrative functions of that office were transferred to a regular civil servant known as the divisional revenue officer (D.R.O.). Nor were the authority and influence of the family destroyed by this last reorganization, for several members have since served in the area as D.R.O.'s (cf. Leach 1961a, p. 29). Moreover the family has also been prominent in electoral politics, providing members of parliament and cabinet ministers in the governments of both D. S. Senanayake and his son, Dudley Senanayake.

Leach has pointed out that in colonial times "although the Ratemahatmaya was held responsible for law and order within his district, he was provided with very little administrative apparatus through which he might legitimately assert authority" (ibid., p. 69). Each Ratemahatmaya's district (*palata*) was divided into several subdistricts (*korales*), each of which was under the authority of an official known as a Korala. Each *korale* was in turn divided into several *tulanas*, each under a headman known as a Lekama or, later, an Arachchi. The principal instrument of local government became the village tribunal, whose area of jurisdiction was that of the *korale*. Established by the British under the Village Communities Ordinance of 1871 in a self-conscious attempt to revive the Kandyan Sinhalese *gamsabha* (village court), the village tribunal enjoyed both administrative and judicial functions (Goonesekere 1958), although these later became separated, the former being taken over by the village committee and the latter by the rural court. Leach argues that "since . . . the Village Tribunal covered one whole *korale*, the Korala was the key official in the day-to-day running of the administration. In the last analysis, the power of the Ratemahatmaya depended on his ability to keep control of the various Korala" (1961a, p. 76).

Leach contends that this was largely achieved by the Ratemahatmaya's control of the system of *variga sabha* (caste courts), which functioned alongside the village tribunals, but which the British did not formally recognize. Appointment to the *variga* courts of all castes was in the hands of the Ratemahatmaya, who also had the right to confirm or deny the courts' decisions. Moreover, Leach argues that although "most of the cases which came before the *variga* court were formally concerned with issues of caste and sex . . . the difference [between these and] most present-day disputes . . . internal to the village community [which] have their focus in some kind of quarrel over rights to irrigation water [is] more apparent than real" (ibid., p. 71). In practice "the *variga* court dealt with nearly all disputes that might arise between members of the same village community, while the Village Tribunal concerned itself with major crimes, disputes between villagers and the Crown, and property disputes between members of different *variga*" (ibid., p. 70).

Not only was the *variga* court an important judicial institution in its own right but the Ratemahatmaya's control of it enabled him to contain the potentially independent authority of the Korala. The latter, like the Lekama or Arachchi below him, was appointed by the British administration after consultation with the leading villagers of the district in which he would hold office. Leach shows that these leading villagers were themselves likely to be officeholders in the *variga* court system and therefore selected by the Ratemahatmaya. They could recompense the Ratemahatmaya for their coveted titles by approving only those candidates for the office of Korala whom the Ratemahatmaya himself recommended.

A further point in Leach's argument must be modified before being applied to the particular case of the Veddas. He is concerned to show that it was to the Ratemahatmaya's advantage vis-à-vis the Korala that while the constituent communities of a single *variga* are not normally contained within a single *korale* they are confined within a single Ratemahatmaya's *palata*. This may be the case with communities of the numerous Goyigama caste, which is divided into a number of mutually exclusive *varigas*, but the Anuradhapura Veddas, by contrast, form a single *variga*, which is dispersed among several Ratemahatmayas' districts. Although this appears to raise the prospect of conflict between Ratemahatmayas in the disposal of offices in the Vedda *variga* court, it does not seriously affect the political argument. In the first place the evidence of recorded meetings of the Vedda *variga* court suggests that representatives from all the widely dispersed Vedda communities did not attend, but only those members who lived relatively close at hand. The meeting of the Vedda court described by Leach (1961a, pp. 307-9) provides an instance of this. The members of the court represented only four communities, and all lived within five or six miles of the village in which the case was being heard. Their villages were all contained within a single *palata*, but were divided among two *korales*. Secondly, and perhaps more importantly, in all districts the Veddas have formed a small and backward minority whose political strength cannot rival that of the more prosperous Goyigama. No Vedda, for example, was ever appointed to the office of *tulana* headman, let alone to that of Korala.

At about the time that the office of Ratemahatmaya was replaced by that of D.R.O. the office of Korala was also abolished and the village tribunal was replaced by the rural court under the presidency of a regular stipendiary magistrate. Leach's argument culminates in the demonstration that it was precisely from this time that "the Rate-mahatmaya lost interest in the maintenance of . . . *variga* institutions" (ibid., p. 78) and that the *variga* court system began to decay.

At the present time the lowest salaried officer in the local administrative bureaucracy is the Gramasevaka, the title now given to the former Lekama or Arachchi, the *tulana* headman. The duties of the Gramasevaka, who may be responsible for up to twenty villages, are mainly clerical. Births and deaths, for example, must be reported to him, and disputes can be referred to him and entered in his official diary, but he has few powers of administrative decision. He does not normally play an active part in the day-to-day affairs of the villages in his division.

In most cases, then, the officeholders and unofficial leaders within a village are not outsiders imposed by government authority but are the products of political processes inside the community itself. In Kandyan and early colonial times village leadership was evidently provided by the Gamarala, whom Ievers describes in his *Manual of the North-Central Province* as "the hereditary chief cultivator of the village" (1899, p. 172), and of whom he writes: "In each village the Gamarala was and is still the chief man" (ibid., p. 61). In Codrington's account of the proper procedure for founding a new village, obtained from informants in 1909, it appears that the Gamarala was originally elected (Codrington 1938, p. 63), but thereafter the office was hereditary. The Gamarala enjoyed a particular holding in the village lands, known as the *gam-vasama*, which was inherited in the normal way, and whoever held the *gamvasama* was, ipso facto, entitled to the office of Gamarala. Leach emphasizes that a village often contained more than one Gamarala because village lands are commonly divided into a number of *baga* (sections), over each of which a Gamarala presides. On the other hand, on the basis of essays on various aspects of social life in the North-Central Province written in competition in the 1930s, Pieris asserts that "when the Gamarala was a man of authority, a village having more than one headman always recognized the superior authority of the chief Gamarala (*pradhana gamarala*)" (Pieris 1956, p. 236).

The basis of land tenure in the traditional and ideal scheme of Kandyan feudalism was the provision of certain services known as *rajakariya* (king's duty).[3] A full analysis of this institution would require a comprehensive examination of the Kandyan state for, as Pieris remarks in his account of *Sinhalese Social Organization*, it was "on this system of service tenures [that] the machinery of state administration largely hinged" (ibid., p. 95; see also Obeyesekere 1967, pp. 215-21; Leach 1961a, pp. 165-68). Suffice it to say here that all tenures were deemed to derive ultimately from the king, though often through one or more intermediaries, and that all land was held in return for the execution of certain economic, political, and ritual duties, the nature of which depended in part upon the tenant's caste status. In Nuvarakalaviya the economic aspect of *rajakariya* included the proper maintenance of the village irrigation system.[4]

In this perspective the Gamarala may be seen as the chief tenant of a village or of a section (*baga*) of a village, holding his land directly from the king, or from a temple priest, or from an aristocratic landlord. His fellow villagers may likewise be seen as the Gamarala's subtenants, on whom he could call in the execution of his duties and with respect to whom he enjoyed certain privileges in landholding and cultivation (Pieris 1956, pp. 238-39, 246; Leach 1961a, pp. 151-55, 166-68).

3. There are of course important differences between Kandyan society and that of medieval Europe, but there are also sufficient structural similarities to justify following Leach (1959) and Obeyesekere (1967, pp. 14-16, 215-21) in describing the Kandyan kingdom as a feudal society. Pieris (1956) provides a recent account of Sinhalese social organization in the Kandyan period. D'Oyly (1929) and Hayley (1923) are important earlier sources.

4. It may be worth noting that caste profession neither is nor was a full-time economic occupation. The Goyigama (Cultivator) caste people have no monopoly on paddy cultivation. Members of the service castes in Anuradhapura District, such as Washermen and Drummers, may pursue their traditional callings, but they live in their own tank villages and devote the greater part of their time to agriculture. Likewise Blacksmiths and Potters, who may devote more time to their special crafts, also inhabit their own villages and cultivate land that, in Kandyan times, would have been held partly in return for the execution of their caste professions.

The implementation by the British of the Paddy Lands Irrigation Ordinance of 1856 and its successors required the appointment of an irrigation headman in each village.[5] Ievers notes that "the irrigation headman . . . was generally the Gamarala, and continues to be so under the title of Vel Vidane" (1899, p. 62). Leach confirms that "in Pul Eliya, down to 1926, the office of Vel Vidane was always held by someone who was simultaneously entitled to call himself Gamarala" (1961a, p. 154). Authority, however, now resided almost exclusively in the former office. The Vel Vidane was made responsible for what had formerly been the economic aspects of *rajakariya*, which the ordinance determined to be owed directly to the state. He was thus required to execute government regulations concerning irrigation practices. He personally controlled the operation of the sluices. He presided over the meeting of cultivators that determined the fields to be cultivated in a particular season. He supervised the cultivators' performance of their duties to clear irrigation channels, build protective fences and watch-huts, and he could bring those who neglected these duties before the village tribunal. He made all necessary clerical returns to the government, and himself received a commission of 1½ percent of the produce.

Although the Vel Vidane's official duties were thus concerned with agriculture, their scope afforded him a sufficient basis of authority from which to influence and even direct nonagricultural affairs within the village. Moreover it seems commonly to have been the case that the Ratemahatmaya, or later the D.R.O., who was after all responsible for several scores of villages, habitually turned to the Vel Vidane as the sole authoritative representative of his community. By the skillful presentation of himself as such to his superiors, and as the local embodiment of governmental authority to his fellow villagers, the Vel Vidane was able to achieve that domination of his community that led Leach to describe his office as "dictatorial" (1961a, p. 154).

In theory the Vel Vidane was elected by his fellow villagers, but the long association of the offices of Gamarala and Vel Vidane in the hands of the same individual suggests that other, more traditional, factors may have diverted the operation of an ideal scheme of representative democracy. But if the details of how a Vel Vidane acquired office remain obscure, the evidence is plain enough that once having obtained office he was reluctant to abandon it, and that his period of tenure was characteristically marked by his own rising prosperity (see below, chapters 5, 6, and 7; cf. Leach 1961a, pp. 28, 193).

As the independent authority of the Vel Vidane's office became

5. See Roberts (1967) for an analysis of these ordinances, and Roberts (1973) for a more general account of land problems and policies in the nineteenth century.

recognized, so that of the Gamarala declined. At the beginning of the present century, when the British surveyed the area and definitively settled land categories, most tanks were deemed to be crown property. This established the villagers as tenants of the crown with respect to their water supplies and was consistent with the irrigation ordinance's assertion that obligations related to irrigation practices were owed directly to the state. At the same time the paddy fields of most villages were determined to be private ancestral property, a decision that destroyed the last vestiges of the Gamarala's intermediate feudal status between his fellow villagers and some superior landlord. His economic responsibilities having been already transferred to the Vel Vidane, he was left with little more than an hereditary title that incurred a few ritual duties within the village. These duties were still imposed in Pul Eliya in 1954 (Leach 1961a, p. 167), but I found no evidence of their present performance in any Vedda village.

This difference should not encourage the speculation, permitted perhaps by the ambiguous position of the Veddas in the Kandyan caste and feudal structures, that the office of Gamarala was of less moment among them than among the Goyigama, or even that it was not recognized at all. Official nineteenth-century records listing the names of Vedda cultivators in particular villages belie this (e.g., Sri Lanka National Archives file 20, vol. 27). The title was also frequently invoked in genealogies obtained in 1970, and in the village with which I am most familiar is today claimed by a member of the cultivation committee (see below) who is commonly referred to as the Vidane and who holds a section of the paddy fields identified as the *gamvasama*.

The rule of the Vel Vidane was formally ended by the Paddy Lands Act of 1958, which transferred his official functions to a new, elected body known as the cultivation committee. The intended scope of this ambitious piece of legislation is indicated in its schedule:

An Act to provide security of tenure to tenant cultivators of paddy lands; to specify the rent payable by tenant cultivators to landlords; to enable the wages of agricultural labourers to be fixed by Cultivation Committees and agricultural labourers to be appointed as tenant cultivators and collective farmers; to provide for the consolidation of holdings of paddy lands, the establishment of collective farms for paddy cultivation, and the regulation of the interest on loans to paddy cultivators and the charges made for the hire by cultivators of implements and buffaloes; to make provision for the establishment of Cultivation Committees; to specify the powers and duties of such Committees . . . to abolish the liability of proprietors to pay remuneration to irrigation headmen. . . . [Paddy Lands Act, 1958, no. 1, p. 3]

Much of all this either did not apply or has not been made to apply to the Vedda villages of Anuradhapura District. Relations between landlords and their tenant cultivators remain much as they were previously. Cultivation committees do not fix agricultural wages. Committee members are unaware of many of the powers conferred upon them by an act that seems designed to facilitate the development of cultivation committees into the executive committees of collective farms. Injunctions on the cultivation committee to ensure "that paddy lands are row-sown or transplanted . . . that the fertility of the soil of paddy lands is improved and maintained by the application of fertilizers in adequate quantities . . . that paddy lands are kept free from weeds . . . ," and so on (Paddy Lands [Amendment] Act, 1964, no. 11, section 36A) have had little visible effect in the Vedda villages. Nevertheless, the cultivation committees are in operation, and they do perform the functions previously entrusted to the Vel Vidane. Even if the full potential of their establishment for social change is as yet unrealized, their introduction is a sufficiently radical departure from earlier practice to merit some close inspection.

The area of a cultivation committee's jurisdiction is decided within the official bureaucracy. The committee is composed of twelve members who are elected for three years. Members do not represent wards or constituencies within the committee's area of jurisdiction. Each elector is entitled to cast his twelve votes for any properly nominated candidates, although he can only vote once for any particular candidate.

The Paddy Lands Act prescribes that cultivation committee members "shall be elected by the qualified cultivators of paddy land wholly or mainly lying within the local jurisdiction of [the] Committee from among themselves" (Paddy Lands [Amendment] Act, 1964, no. 11, section 25). " 'Qualified cultivators' mean owner cultivators, tenant cultivators or collective farmers, who are citizens of Ceylon" (ibid.). " 'Cultivator,' with reference to any extent of paddy land, means a person who, by himself or *by any member of his family* carries out on such extent—(a) two or more of the operations of ploughing, sowing and reaping and (b) the operation of tending or watching the crop" (Paddy Lands Act, 1958, no. 1, section 63, as amended by Paddy Lands [Amendment] Act, 1961, no. 61, section 9; emphasis added). It may be noted at once that although land is usually managed by men, and women work only in the fields at harvest, this formula gives full voting rights to those female owners and tenants whose holdings, as is commonly the case, are worked by their spouses and sons.

The following description of the one election I was able to observe shows the practical application of these rules.

The former Vel Vidane of Kukulewa, a Vedda village, was respon-

sible only for the paddy lands within Kukulewa itself. The Mekichchawa
Cultivation Committee, however, also contains three neighboring
villages of different caste affiliation within its area of jurisdiction. This
feature is common, but the case is unusual in that the Vedda village is
here the largest of the four, providing about 40 percent of the electors.
The three other villages are all Goyigama communities, but they belong
to two different *varigas*.

The failure to divide the committee's area of jurisdiction into a
number of constituencies encourages the formation of alliances between candidates from different villages. A man cannot expect to be
elected solely by the votes of his own community, and he is likely to
be more or less unfamiliar to a number of voters in villages of foreign
variga. He therefore seeks the public endorsement of respected figures
in such villages, many of whom will themselves be candidates.

No public meetings were held prior to the Mekichchawa elections,
but for several days small groups of candidates, their friends, and
sponsors could be observed canvassing in the several villages. Candidates from foreign villages were introduced and recommended by their
allies in the village being canvassed, and voters were asked to pledge
their support. In some cases pledges were encouraged by the generous
dispensation of home-brewed liquor, and private accusations of bribery
were not infrequent. Canvassing appeared to be directed exclusively to
men, although it might have been expected that in a society in which
the rule of inheritance is bilateral, women would comprise a significant
proportion of the electorate.

Female owners and tenants are, however, a minority, despite the
ideal rule of inheritance. This is a result not only of deviations from the
rule but also of the substantial grants of land made in recent years
under the Land Development Ordinance, most of which have been
made to men. Moreover, candidates for office are deterred from solicit-
ing female votes both by cultural rules governing interaction between
the sexes and by the widespread male belief that women cast their votes
in accordance with their husbands' directions. It was impossible to
assess the accuracy of this belief because the ballot was secret.

The election took place only a month after I began field work and
I was not at the time familiar with the subtleties of political alliance
and division within the communities. The candidates grouped themselves into two opposed parties, the term *party* being quite appropriate
because, as I later discovered, the groupings largely reflected the candidates' loyalties to the two major national political parties. Most of one
group were supporters of the U.N.P. (United National Party); most of
the other were supporters of the S.L.F.P. (Sri Lanka Freedom Party).

The election itself, however, did not appear to be contested by appeal to national party loyalties, and the formal electoral machinery certainly made no provision for this.

Informants more commonly described the contest as one between the incumbent members and their opponents. This prompted some critical discussion of whether the incumbents had justified their tenure of office, but it also permitted some lively and unflattering speculation concerning the intentions of the opposition, particularly with respect to the committee's bank account.

The election itself was conducted in Kukulewa by officials of the Department of Agrarian Services. Two police constables were also in attendance. When the presiding officer called for nominations, one man stepped forward to nominate ten candidates, nine of whom were members of the previous committee. Three former members had decided not to run for re-election, and one new candidate was included. The opposition then nominated eleven candidates. All twenty-one candidates were men.

The opposition party in Kukulewa itself was chiefly organized by H. V. Bandathe, the former Vel Vidane. This man had held office for thirty years and had then sat on the first cultivation committee, but had subsequently resigned under threat of removal for dereliction of duty. In promoting his candidates in Kukulewa he emphasized that the Vedda village was underrepresented on the committee and that he intended his ticket to redress the balance. But the potential candidates he approached fell away and in the end the only Kukulewa villager on the opposition ticket was his own son. The incumbent party, by contrast, included three Kukulewa villagers, one of whom was a close classificatory son of the former Vel Vidane (his mother's sister's son's son). This alignment suggested a certain lack of enthusiasm for the opposition, which was amply confirmed in the election results. All ten of the incumbent party's candidates were returned, leaving only two seats for the most popular among the opposition.

There was a heavy turnout of voters, estimated at more than 80 percent of those qualified. Women appeared to figure disproportionately among those who failed to vote. When the results were being tabulated it became clear that most voters had followed party lines, but that a number had cast only a few of the twelve votes to which they were entitled, perhaps restricting themselves to candidates from their own villages.

After the results were announced the new committee immediately went into session and elected its president, secretary, and treasurer. Subsequently the traditional meetings of cultivators were held in each village to decide, in view of the current water level in the tank and the likelihood of further rain, which fields to cultivate in the coming season, what methods of cultivation to employ, and the dates by which the several agricultural operations were to be completed.[6] The secretary was the only committee member, other than those who held land in the village in question, to attend these meetings. The full committee thereafter met at monthly intervals during the cultivation season to discuss directives and recommendations from the Department of Agrarian Services, whose local officers sometimes attended themselves, and to initiate and debate proposals to improve the practice of cultivation. The committee also attempted to resolve minor disputes between cultivators and considered action against those who had neglected their *rajakariya*. If a committee's warnings to such offenders are ignored it can bring a case against them in the rural courts. Likewise, if the informal procedures of the committee fail to settle a dispute over water rights, for example, or the division of an inheritance, either party can bring an action in the courts.

The Mekichchawa Cultivation Committee also appointed agents from among its members to take particular responsibility for each of the blocks of paddy land within its jurisdiction. The most senior of the three Kukulewa members was appointed agent for the ancestral fields and the other two divided the three other blocks of land in the village between them. One of the agent's responsibilities is to collect the "acre levy" of six rupees paid to the government on each cultivated acre. In compensation for his efforts the agent receives 40 percent of the amount he collects, while the secretary, who has more extensive duties than other committee members, retains a further 10 percent.

In this respect, as in others, the system of cultivation committees retains its links with earlier practices. The agent does not receive a fixed proportion of the produce, as did the Vel Vidane, but like the latter his fees are directly related to the extent of cultivation. Again, the traditional practice of holding cultivators' meetings at the beginning of the season is carried over under the new system. We have seen too that in the case of Kukulewa, which is in this respect typical, although the cultivation committee embraces several villages the individual agents responsible for particular blocks of land are men of the village in which the land is situated. Kukulewa is not typical, however, in the fate that has befallen its former Vel Vidane. Many other Vel Vidanes have

6. It will be understood that since paddy cultivation requires different quantities of water at the various stages of the plant's growth, the cultivation of all plots using the same irrigation channels must be closely coordinated.

continued to serve as elected members and officials of their cultivation committees.

Such evidence of continuity should not obscure the fundamental changes the new system implies. The establishment of cultivation committees challenges the substantial autonomy of the individual village, which was earlier preserved through the mediating offices of the Gamarala and the Vel Vidane. The lingering feudal associations of the former offices, most strikingly expressed in the Gamarala's ritual obligations, have now given way to an institution more fitted to the bureaucratic character of the modern state and more appropriate to its ideal of representative democracy.

Other changes that have been noted point in the same general direction. The ritual dimension of *rajakariya* has been stripped away and the personal nature of the *rajakariya* relationship, linking a particular cultivator with the particular landlord to whom his service was due, has been removed. What remains is a rational economic and contractual relationship between the cultivator and the state, seen in this context as the landlord of his irrigation works. Similarly the replacement of the Ratemahatmaya by the D.R.O., and of the Gamarala by the Vel Vidane, as indeed also the collapse of the *variga* courts as judicial institutions, represent the withdrawal of a rule of kinship from operation in the administrative domain.

It will not be necessary to describe in detail all the other administrative developments that have had an effect on the village society. For the most part they have shared a similar character, but either their import has been less or they are themselves less relevant to my subject. For example, the village committee is an elected local government body with an area of jurisdiction comparable to that of the former *korale*. Its effective powers are few and it plays little part in village life, but insofar as it does have responsibilities regarding the building and maintenance of minor roads and culverts, wells, cemeteries, and sanitary reserves, to that extent the autonomy of the village is again reduced.

Nevertheless it is important to bear in mind that the period covered by this study has been one of major change in the national society. Great events in the history of Sri Lanka, such as the establishment of parliamentary democracy and the attainment of independence within the Commonwealth are largely ignored here, but in recent years the Veddas have had to adapt to a wide variety of exogenous changes that have affected their daily lives in numerous ways. Any analysis of their social organization must assess the impact of such developments as improved communications, the construction of schools and medical facilities, attempts to eliminate malaria, governmental efforts to restore the major irrigation works of the Anuradhapura kingdom and to install new colonies of pioneer cultivators, and the tentative establishment of light industries in the region. All these developments are discussed later as they impinge upon my central theme, but my treatment of them is in no way exhaustive. Other exogenous factors, the impact of which has been more direct and decisive, such as changes in the system of land tenure, governmental assistance in the expansion of paddy cultivation, and the spread of the cash economy, receive more detailed attention in the next two chapters, in which the emphasis switches from the administrative structure to matters of kinship and economic organization.

3

Land Categories and Kin Groups

VILLAGE LAND CATEGORIES

All but five of the forty-six villages, whose inhabitants make up the overwhelming majority of the Vedda *variga*, lie within Nuwaragam *palata* and Hurulu *palata* in Anuradhapura District, an area of approximately twenty-five hundred square miles. Of the remainder two are in Vavuniya District, two in Trincomalee District and one in Polonnaruwa District (map 2.1). The most widely separated villages are sixty miles apart. The Vedda *variga* is thus very much more widely dispersed than the Goyigama *variga* described by Leach (1961a, pp. 22, 83).

The Veddas refer to their settlements by the term *gama*. Although I translate this term as "village," it is important to recognize, as Obeyesekere has pointed out, that one of the etymological meanings of *gama* is "a collection of land holdings" and that its core meaning is "estate" (1967, pp. 12-14). It might then be anticipated that where a village contains more than one tank (*wewa*), each with its associated paddy fields, it will be thought of as comprising more than one *gama*. Veddas admit this possibility in principle, but the normal practice in such cases is to specify that a single *gama* includes more than one *wewa*. This usage has both physical and social references that are generally in accord with one another, as well as with the administrative unit that is also called a *gama*. In other words what I describe as a village in most cases corresponds not only to the administrative division known as a *gama* or village, but also to what the Veddas call a *gama* when they are

58

referring to a distinct parcel of land occupied by a community of people who stand in a particular relationship to one another and to the land itself. There are, however, some marginal and exceptional cases. In recent years a number of small and long abandoned tanks have been restored, often by individual effort, and new paddy fields brought under cultivation. If the pioneer cultivator has not shifted his residence I treat the new estate as part of the former village, even if it lies outside the *gama* as defined by the administration. If, however, the pioneer has moved his residence to the new estate in a self-conscious attempt to found a new community, I treat the new settlement as an independent village, even if it lies within the boundaries of the present *gama* as defined administratively. Thus, to take the extreme case, S. Herathamy, formerly of Kuda Tammanawa, has recently established a new settlement, lying within the administrative boundaries of Kuda Tammanawa but spatially separated from the other houses of the village and has given it the name of Heratgama. Although the settlement contains only a single household it does comprise a distinct estate and a distinct community. I therefore respect the disengagement that the name *Heratgama* implies and treat it as a separate village from Kuda Tammanawa.

One effect of this procedure is that the forty-six villages composing the *variga* are communities of extremely variable size. Their populations range between 8 and 552 (table 3.1), with an average of 144 and median of 115.

TABLE 3.1

POPULATION OF VEDDA VILLAGES, 1970

Population	Number of Villages
1-50	15
51-100	7
101-200	10
201-300	8
301-400	4
401-500	1
501-600	1

Although it is obvious that a village containing only one or two households differs in at least one important respect from a village of ninety households, it is no less true that a common culture, participation in the same network of social relations, and similar ecological circumstances impose a certain uniformity on all the villages. Common patterns of village topography, settlement, land use, household formation and composition, kinship rules and behavior, and economic occupations are shared by all the Vedda villages, whatever their size.[1]

The layout of Vedda villages observes the general pattern of the area, which is by now well understood. Ievers (1899), Codrington (1938) and Pieris (1956) provide synthetic descriptions that are balanced by Leach's detailed analysis (1961a) and Yalman's briefer account (1967, pp. 247-62) of specific Goyigama villages. Apart from a recent change in the location of house sites, to be discussed below, much of Rhys Davids's description still holds good: "Each village consists, firstly, of the tank and the field below it; secondly, of the huts of the shareholders hidden in the shade of their fruit trees, either under the bund or along the sides of the field; and thirdly, of all the waste land lying within the boundaries of the parish or village" (1871, p. 90).

The fundamental categories of land are *mada idam* (paddy land or mud land) and *goda idam* (high land). The latter is not necessarily of any great elevation; it is simply land that is not, or cannot be, irrigated. Accordingly *mada idam* includes not only paddy land proper but also other wet lands, such as the house-site area in Pul Eliya that lies between the tank and the paddy fields (Leach 1961a, p. 54, and maps B and C, pp. 44-45). Cutting across this classification is a tripartite division according to the terms of tenure. Here the categories are *paraveni* (ancestral), *sinakkera* (freehold) and *badu* (lease). Use of these terms is not always consistent with present practice. For example, a block of paddy land that is immediately adjacent to the main field in Kukulewa is called *goda akkera*. The latter term indicates that it is freehold "acre land" (*sinakkera*), the former that it was previously unirrigated high land (*goda idam*).

Paraveni property comprises those house sites, gardens, and paddy fields that were in use when the colonial government surveyed the area at the beginning of the present century. Such lands were treated as ancestral private property. All other land and most village tanks were deemed to be crown property. Subsequently villagers were enabled to purchase plots of crown lands either for new house sites or in order to "asweddumize" them, that is, to develop them into permanent paddy

1. In this and the following chapter the general process of Vedda village life is described with disproportionate reference to Kukulewa, the village in which research was most heavily concentrated. In putting together a synthetic account of Vedda kinship and economic organization, the richness and depth of the Kukulewa data outweigh Kukulewa's atypical size (largest of all the Vedda villages). The Kukulewa facts can still be used to illuminate very general aspects of Vedda social life, while the peculiarities of individual villages, including their distinctive demographic histories, will receive the attention they deserve subsequently.

fields.[2] Land thus acquired is freehold and is called *sinakkera* in recognition of its administrative measurement in quantities of acres, roods, and perches.[3]

Since the Land Development Ordinance of 1935, however, it has no longer been possible to acquire *sinakkera* land from the government.[4] Crown land is now granted to villagers only on permanent lease (*badu*), under conditions that are compared unfavorably with those governing *sinakkera* and *paraveni* property. In the first place villagers fear eviction from their *badu* lands. Second, tenancy involves the payment of an annual rent. Third, the tenant does not enjoy the same legal freedom to mortgage his holding (L.D.O., 1956 Revision, section 43) that is available with respect to freehold land. Fourth, the tenant is required to nominate a single heir to his holding (L.D.O., 1956 Revision, section 81), a regulation that reflects governmental concern to prevent the excessive fragmentation of holdings, but directly contradicts the cultural rule of equal inheritance by all children. The Veddas have devised a number of schemes for evading what is to them an objectionable restriction, but as most *badu* lands have been obtained since 1950 and have not yet been subject to inheritance, it is too soon to tell whether such schemes will, or can, be effectively practiced.

Legal changes regarding land tenure thus provide a crude index to the expansion of paddy cultivation in the villages. With few exceptions *paraveni* land is land that was cultivated prior to 1900, while *sinakkera* and *badu idam* represent accretions between 1900 and 1935, and 1935 and the present, respectively. The present holdings of paddy land in Kukulewa comprise 33 acres of *paraveni* land, 33 acres *sinakkera*, and 64 acres *badu idam*.[5] This expansion of cultivable land can be

2. "Asweddumize" is a Sinhalese-English term used to describe the process whereby previously unirrigated land is turned into permanently cultivable paddy land.

3. 40 perches = 1 rood; 4 roods = 1 acre.

4. Leach's analysis of the Pul Eliya land map (1961a, pp. 43-66) includes an assessment of the motives behind this and other changes in government policy.

5. These figures are not in fact the total of all registered holdings in the village. First, I have omitted the lands under two small tanks that have long since passed into the hands of neighboring villages. Second, I have included only those fields that were cultivated at least once during the period of research. The plots thus excluded are of two types: (a) those that are not at present accessible to irrigation and (b) plots recently acquired that have not yet been asweddumized. If these fields were included the Kukulewa totals would be 33 acres of *paraveni* land, 40 acres *sinakkera*, and 98 acres *badu idam*.

I am unfortunately unable to present comparable statistics for all the other villages. Our brief visits to the villages did not permit us to determine which holdings were genuinely and regularly cultivable, and the informants were inclined, if

compared with the growth of population, which in Kukulewa increased from 215 in 1901 to 552 in 1970, indicating a rise in the per capita holding of paddy land from 0.15 acres to 0.24 acres. There is a good deal of variability among the villages in both the rate of population growth and the expansion of the area under paddy cultivation. The figures for Kukulewa are typical only in the sense that a significant expansion of both population and paddy cultivation has been the common experience of almost all the villages.

One result of bringing more land under paddy cultivation has been the breakdown of the traditional formula: "one village-one tank." Many of the larger villages now contain several independent blocks of paddy land. New irrigation works have been constructed and abandoned ones restored, partly by private initiative but also with government assistance and encouragement. Most of this work having been done in the last twenty or thirty years, the fields under these irrigation works are typically *badu idam*. Some of the land thus granted is well irrigated but much of it is extremely marginal.[6]

With few exceptions, inherited paddy land is physically divided among the heirs and at any one time is likely to be the recognized property of a single individual. By contrast rights in a *paraveni* house-site plot, which is usually also *mada idam* (mud land), are commonly shared among a number of individuals, only a few, or in the present even none, of whom actually reside on it. If both a man's parents were natal members of the village in which he lives, he may inherit rights in two different house-site plots. If his wife's parents also married endogamously within the same village, he may even have a choice of four residential sites. Whichever he chooses, his children will inherit rights in all four sites, and so on. Such rights are not contingent upon residence

---

they thought the anthropologist was unable or unlikely to check, to describe as *paraveni* lands that were really *sinakkera* or even *badu*. That they should wish to present their holdings as ancestral will not surprise readers of *Pul Eliya* (Leach 1961a). An accurate assessment of their claims would have been possible if we had consulted all the various official records concerning the villages, but we did not find time for this lengthy business. Nevertheless in later chapters I make some general inferences about the expansion of paddy cultivation over the last forty years based largely on the distinction between lease (*badu*) land and freehold (including both *paraveni* and *sinakkera*) land, which was relatively less difficult to determine.

6. This suggests another reason why *badu idam* is less highly valued than *paraveni* and *sinakkera* lands. Comparison of the figures given for all registered paddy land in Kukulewa with those for the land that is actually cultivated will show that *badu idam* accounts for nearly the whole difference and that one-third of the *badu idam* is not being cultivated at all. But, as I emphasize in the text, it is by no means the case that all *badu idam* is unproductive or uneconomical to cultivate (cf. Leach 1961a, pp. 50-52).

or any other factor beyond the heir's memory, which, however, does not often extend any further back than his grandparents.

House-site plots do eventually become divided, but not as rapidly as paddy landholdings. Thus while the common occupation of paddy land is usually a brief phase in the ongoing process of land tenure, concurrent and prolonged occupation of a single house-site plot or compound (*vatta*) by a number of related but independent households is, or was, the normal practice. But it is doubtful that compounds and their associated compound groups ever enjoyed the crucial structural significance that they assume in Pul Eliya, where rights in a *paraveni* house site are intimately involved with the possession of ancestral paddy land and with accepted membership in both the local community and the *variga* as a whole (Leach 1961a, p. 193 et passim). Perhaps this reflects the possibility that paddy cultivation has been less crucial in the Vedda than in the Goyigama economy. Certainly the government program to encourage villagers to move their dwellings away from the typically damp and unsanitary conditions of *paraveni* house-site areas has not encountered the resistance among the Veddas that Leach predicted for Pul Eliya (1961a, pp. 60, 304).[7]

Few *paraveni* house-site areas have been totally abandoned by the Veddas, but most now contain only a minority of the dwellings in the village. The congregation of more than one household in a single compound is more common in the ancestral area than elsewhere but such compound groups rarely contain more than two or three households. Most villagers have responded to the government's promise of a building subsidy and have moved in the last fifteen to twenty years into new houses on one-acre plots of *badu* land obtained from the crown. The new house sites are *goda idam* (high land) plots, and are usually stretched out along either side of whatever cart tracks or paths pass through the village. Because the one-acre plots are also a good deal larger than the average traditional compounds, one result has been the widespread dispersal of the traditionally closely clustered settlement.

Vedda villages contain few buildings that are not private houses. Some shops are separate structures, but many are also dwellings. Some of the larger villages contain a school and a house for the schoolteacher. Only one has an active Buddhist temple (*vihara*). No cooperative stores, dispensaries, or local government offices are located in Vedda villages.

Apart from house sites, the few public buildings, tracks, and foot

---

7. Government officials admit that this program has indeed encountered considerable resistance. Casual comparison with villages of other *variga* tends to confirm that the Veddas have been distinctly forward in moving their house sites. A brief excursion to Pul Eliya in 1969 suggested that most dwellings were still located in the traditional house-site area.

paths, the remainder of the high land within the villages is given over to scrub jungle. It is classified as waste land and remains crown property. It is used for chena (slash-and-burn) cultivation, forage for cattle and goats, occasional hunting, the collection of house posts, wattle, firewood, and some wild plants that are valued for food or medicine, disposal of the dead, reputed acts of illicit copulation, and the performance of other bodily functions. The more economically significant of these activities will be discussed later. But first I describe kinship and domestic organization within the villages.

THE *VARIGA*

The inhabitants of the forty-six Vedda villages form a single *variga* and consider one another to be their kinsmen (*nayo*). The Anuradhapura Veddas claim a remote common ancestry with the Veddas of the Veddaratta, but, although they will admit the latter to the same caste (*jati*) as themselves, they assign them to a different *variga*. There is in any case no direct contact between the two groups and, with certain exceptions, the Anuradhapura Veddas' relations of kinship and marriage are confined within their own forty-six villages. In other words the Anuradhapura Vedda *variga* is ideally, and to a large extent in practice, an endogamous group. Kinship is bilateral, and equal importance is attached to both patrilateral and matrilateral relatives. Membership in the *variga* is acquired by being the recognized child of parents both of whom are themselves *variga* members. There is no hint of the proliferation of exogamous matrilineal clans, also called *waruge*, which the Seligmanns (1911) described for the classic wild Veddas.

Leach claims that "the Nuvarakalaviya *variga* is a relatively corporate type of social group [not only because] its representative leaders (the members of the *variga* court) ultimately decide who is and who is not a member of the group but also because the *variga*, as an aggregate, has title in all the lands of all the villages comprising the *variga*; furthermore *variga* membership is directly linked with this title in land" (1961a, pp. 78-79). It will be seen that the first feature qualifies the *variga* as a corporation by Weber's (1947) criteria while the second is reminiscent of Maine (1888), although, as Fortes has recently emphasized, "in his [Maine's] view . . . rights and duties, office and property, are not the forces that generate corporations but the vehicles and media through the agency of which corporations express their intrinsic perpetuity" (1969, p. 293). Maine's concern with the perpetuity of corporations may in fact be more appropriate not only to the Vedda case, but also to the Goyigama *variga* described by Leach, than is an emphasis on property, because it is not at all clear in what sense "the *variga*, as an aggregate, has title in all the lands of all the villages comprising the *variga*." This is Leach's claim, but he also acknowledges that "the ownership rights of individual Sinhalese are, in theory, almost unconditional" (1961a, p. 132). His detailed analysis shows not only that paddy land in Pul Eliya is owned by individual *variga* members but that it is often sold by them to traders who are outside the *variga* (ibid., p. 174). That such land is soon bought back by other *variga* members evidently depends as much on the traders not being cultivators (ibid., p. 132) and on the informal sanctions that villagers can bring to bear on nonresident owners (ibid., p. 252), as on any notion that the *variga*, as an aggregate, has title to the land. Certainly the *variga* court in its heyday controlled membership of the group, and could thus ensure that at any one time there was an approximate fit between group membership and the possession of land in any village occupied by *variga* members. But Leach makes clear that this was achieved by manipulating membership, not by the direct control of property (ibid., p. 95).

The Vedda evidence is particularly striking on this point. In the last eighty years, and doubtless also earlier, a number of villages that were formerly in Vedda hands have passed completely to members of other *varigas* and are no longer inhabited by Veddas. This has been the cumulative result of individual transactions by the former Vedda owners. There is no evidence that the *variga*, as a whole, was ever involved.

The Vedda *variga* is not, then, a property-holding corporation. Nor has it, since the decay of the *variga* court system, enjoyed representative leadership. If the *variga* in its present form is to be considered corporate at all, it must be on the basis of its intrinsic perpetuity, achieved by "exclusive recruitment to restricted membership that carries actual or potential equality of status and mutuality of interests and obligations in its internal affairs" (Fortes 1969, p. 306). This is a matter of descent.

The concepts of descent and descent group have received a good deal of attention in recent years (see Fortes 1969, chap. 14, for a review and a further contribution). Much of the debate has focused on the applicability of these concepts to societies lacking a strictly unilineal rule, and should therefore be relevant to the case of the bilateral Veddas. Some critics (e.g., Leach 1962) have urged the retention of the usage established by Rivers (1924, p. 86), whereby descent is restricted to the regulation of membership in unilineal groups. It is argued that the discrete and nonoverlapping groups produced by automatic recruitment on the basis of birth alone are qualitatively different from those that have been called nonunilinear descent groups. Others have claimed that the latter are "comparable" (Davenport 1959,

p. 562) or "analogous" (Goodenough 1955, p. 72) or "functionally equivalent" (Firth 1963, p. 32) to the classic unilineal descent groups. They emphasize not only that nonunilineal descent groups are undoubtedly groups of genealogically connected kinsmen but that they also may act corporately to perform the functions that are elsewhere attributed to unilineal groups. The issue is thus one of recruitment, discreteness, and the degree of choice in affiliation, for it is recognized that membership of nonunilineal descent groups is commonly not adequately defined by rules of kinship alone. Firth, for example, writes that "in Polynesia descent, i.e., membership of a named kinship group, is usually not unilateral, but is conditioned to a large extent by residence" (1957, p. 4). Likewise Davenport states that "residence and social participation with a [nonunilineal descent] group frequently serve as either contingent or final factors in fixing present affiliation and that of descendants" (1959, p. 562; see also Keesing 1975).

Concern with the basis of recruitment, and hence with the discreteness of descent groups, is common in discussions of their corporate character, whether one prefers Maine's, or Weber's, or anyone else's model of a corporation.[8] And while it is evident that corporate groups of kinsmen need not recruit their membership on the basis of kinship alone, one may agree with Fortes that the rule of recruitment is a significant factor. It is for him a "crucial distinction . . . that 'descent groups' are closed by genealogical or quasi-genealogical criteria, whereas 'cognatic groups' are open by genealogical reckoning and are closed by non-kinship boundaries" (1969, p. 287).

But where do the Veddas fit into all this? Fortes has departed from Rivers to the extent that his genealogical criteria are not specifically unilineal. This admits the possibility, which he acknowledges, that certain groups in which the reckoning of kinship is cognatic may qualify as descent groups but not as cognatic groups. One such group is the Vedda *variga*, which is closed by the combined kinship criteria of bilaterality and endogamy.

It remains to take account of Leach's statement, made in connection with the very similar Pul Eliya *variga*, that "relationships of *descent* are not involved at all since there are no unilineal descent groups in which the individual automatically acquires a membership by virtue

8. It may be worth noting in this connection that the question of discreteness has nothing to do with that of overlapping membership, with which it appears to have sometimes been confused. It is evident that a group may yet be corporate and discrete where all its members also belong to other groups, each of which is likewise corporate and discrete, as in a system of double descent. Multiple membership is also possible in different corporations operating in the same field, as in the Western business world.

of his birth" (1961a, p. 95, emphasis in the original). This reiterates the contention that descent should be defined unilineally, to which Leach indicates elsewhere (1962, pp. 130-32) that he adheres on the grounds that in practice only a unilineal rule assigns a person, by virtue of birth alone, to unambiguous permanent and involuntary membership of a discrete, sectional grouping within the total society. The point is that in the statement quoted above it is the *variga* that is being considered as the total society. There are indeed no descent rules, unilineal or otherwise, that by themselves produce discrete, sectional groupings *within* the *variga*. But it may yet be useful to consider the *variga* itself as a descent group in relation to other groups recruited on the same or a similar basis.

Finally, it must be emphasized again that the corporate activities of the Vedda *variga* are severely circumscribed. It does not hold or control material property and it no longer has a representative and executive leadership. It does, however, restrict and perpetuate its membership by a precise rule of recruitment, which also defines the proper boundaries of kinship and marriage. As a group of kinsmen, who thereby enjoy "equality of status and mutuality of interests and obligations" (Fortes 1969, p. 306), the Vedda *variga* is thus distinguished from all other comparable groups. Even these features, which are among what Fortes calls "the bare essentials [of] corporateness" (ibid.), have been placed in jeopardy by the decay of the *variga* court, the representative institution. There is now no formal instrument to control recruitment and ensure the closure of the group, but only a persistent attachment to the ideology of *variga* endogamy, supported in some instances by the application of informal ad hoc sanctions.

KINSHIP AND MARRIAGE

As speakers of the local dialect of Sinhalese, the Veddas use a Dravidian system of kinship terminology. Classifications of terminological systems based on cousin terms (e.g., Murdock 1967, p. 158) do not distinguish Dravidian from Iroquois systems, although it is by now understood that the two are radically different (Lounsbury 1964; Kay 1967, pp. 83-85; Buchler and Selby 1968, pp. 233-46). Differences appear both in the classification of kinsmen beyond the range of first cousins and in the treatment of affines. There have been a number of recent descriptions of Sinhalese kinship terminology (Obeyesekere 1967, pp. 248-53; Yalman 1962, pp. 558-59; 1967, pp. 210-12; Leach 1960, pp. 124-26; 1961a, pp. 125-28; Tambiah 1958, p. 22; Pieris 1956, pp. 212-15) and my own treatment will therefore be as brief as possible.

Sex is distinguished throughout, generation as far as the grand-

parents and grandchildren. In Ego's own generation, and in the generation immediately senior and junior to him, kinsmen of the same sex are
divided into two classes. This is sometimes presented as a distinction
between "parallel" and "cross" relatives, sometimes as a distinction
between "kin" and "affines." In Ego's own generation the age of
parallel kin relative to Ego is specified. In the immediately senior
generation the age of parallel kin relative to the relevant parent is
specified.[9] The terms applied to consanguines are also applied to affines
consistently with marriage between cross-cousins. Thus, for example, a
man applies the same term towards his mother's brother and his wife's
father, the same term towards his father's sister's son and his wife's
brother, and the same term towards his sister's own son and his daughter's husband. These rules distribute kinsmen among twenty-two
categories as shown in table 3.2.[10]

These terms are employed beyond the range of first cousins according to the same logic that operates within that range. A "male cross-
cousin" of my cross-cousin is, ipso facto, either my "elder brother" or
my "younger brother." Any "son" of my maternal uncle is my "male
cross-cousin." Any "nephew" of anyone I call "elder brother" is my
"nephew," and all his "brothers" are also my "nephews," and so on.

9. In Ego's own generation the specification of relative age is achieved by the
use of radically different terms; in the senior generation only prefixes are used (see
table 3.2).

10. In order to save the reader the trouble of learning Sinhalese kinship terms I
shall use the English terms in the right-hand column of table 3.2 as follows. If a term
such as *elder brother* or *maternal uncle* appears without the use of quotation marks
it is to be understood, as in the common English usage, to refer to the primary kin
so designated. If, however, it appears in the form *"elder brother"* or *"maternal
uncle"* it is to be understood in the sense anthropologists describe as classificatory. I
shall sometimes further emphasize the distinction between *"cross-cousins"* and
cross-cousins by describing the latter as first cross-cousins. Alternatively, when I
want to specify a genealogical relationship, I shall make use of the accepted symbols *F*
(father), *M* (mother), *B* (brother), *Z* (sister), *S* (son), *D* (daughter), *H* (husband), *W*
(wife), and compounds thereof. Thus FZD and MBD will be described as cross-
cousins or first cross-cousins but not as "cross-cousins." With respect to cross
kinsmen of the speaker's own and parental generations this corresponds to the
Vedda use of the expression *ävässa* (essential, close). Veddas sometimes refer to
their MBS and FZS as *ävässa massinā*, and to their MB as *ävässa māma* or *māmandi*. They do not so refer to more remote "cross-cousins" or "maternal uncles."

Further, I shall normally translate *māma* as "maternal uncle" rather than
"father-in-law," *massinā*, as "male cross-cousin" rather than "brother-in-law," and
bāna as "nephew" rather than "son-in-law"; similarly with terms for female "cross"
relatives. I may also omit the sex indicator from "cross-cousin" where the context
makes it unnecessary and the qualifiers "elder" and "younger" from "brother" or
"sister" where both *aiya* and *malli* or *akka* and *nangi* are included in the reference.

TABLE 3.2

Categories of Vedda Kinship Terminology

Generation	Male Cross	Male Parallel	Female Cross	Female Parallel
G^{+2}		A		B
G^{+1}	C	D E F	K	G H J
G^{0}	L	M N	R	P Q
G^{-1}	S	T	V	U
G^{-2}		W		X

Category	Kinsmen Included	Sinhalese Term	Closest English Equivalent
A	FF, MF	sīya, kiriappa, *attappa*	grandfather
B	FM, MM	achchi, kiriamma, *attamma*	grandmother
C	MB, FZH; WF (male ego) HF (female ego)	māma	maternal uncle and/or father-in-law
D	FeB, MeZH	*loku appa,* loku tatta	father's elder brother
E	F	appa, *tatta*	father
F	FyB, MyZH	bāppa	father's younger brother
G	MeZ, FeBW	loku amma	mother's elder sister
H	M	amma	mother
J	MyZ, FyBW	balamma, *punchi amma*	mother's younger sister
K	FZ, MBW; WM (male ego) HM (female ego)	nända	paternal aunt
L	FZS, MBS, ZH; WB (male ego) HB (female ego)	massinā	male cross-cousin and/or brother-in-law
M	eB, FBS, MZS	aiya	elder brother
N	yB, FBS, MZS	malli	younger brother
P	eZ, FBD, MZD	akka	elder sister
Q	yZ, FBD, MZD	nangi	younger sister
R	FZD, MBD, BW; WZ (male ego); HZ (female ego)	nāna	female cross-cousin and/or sister-in-law
S	DH; ZS (male ego); BS (female ego)	bāna	son-in-law and/or nephew
T	S; BS (male ego); ZS (female ego)	puta	son
U	D; BD (male ego); ZD (female ego)	duva	daughter
V	SW; ZD (male ego); BD (female ego)	lēli	daughter-in-law and/or niece
W	SS, DS	munuburu	grandson
X	SD, DD	minibiri	granddaughter

NOTE: Where Sinhalese has alternative terms, the one most commonly employed by the Vedda is italicized.

Taken in conjunction with the rule of *variga* endogamy and the recognition of common kinship within the *variga*, it follows that all Veddas,
but no others, can be assigned to one or other of the kinship categories.
All that is necessary is to establish and agree upon the intervening links
that determine whether a fellow Vedda is a "maternal uncle," a "cross-
cousin," an "elder brother," a "younger brother," a "nephew," or
whatever. Since genealogical knowledge rarely extends more than two
generations back, if two Veddas do not share a common grandparent
their kinship relationship is usually calculated laterally. Thus Banda
says that Herathamy is his "male cross-cousin." The anthropologist,
who already knows that none of Banda's sibling group is married into
Herathamy's sibling group, asks Banda if Herathamy is either his MBS
or his FZS. Banda denies this. What then is the relationship? Banda
cannot specify a genealogical connection but says that his father calls
Herathamy's mother "younger sister"; Herathamy is therefore his
"male cross-cousin."

In this way a Vedda is normally able to assign every other member
of his village to a particular kinship category. He is often able to do the
same for the inhabitants of other Vedda villages that are nearby or with
which he has close kinship ties. But the inhabitants of more distant
villages will be largely or totally unknown to him, and he will refer to
them simply as *apee nayo* (our kinsmen). This provides a reservoir of
kinship that may be tapped as the occasion demands as, for example,
when a man migrates to another village or when he marries.

It will be evident that given the rule of endogamy, the maintenance
of a single terminological grid into which all kinship relations can be
precisely and unambiguously fitted is dependent upon marriage taking
place between the proper categories of kin, that is, in Vedda as in other
Dravidian systems, between "cross-cousins."[11] Just as the terminological

11. Since Yalman has been criticized for his very similar statement that "[Dra-
vidian] terminology is highly systematic, and all the terms imply bilateral cross-
cousin marriage, and such marriage is essential if the categories of kinship are to be
kept in order" (1962, p. 548), I should perhaps emphasize that my own statement
refers only to the logic of the terminology and does not imply either that the
Veddas do marry their cross-cousins or that they do in fact keep their kinship categories in order. These are substantive matters, which will be discussed shortly.
Yalman's critics have shown that he does not consistently observe this distinction
and that "he makes the transition from terminological rules to the way in which
they are applied on the ground, from cross-cousin marriage embedded in the terminology to actual marriage contracts, as if these two levels were congruent" (Tambiah 1965, p. 135; see also Dumont 1964, pp. 77-78, and Obeyesekere 1967,
pp. 248-51). It is however only partly on account of this failure that Yalman's
proposition "that the main function of the Dravidian kinship categories is to
regulate marriage and sexual relations inside bilateral and largely endogamous
'kindreds' " (1962, p. 548) is inapplicable to the Vedda situation.

distinctions based on sex, generation, and relative age closely follow the guidelines of nature, whereas that between "cross" and "parallel" kin is more purely cultural, so the introduction of new kinsmen by the natural process of birth presents no terminological problems, whereas the cultural process of marriage, if unrestricted, threatens to disturb what has been recognized for a hundred years as "the rigorous precision" of Dravidian terminology (Morgan 1871, p. 394). For the "error" committed by the marriage of two people who are not "cross-cousins" is cumulative. Children of such a marriage will be able to place their kinsmen in two different categories according to whether they trace the connection through their father or through their mother. It requires only a limited number of such "wrong" marriages before a man can apply more than one term to the majority of his kinsmen with equal plausibility. The smaller the range of kin within which marriage takes place the fewer the number of wrong marriages that are needed to bring about this state of affairs.

The practice of Vedda kinship abounds with this kind of indeterminacy. The terminology encourages one to predict the kin term employed by a man for a woman from the term he applies to her husband. If I call a man "nephew," his wife is my "daughter"; if I call him "maternal uncle," his wife is my "paternal aunt," and so on. Yet to record the terms used by Kukulewa villagers to refer to the married people of the village is to discover that in approximately 30 percent of the cases the terms used for a man and his wife are inconsistent according to the principles of the terminology as it is understood both by the analyst and the Veddas themselves. Inconsistencies are particularly evident in the informant's own generation and in that immediately below him. Men tend to demote the wives of their generational equals to the junior generation, or alternatively to raise the husbands of their junior kinswomen to their own generation. Thus the wives of "younger brothers" and "cross-cousins" (but rarely "elder brothers") may be called "daughters" or "nieces." Among female informants a preference for "parallel" over "cross" kinsmen, which is also observable among male informants, is more pronounced. It will be understood that the perfect functioning of the terminological system would furnish each individual with an equal number of cross and parallel kinsmen, subject only to random demographic fluctuations. Yet Kukulewa women claim twice as many "elder sisters" and "younger sisters" as female "cross-cousins" and only a slightly smaller preponderance of "elder brothers" and "younger brothers" over "male cross-cousins."

Some kind of flexibility is plainly necessary. The terminology is pervasively hierarchical. The sexes, as well as the generations, are superior and inferior. Among parallel kin the specification of relative age expands the classes of the hierarchy. The only reciprocal terms are those used by "cross-cousins" of the same sex. Only those who give and take in marriage are equal, and they must be. Relations within the hierarchy imply some combination of formality, respect, avoidance, rivalry, and claim, but their ideal or extreme expression is approached only by close kinsmen. This is sometimes signaled in the terminology itself, as when a man addresses as *māmandi* a *māma* (maternal uncle) upon whom he intends to exert the full claims of a sister's son. If the full complement of formal and respectful behavior was required in all encounters between those who call one another "elder brother" and "younger brother," say, or "maternal uncle" and "nephew," ordinary social life would be hopelessly circumscribed. It would, for instance, be impossible for more than two kinsmen to gather together on a basis of equality. Only those of the same generation are equal, and within the generation only those who call one another "cross-cousin." But if a third man joins two "cross-cousins" and is himself to be "cross-cousin" to one of them, he must be "elder brother" or "younger brother" to the other, according to the logic of the terminology. In practice the easy and informal associations of groups larger than two is frequent, and men treat their distant "father's younger brothers," "elder brothers," "younger brothers," and "male cross-cousins" with equally casual familiarity.

The practical flexibility with which the formal rigor of the terminology is softened also permits kin term usage to accommodate itself to biological and social realities. A man's "maternal uncles," "sons," and "nephews" who are approximately the same age as himself can be converted into more appropriate "elder brothers" or "younger brothers" or "cross-cousins." Likewise a relatively powerful and wealthy man may welcome the freedom to convert a client supporter from a "male cross-cousin" into a "nephew."

Some of this flexibility derives from previous marriages between parties who were not "cross-cousins," or who also stood in some other relationship. This causes no difficulties in everyday life and may even be said to facilitate social relationships, but in the context of further marriage arrangements its function is somewhat different. Here it can, and commonly does, provide the idiom in which a proposed marriage is approved or opposed. The underlying grounds for opposing a particular marriage may be various, but a critic can nearly always phrase his objections, unless the parties are first cross-cousins, in terms of the illegitimacy of the proposed union.

The Case of N. Piyaratne's Marriage

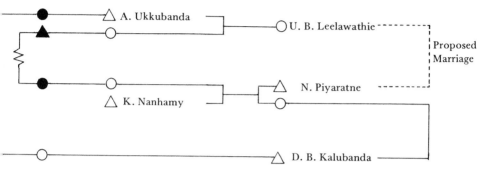

Fig. 3.1. The Proposed Marriage of N. Piyaratne

N. Piyaratne has persuaded his father, K. Nanhamy, to arrange a marriage for him with A. Ukkubanda's daughter Leelawathie. Nanhamy's son-in-law, D. B. Kalubanda, expresses his opposition to this marriage on the grounds that he and Ukkubanda are "brothers," being the sons of two sisters. But Kalubanda is Piyaratne's brother-in-law, being married to his sister, and therefore Ukkubanda is also Piyaratne's "brother-in-law" or "male cross-cousin." In that case Ukkabanda's daughter is Piyaratne's "niece." Kalubanda goes on to say that if it is correct for a "maternal uncle" to marry his "niece" then Piyaratne should marry his (Kalubanda's) daughter when she comes of age. Nanhamy counters that it is only on account of Kalubanda's marriage that Piyaratne is Leelawathie's "maternal uncle." If the relationship is traced through Leelawathie's mother, who is "cross-cousin" to Nanhamy's wife, then Leelawathie is Piyaratne's "cross-cousin," and the marriage is correct.

One way to avoid this kind of embarrassment is to find a wife in a distant village with which recent kinship and marriage ties have been minimal. Here a man will be able to address as "cross-cousin" the father of the girl he wants as his son's wife with little fear of contradiction. Alternatively and even more safely he can go to the opposite extreme and arrange a marriage for his son with his sister's daughter, or his wife's brother's daughter. In such cases of first cross-cousin marriage, the undisputed sibling bond between the father of one party and the mother of the other banishes any suspicion that the other two parents may not be "brother" and "sister."

It thus appears that beyond the range of first cousins, the categories of kinship can usually be manipulated to confirm the propriety of any marriage that is strongly desired. But they equally provide ammunition for its opponents. The kinship terminology is not then a rigid system to which its users are enslaved, but a flexible idiom that expresses a scheme of proper and permissible conduct but is adaptable to circumstance and ambition.

If the propriety of many marriages can be challenged, there are yet very few that are so offensive as to be intolerable to the community. "Wrong" marriages of the type so far discussed, between a man and his "niece" or a distant "younger sister" or "daughter" may be deplored and criticized, but once established they are accepted in the normal course of events. More extreme violations of the rules are possible, however, which cannot be accommodated so comfortably.

In former times offenses against the caste order were dealt with by the *variga* court. Leach's analysis of the Pul Eliya *variga* court (1961a, pp. 67-79) is fully applicable to the Vedda court, which seems to have operated in precisely similar fashion. Charges and judgments were each of two kinds. The accusation might be either incest (union with too close a kinsman) or exogamy (union with someone who was not a kinsman at all, i.e., not a Vedda), and the judgment might be either expulsion from the *variga* or the imposition of a fine. Leach argues that "payment of the fine then constituted a purging of the offence, and in the case of exogamy offences was tantamount to a *variga* admission fee" (1961a, p. 72).

The only cases that are recalled by Veddas (in Kukulewa) today are accusations of exogamy, although the court's competence to hear charges of incest is fully recognized. Incest here has a wide definition, including all unions between kinsmen who are not "cross-cousins." It is likely that most marriages of this kind were between quite distant kinsmen and were accommodated, in the past as today, without recourse to the *variga* court, though the threat of court proceedings may have made them less common. Moreover it is claimed that after the offender had paid his fine, any reference to the impropriety of the former relationship was itself punishable by a fine equal to that imposed on the original offender. The fine, in short, purchased the correct "cross-cousin" relationship, and the latter was retroactive. On the other hand the suggestion of union with a close kinswoman in a wrong category, for example, a mother's sister's daughter, or a brother's daughter, provokes horrified outcries against incest, and has probably always been extremely rare. Certainly no such cases are publicly admitted today nor have any been uncovered in the exhaustive collection of genealogical data.

The failure to recollect any cases of incest, and the further absence of any judgments of innocence followed by acquittal, suggest that a main function of the court was, as Leach claims, to regulate admission to the *variga*. The court was less concerned with the impartial judgment of sexual morality than with the formal adjustment of social relationships where facts and ideals were in disturbing contradiction. Yet to argue, as Leach does, that "the court's interest in sexual morality was distinctly hypocritical" (1961a, p. 72) would be to underestimate, at least among the Veddas, the community's interest in preserving its purity. This is not of course the villager's sole or even primary concern, but it persists long after the court has ceased to function.

The case history of figure 3.2 illustrates some of the factors at work in cases of cross-caste liaison and *variga* admission.

The Case of the Fernando Family

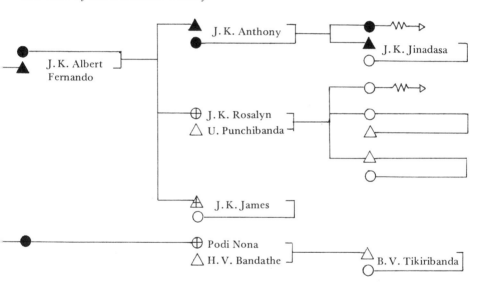

Fig. 3.2. The Fernando Family

[NOTE: In this figure *only*, symbols should be interpreted as follows: △ ○ Veddas by birth; ▲ ● non-Veddas; ⚠ ⊕ those who changed caste or whose status is marginal]

J. K. Albert Fernando was a Karaava (Fisherman) caste Christian from the Colombo area who came to Kukulewa in about 1920 as a worker for the survey department. He settled in the village with his wife, who was of the same background, and raised two sons, J. K. Anthony Fernando and J. K. James Fernando, a daughter, Rosalyn, and his sister's daughter, Podi Nona. Podi Nona was married to Herathamy Vidane ge Bandathe, who was Vel Vidane of Kukulewa and the most powerful man in the village between 1930 and 1960. Bandathe went before the *variga* court and paid the prescribed fine. This marriage produced one child, B. V. Tikiribanda, who grew up to marry a woman from the Vedda village of Katamankulama. He and his wife and children, none of whom is yet married, continue to reside in Kukulewa, and are respectable members of the community.

Albert Fernando's daughter, Rosalyn, formed a liaison and set up house with U. Punchibanda, son of Ukkurala Vel Vidane, a leading figure in the village and a member of the *variga* court. The match was strenuously opposed, and although the couple lived in Kukulewa, they were for a while ostracized. Later there was a reconciliation, the case went before the *variga* court, and Punchibanda, assisted by his father and the Fernando family, paid the fine. Thereafter the marriage was recognized, and Rosalyn's children, like Podi Nona's, are fully accepted as Veddas. Two of them have married within the village and a third into the nearby Vedda village of Elapatgama.

Albert Fernando's eldest son, Anthony, grew up in Kukulewa, but went away during World War II to work as a delivery boy in Trincomalee. Later he returned to Anuradhapura, where he married a woman from the Low Country, and then settled down in Kukulewa, where he opened a shop. His business prospered and he acquired paddy land, partly from his mother who had also been a shopkeeper, partly by purchase and partly on mortgage. But after some years his shop failed, the result, he claims, of the heavy medical expenses he bore on behalf of his mother and sister. Others attribute the failure of his shop to a successful boycott organized in opposition to an affair (which still continues) he had begun with a woman of the village. For the last ten years, while continuing to own paddy land, Anthony has worked as a laborer for the village committee, a coveted job he obtained through the influence of his "elder brother," H. V. Bandathe Vel Vidane, whose close political ally he is, and through his own outside contacts. He is not, however, accorded kinship by the vast majority of villagers, who, if they wish to be respectful, will address him not by any kinship term but by the trader's honorific, *mudalali.* Two of Anthony's children are married. His eldest daughter married an outsider and has left the village. About five years ago his eldest son, Jinadasa, married a girl of the village by whom he has had three children. The marriage appears to be stable, but it caused great offense at the time and is still presented as a prime illustration by villagers propounding the thesis of the contemporary abnegation of moral standards. The family is not visited by many villagers. Jinadasa himself is away from the village a good deal of the time, working in Anuradhapura, and is thinking of moving his family away permanently.

Albert Fernando's younger son, James, has always lived in Kukulewa, and his career has more closely approximated that of the average villager than has his elder brother's. He works as a cultivator and casual laborer, has never engaged in trade, and does not boast a range of outside connections like those of Anthony. His wife is a Vedda by birth, kinswoman of other villagers, but adopted in infancy by a Goyigama family. Kinship is extended to James by many who deny it to Anthony. James has two surviving sons, both teenagers. One fits comfortably into the life style and company of his age mates, the other is one of only two village children attending high school, and may be destined for a career outside the village. He would like to become a schoolteacher.

It would be rash to infer any general trends from this single case. One might be tempted, on the basis of the more complete admission into the *variga* of the two women, Rosalyn and Podi Nona, in comparison with Anthony and James, to suppose that the Veddas are more willing to accept foreign wives than to grant sexual access to their women to foreign men. This might then be taken as an instance of the general rule that "purity of caste must be maintained especially by the purity of its women" (Yalman 1963, p. 48; see also Stevenson 1954; Yalman 1960; Leach 1961a, p. 74). But a number of instances will be cited later in which foreign men have settled down comfortably with Vedda wives in other Vedda villages. A full analysis of these cases would require an assessment of the ideology of caste, the extent of Vedda commitment to the ideas of ritual purity and pollution, their differing status relations vis-à-vis other caste groups and particularly their sense that only the Goyigama are of approximately equivalent status to themselves, the few but significant cases of the related phenomenon of cross-caste adoption, of which James's wife provides an instance, and sundry other matters that extend far beyond the scope of the present inquiry. I therefore confine myself for the present to a few general observations. Recruitment of both foreign men and foreign women into the Vedda *variga* is possible but infrequent. Admission is rarely achieved without opposition and, since the collapse of the *variga* court system, has often been only partial, blurring the boundaries of the kin group. Acceptance is easier and more complete if the foreign spouse has no nearby kinsmen of his own. The frequency of cross-caste unions appears to have increased in the generation since the court system ceased to operate, but may also be related to the large-scale immigration into the area of Sinhalese from outside Anuradhapura District, often in connection with one or other of the government's major colonization schemes, which has occurred during the same period. But part of this apparent increase is probably also due to the tendency for Veddas who have married foreigners and moved away from their native village to be dropped from their former kinsmen's genealogies.

Most marriages, however, take place between recognized members of the *variga*. Vedda descriptions of the means by which marriages are negotiated and the ceremonies accompanying them closely resemble the accounts of formal Sinhalese marriages provided, for example, by Yalman (1967, pp. 161-67). Marriages should be arranged by the parents of the bride and groom, or by the parents' representatives. The initial advances should be made by the groom's family, following which a prescribed sequence of negotiations, visits, commensality, and gift exchange culminates in the wedding itself. Man and woman both enjoy the right to refuse a prospective spouse whom their parents have selected, but the initiative properly resides with the parents.

Most informants claim that their marriages were arranged by their parents and were marked by considerable feasting and gift exchange, but such accounts are largely fabulous. Certainly a number of marriages, particularly those between members of distant villages, are arranged by the parents, and parental control may have been more direct in an earlier age when, as is claimed, girls were married shortly after puberty and their husbands were only a few years older. But today girls are often in their late teens and boys in their twenties before they marry, and they are in practice rarely the passive recipients of a marriage fate determined only by their parents. They have plenty of time in which to discover a preference among members of the opposite sex, even though adolescent social life is for the most part sexually segregated. Boys and girls express their preferences in a variety of courtship procedures leading from "accidental" encounters at the well, the tank, or the house of a common kinsman, to the secret exchange of love letters and clandestine meetings in the jungle. Meanwhile they do not neglect the home front, and by the incessant advocacy of their loved one, the tearful rejection of all others, and the persuasive threat of suicide, they often achieve marriage earlier and to a different spouse than their parents had intended. In such circumstances it may be difficult to maintain even the appearance of formal propriety.

The Case of the Marriage of P. Heratbanda and U. B. Podimenike

P. Heratbanda wanted to marry U. B. Podimenike, who is his father's half-sister's daughter. His father, B. Punchirala, opposed the marriage on the grounds that Heratbanda was too young and too lazy. He wasn't ready to settle down in marriage. Punchirala said that Heratbanda, who had always been an obedient son, suddenly became boisterous and trouble-some, ignoring his parents and staying away from home. Punchirala was at a loss to understand his son's behavior and sought the advice of his elder brother, B. Undiyarala. Undiyarala questioned Heratbanda and discovered that he was anxious to marry A. Ukkubanda's daughter Podimenike. Undiyarala then went to Ukkubanda, his half-sister's husband, and asked if the marriage was agreeable to him. They decided that Heratbanda should come to live in Ukkubanda's house, where his prospective parents-in-law could ascertain his character and determine whether the couple were well suited to one another.

Heratbanda lived in Ukkubanda's household for about two months. During this time he was not allowed to approach Podimenike. Even if he wanted no more than a cup of tea he was obliged to ask her mother or sister, not Podimenike herself.

The marriage was eventually scheduled for the middle of January, but at that time Podimenike's elder sister produced a child who was stillborn, and the wedding was postponed. Punchirala wanted to put off the marriage for a year because he could not afford to celebrate it on the proper traditional scale on account of the crop failure that season.

Heratbanda was, however, impatient. He quarreled with Ukkubanda and left his house. Rumors reached Punchirala and Undiyarala that Heratbanda was threatening to kill himself by drinking insecticide. They conferred, confirmed that Ukkubanda still approved the marriage, and brought Heratbanda back to his father's house, where they informed him that he could bring Podimenike if he wanted. Heratbanda agreed and Punchirala informed Ukkubanda that a party would be coming to collect Podimenike and bring her to his house. Punchirala sent S. Menikrala (his half-brother), A. Muthubanda (his "nephew"), and K. Gunadasa (his sister's son) to collect the girl. When they returned with the girl, Ukkubanda accompanied them, in violation of the rule that the parents of the bride do not accompany her to the bridegroom's house.

For a few days after this Punchirala maintained that the marriage was not yet consummated. He claimed the Podimenike was only serving Heratbanda's meals and that they had not yet had sexual relations. For the marriage to be finally consummated they must wait for an auspicious day and obtain the services of the ritual washerman. Punchirala discovered that the third day after Podimenike's arrival was auspicious and he then presented her with a sari, a slip, and other clothes. He acknowledged that these were insufficient; he should have given jewelry as well. "Usually," he said, "we take the clothes and jewelry to her house on an auspicious day. But we had no time and didn't do all these things." No washerman came.

Punchirala also began to build a house for Heratbanda and Podimenike in his compound and asserted that the marriage would not be consummated until the house had been completed and the couple moved into it on an auspicious day. But he later admitted, shamefacedly, that the couple had been having sexual relations since the very day that Podimenike was brought to his house.

RESIDENCE AND HOUSEHOLD COMPOSITION

Social anthropologists have still not agreed upon a standard terminology to describe patterns of postmarital residence, and current terms are, in any case, inadequate to the requirements of this thesis. In addition to distinguishing between, for example, "virilocal" and "uxorilocal," I need to make distinctions both between norms and practice and according to whether the reference is to the village or to the household. My usage is as follows.

When two Veddas marry who are natives of the same village, the norm is that they continue to reside in their native village. I describe this norm, and its practice, as *duolocal* residence to emphasize that the couple lives in the native village of *both* the husband and the wife. The point of reference here is the village.

When two Veddas marry who are natives of different villages, the norm is *ambilocality*, which I define, from the village perspective, as residence in either the husband's village or the wife's village. When this norm is put into practice, the actual residence is either *virilocal* or *uxorilocal*, terms that I use in the standard manner.

Neolocal residence is not normatively sanctioned but is practiced in a small number of cases. In reference to the village, a statement of *neolocal* residence indicates that a couple is living in the village of neither the husband's nor the wife's parents.

I emphasize that where the village provides the point of reference, statements of duolocal, ambilocal, virilocal, uxorilocal, and neolocal residence specify only the *village* of residence. Except in the case of neolocal residence, where household separation is logically entailed, they say nothing at all about whether the younger couple does or does not share a household, a house, or a compound with either set of parents. Such a specification requires a shift to the household perspective.

If a man marries, say, his MBD, and both his own parents and those of his wife live in the same compound, then the norm of initial residence, from the household as well as from the village perspective, is *duolocality*. This is practiced when the young couple settles in the compound of both the husband's and the wife's parents. But both the opportunity and the practice of such residence are rare. Much more commonly, when a man marries a woman of his own village, his own and his wife's parents live in different compounds. From the village perspective, as I have noted, the residential norm in this case is still described as duolocality, but from the household perspective it is *ambilocality*, that is, residence in the *compound* of either the husband's or the wife's parents. Again, the actual residential practice is either *virilocal* or *uxorilocal*.

Thus, maintaining the household, or compound, reference, the norm of initial residence is duolocality where it is possible and ambilocality where it is not. Practice of these norms leads to duolocal, virilocal, or uxorilocal residence. Note that I have specified *initial* residence. It is expected that mature couples will move away from their parents to establish *neolocal* residence that, from the household perspective, specifies residence in the compound of neither the husband's nor the wife's parents. This residence is also practiced, in violation of cultural norms, by some couples from the beginning. Note that from the household perspective neolocal residence can include either residence in the same village as one or both sets of parents or residence in a separate village.

My use of *ambilocality* is based on that of Fox (1967, p. 85) and Harris (1971, p. 623). This usage corresponds to Murdock's "bilocal" residence (1949, p. 16), but I prefer to follow Harris (1971, p. 625) and reserve the latter term for those societies, of which Dobu is the most famous (Fortune 1932), in which couples regularly shift their residence between the husband's group and that of the wife. Thus, with respect to norms, *ambilocality* implies a choice that is absent from *bilocality*. For my own purposes, *ambilocality* is adequate to describe Vedda norms, but in examining residential practices it will be necessary to break it down into its components; that is, where the reference is to residential practice, the frequency of ambilocal residence is equal to the sum of the frequencies of virilocal and uxorilocal residence.

My usages are summarized in table 3.3. The text will indicate whether the reference being adopted is that of the household or the village.

TABLE 3.3

RESIDENCE PATTERNS AND TERMINOLOGY

Norm	Practice
Village Reference	
Duolocal (where possible)	Duolocal
Ambilocal	{ Virilocal { Uxorilocal
	Neolocal
Household Reference	
Duolocal (where possible)	Duolocal
Ambilocal (young couples)	{ Virilocal { Uxorilocal
Neolocal (mature couples)	Neolocal

One of the topics discussed when a marriage is being negotiated is the couple's postmarital residence. Both sets of parents are expected to want their married children to reside near them, but the bride's parents are also expected to give way and allow their daughter to move away at marriage if the husband's people insist and if they can convince the girl's parents that she will be well cared for. Residence is thus a matter of choice and negotiation, not automatic prescription. The statistical outcome of a large number of such choices will be analyzed in later chapters, where I discuss the process of village development, for a village must be able to attract spouses who will settle in it if it is to maintain itself through the generations. Here my intention is simply to indicate some of the factors that impinge upon the various options and to illustrate their relative strength by presenting the data from a single village.

One solution to the residential problem, which many favor but which is less frequently available in the smaller communities, is marriage within the village. Thirty-three of the current marriages (37.5 percent) in Kukulewa, the largest Vedda village, are of this type.[12] Of the other fifty-five marriages, those in which only one of the parties is a native of Kukulewa, thirty-eight (43.2 percent) are virilocal and seventeen (19.3 percent) are uxorilocal. Other accounts of Sinhalese social organization have concluded that, in Leach's words, uxorilocal marriages "are, by and large, those of overprivileged females or of underprivileged males" (1961a, p. 85) and that the uxorilocal husband has low status in his in-laws' household, but the Vedda evidence shows no very marked differentiation. Certainly the proverb enjoining the man who lives at his wife's place "to have constantly ready . . . a walking-stick . . . and a torch, that he may be prepared at any hour of the day or night . . . to quit the house on being ordered" (D'Oyly 1929, p. 129, quoted in Pieris 1956, p. 204) is well known, and some Veddas assert that only a very poor man would accept this position, but others deny that uxorilocal residence is degrading.

This is largely a matter of property and inheritance.[13] Whereas the ideal rule is that all children should inherit equally, in practice paddy land, which is the most substantial form of property, passes almost exclusively to those children, both male and female, who continue to reside in their native villages. Few Vedda villages are so close to one another that a man can live in one and work land in another (cf. Leach 1961a, pp. 86-87). In wealthier Sinhalese communities a woman who is married out may receive a dowry (*davadda*) of cash, jewelry, and

12. These statistics, and those on household composition that follow, are derived from a census taken in 1968 and do not exactly correspond with those presented in the later discussion of all the Vedda villages and in the analysis of household involvement in paddy cultivation, which are derived from a census taken during the 1969-70 cultivation season.

13. Throughout this work I follow Tambiah in using "the word inheritance in a general sense to denote both property transmission or transference *inter vivos* and intestate succession" (1965, pp. 148-49).

other movables in lieu of inheriting land (Leach 1961a, pp. 135-36; Obeyesekere 1967, pp. 43-44), but dowry is not significant among the Veddas. Men and women who move away from their natal village at marriage do not receive an inheritance at that time, nor do they subsequently exercise more that a residual and symbolic interest in their parents' land.[14] But because the amount of paddy land most Veddas stand to inherit is small anyway, and many of them derive less of their income and subsistence from their own land than from wage labor and chena cultivation, both of which can be done as readily in one's wife's village as in one's own, the choice of residence is not always economically strategic.[15] This is reflected in Vedda usage of the terms *diga* and *binna*, which are commonly translated in the literature as virilocal and uxorilocal respectively, but which also carry fundamental implications with respect to inheritance (Obeyesekere 1967, pp. 44-45). Many Veddas claim to understand the distinction between *diga* and *binna* marriages, but I only heard the terms used when I specifically inquired about them. Then the interpretations informants offered were imprecise and there was no agreement among them as to which term referred to which form of residence.

However, virilocal residence remains twice as common in Kukulewa as uxorilocal residence. To anticipate somewhat, it will be shown that this is a recent trend that is correlated with the expansion of paddy cultivation. Recent allocations of *badu* (lease) land have endowed otherwise landless young men with property, or have at least increased their prospects of inheritance, and it may be inferred that they have been thereby further encouraged to remain in their native villages (cf. Leach 1961a, p. 84).[16]

Yet the same preference for virilocal residence does also recur among marriages within the village. There are fourteen cases of marriage within Kukulewa where both members of both sets of parents also still live in the village. In ten of these the younger couple shares a single household with the husband's parents or lives immediately adjacent to them. In only two cases do they live with or close to the wife's parents. Moreover, in fifteen of the twenty cases of marriages where both the husband's parents also reside in Kukulewa the couple either shares a

14. The latter is expressed, for example, in the gifts of produce from his wife's parental property that a man may expect to receive when he visits her village.

15. This statement is made from the point of view of the individual, or the individual couple. It does not imply that the cumulative effect of many such choices is insignificant at the level of the village or the society at large.

16. The overwhelming majority of *badu* land grants have been made to men, and all have been made to village residents.

household with the husband's parents or are their immediate neighbors. Only eight of twenty-eight couples have chosen to live so close to the wife's parents when both the latter reside in Kukulewa.

Behind the preference for virilocal residence these figures indicate a more general tendency to remain close to any parent. Thirty-seven of the fifty-three couples (69.8 percent) who have at least one parent living in the village either share a common household or live immediately adjacent to a parent. The same pattern emerges when viewed from the opposite perspective. There are sixteen widows in Kukulewa who have not remarried. Nine have joined the household of a married son, but only one has joined a married daughter, and in this case the daughter is herself divorced. Two other widows, one of whom is the other's husband's father's sister, have set up a common household. The other four retain independent households, but none is wholly isolated. Two have a brother and two a married daughter as their immediate neighbors. Only one of these four has a married son, whereas five of the nine who have settled with a married son also have a married daughter. In brief, the widow's preference for her sons' rather than her daughters' company corresponds to the couple's preferred residence close to the husband's parents, and is reflected in a more intimate association when parents and their married sons do live in close proximity; that is, the association is more likely to be contained within a single household than when the parents come together with their married daughters.

Table 3.4 presents a classification of households. Leach (1961a, pp. 89-90), Yalman (1967, pp. 102-4), and Robinson (1968, p. 403) have stressed the significance of commensality and separate cooking facilities in the establishment of marriages and households among the Kandyan Sinhalese, and I follow them here in defining the Vedda household in terms of commensality and the creation of a separate hearth. Among the Veddas, however, a marriage is not always immediately or inevitably signaled by the establishment of an independent hearth, as is shown by the seven cases of joint family households.

For many purposes it is both convenient and appropriate to treat a household as an economic unit, although where two households are contained within the same house the economic border between them may be somewhat indistinct. It is also important to remember that almost all property is individually owned. Cattle, for example, are commonly branded in the names of successive children, and unmarried sons may retain much of their earnings from wage labor for their private purposes. Yet when a woman owns paddy land it is usually managed and cultivated by her husband, and the facts of commensality, common involvement by household members in cultivation, and the

TABLE 3.4

HOUSEHOLD COMPOSITION IN KUKULEWA, 1968

Type of Household	Number (of households)	Percentage	Number (of inhabitants)	Average Number per Household (of inhabitants)
Conjugal family	64	71.1	384	6.0
Joint family	7	7.8	52	7.4
Augmented conjugal family: a	9	10.0	62	6.9
b	1	1.1	11	11.0
Broken conjugal family	6	6.7	20	3.3
Miscellaneous	3	3.3	10	3.3
TOTAL	90	100.0	539	6.0

NOTE: Definition of household types: *Conjugal family*: husband, wife, children (if any). *Joint family*: husband, wife, children including at least one married child with spouse and children (if any). *Augmented conjugal family*: a. husband, wife, children (if any) plus the widowed or divorced father or mother of the husband; b. husband, wife, children (if any) plus the widowed or divorced father or mother of the wife. *Broken conjugal family*: widow, widower, or divorced person with or without children. *Miscellaneous*: (a) a widow with two children and her husband's father's sister; (b) a widow, her divorced daughter, and her daughter's children; (c) a spinster who for many years kept house for her widowed father, who himself recently died.

pooling of resources for subsistence within the household, make it a
suitable unit for both economic and social analysis.

The classification of households in table 3.4 should not be given a
static or rigid interpretation. Conjugal family households provide the
statistical norm, but when viewed dynamically only the three miscellaneous households are abnormal. The other categories simply represent
briefer stages in the developmental cycle of marriages and domestic
groups. The categories of augmented and broken conjugal family households allow for the widow's or divorcée's choice between joining the
household of a married child and remaining independent.[17] Joint
family households are temporary arrangements that end when the
younger couple establishes an independent household.

In their early stages marriages and households are at their most
unstable, and divorce, separation, and change of residence are frequent
among young couples. I have already noted that parents encourage their
married children to continue to live near them. Older people commonly
state that young couples "don't know how to live" or run a household,
and young adults tend to agree that the advice and assistance of parents
who are living close at hand are extremely useful. Young people are
keen to escape the authority of their parents, but they have rarely
been given land by the time they marry, and they often lack the resources necessary to build and furnish a house and to provide themselves with domestic utensils and agricultural tools. They therefore
continue to depend upon the material support of their parents, and
they commonly begin their married life as part of one or other of their
parental households.

Comfortable relations with the parents, however, are hard to
sustain. A young woman's relationship with her coresident mother-in-
law, who supervises and instructs her in her domestic work, is notori-
ously difficult, while a uxorilocal husband must also be prepared to
subordinate himself to his affines. If he lives virilocally a man often
feels stifled by the continued close authority of his father. As for
parents, however much they may have approved the marriage, their
first concern remains for their child rather than for the couple as such.
Thus when a man quarrels with his wife he is likely to find all her close
kin ranged against him. If he is married virilocally her parents will
already be anxious for the welfare of their daughter, now no longer
under their direct protection. If he has settled uxorilocally he has no
close support for himself and few options other than to submit or

17. There are only two cases of widowers or divorced men who have not
remarried.

leave. There is little to inhibit the discontented spouse from rejecting his affines and returning to his parents. The husband's people may feel that to divorce a wife is dishonorable—"it is not right to return soiled goods"—but the wife's parents are very willing to receive her back, and indeed often encourage her to return.

Moreover, in the early stages of a marriage a man and his wife share few economic interests that might serve to mitigate the fickleness of passion. Whatever the pretense of formal propriety and elaborate ceremony, the inception of a marriage involves little in the way of incentives to ensure its permanence. There is no great exchange of property or wealth, and a child's inheritance is not jeopardized if his parents are divorced, or even if they were, according to Sri Lankan law, never married at all. The registration of births is more closely attended to than that of marriages, and is often done earlier.

The frequency of divorce cannot be specified precisely, because a terminated marriage that has produced no children is not easily detected. The parties themselves are usually unwilling to admit its former existence, and it leaves few social traces other than perhaps a mild embarrassment when a former spouse is being discussed, or an otherwise inexplicable reluctance to visit his present home. I was still occasionally learning of previously unsuspected marriages in Kukulewa at the end of my period of research, after two years of ceaseless prying into the people's lives. From what I did learn, and without claiming a specious precision, it seems possible that as many as a majority of adult Veddas have married more than once.

Nevertheless the attempt to sustain a marriage can survive a number of quarrels and even separations. When a girl has left her husband and resumed her former place in her parents' household she may be tempted to start a new marriage, but it is as likely that she will, after a while, again take up with her former husband. Since the man and wife have often chosen the match, although they may scarcely have known one another, there is already an initial commitment. But it is only with the birth of children that a marriage comes into its own and acquires stability. It is around the children that the young couple and their parents come together to consolidate and sustain the marriage. It is not only difficult for a woman with two or three children to acquire a new husband, but her parents will discourage her, for they fear that their grandchildren will become the neglected stepchildren of a new alliance.

Thus while divorce is frequent among young childless couples, marriages that have produced three or more children are almost never willfully terminated. With the appearance of children the man and wife deepen their commitment to the marriage, and in doing so become more tolerant of its occasional abuses. Adultery, for example, is a matter of common gossip. Yet while it provokes the dissolution of many young marriages, among older people it may be passed over with no more than a brief and angry fight, or indeed it may be quietly tolerated and even encouraged. Perhaps it is the same growth of commitment that is revealed when married women are asked how they would like to be reborn in their next life. The vast majority choose to be reborn as men, but whereas the younger women select their father, or sometimes a brother, as their model, the older women are more inclined to name their husband.

A similar pattern is discernible in the custom whereby a virilocal woman returns to her parents' home for childbirth. Women who already have several children do not often observe this practice, but younger women usually do, and may be accompanied on such occasions by their husbands, who may then remain with their affines for an agricultural season or even longer. This custom causes a measure of the residential mobility that is observable among young couples, but does not account for all of it. More powerful than the force of tradition is the difficulty of dealing with parents-in-law, which is reflected in a pattern of shifting residence as young couples move back and forth from the compound or village of the husband's parents to that of the wife's parents, according to which partner can currently get along better with the other's parents.

This pattern of shifting residence betweeen virilocality and uxorilocality is cut across by a tendency to move progressively farther away from either set of parents. If the former pattern reflects "the in-law problem," the latter is an expression of the youthful inclination to be free of all parental authority. A newly married couple, as I have mentioned, often begins by sharing a joint household with either the husband's or the wife's parents. After a while the households split, but the two couples continue to live in the same house. Later a small separate house may be built for the young couple in the parent's compound. Several years may elapse, and a number of children may have been born before the younger couple establishes itself completely independently. Not every couple goes through each stage of this process and there is much variation in the speed and ease with which it is accomplished, but the general trend is apparent from table 3.5, which shows that the more children a couple has the farther away from the parents it is likely to reside.

This process of increasing residential separation between parents and their married children is paralleled by the transmission of property between them. I shall be discussing inheritance and related matters in

TABLE 3.5

RESIDENCE OF KUKULEWA COUPLES WITH AT LEAST ONE PAIR OF PARENTS
ALSO LIVING IN KUKULEWA, AND THE NUMBER OF THEIR CHILDREN

Residential Proximity of Parental and Filial Couples	Number of Cases	Number of Children of Filial Couples	
		Total	Average
Joint household	7	2	0.3
Separate households in same house	3	5	1.7
Separate households in adjacent houses	14	35	2.5
Separate and nonadjacent households	13	43	3.3

NOTE: 1. Where both sets of parents reside in Kukulewa the residential proximity of the closer set is represented. 2. Cases where only a single parent survives are omitted on the grounds that widows and widowers are inclined to rejoin their married children however many children the latter themselves have, and their inclusion would therefore disturb the general pattern which the table is designed to reveal. 3. A joint household is always contained within a single house.

some detail in the next chapter, and it will be sufficient to note here that the transmission of immovable property between the generations is often drawn out over a long period, beginning about the time the eldest child marries and not being completed before the parent's death. Under these conditions the residential separation of parents and their married children not only expresses the degree to which the children have escaped the physical presence of parental authority but also provides an indication of their mutual economic independence.

Accounts of Sinhalese social structure commonly describe kin groups that extend beyond the household, such as the *gedera* (Tambiah 1958; 1965), *pavula* (Leach 1961a; Yalman 1962; 1967), compound group (Leach 1961a), *vasagama* (Tambiah 1965; Obeyesekere 1967), *pelantiya* (Obeyesekere 1967), and so on. With the exception of the *pavula*, Vedda society is, by contrast, characterized by the absence of recognized kin groups between the level of the household and the village community as a whole. No names, for example, are inherited in either the male or the female line beyond a single generation, and there are therefore no large groups of patrilineal or matrilineal kin linked by common possession of an ancestral name.[18] A person's name is simply his own personal name prefixed by that of his father, for example, Banda ge Ukkurala (i.e., Banda's Ukkurala), whose own children will be known as Ukkurala ge Herathamy, Ukkurala ge Ranmenike, and so on.

I have already noted that Vedda compound groups lack the strategic significance that attaches to them in Pul Eliya society. Many compounds do contain more than one household, but in most cases the second household is that of a recently married son or daughter who may be expected eventually to move to an independent site. The official grants of high land, on which most houses are now located, have been made in the last twenty years and it is conceivable that compound groups may yet form on these new sites. But such an outcome is unlikely, for "squatters" who have cleared and settled on adjacent high land since the original allocations have also been able to acquire leases to their compounds. The general trend then is towards the establishment of independent households in individually held compounds. Nineteen of the ninety households in Kukulewa are still located in the

18. This statement requires a minor qualification. Some Veddas lay claim to a high-sounding *vasagama* name, usually Wannisinghe Mudiyanselage (cf. Leach 1961a, p. 75; see Obeyesekere 1967, pp. 14-17, and Tambiah 1965, p. 166, for discussion of *vasagama* names). My impression is that the public display of such a name was felt to be pretentious and somewhat ridiculous, and it was certainly rare. Veddas who bear the same *vasagama* name form a group only in the sense that the name is considered to be the property of all members of the *variga*.

traditional house-site area (*gamgoda*), but only two compounds in the *gamgoda* now contain more than a single household.

The word *pavula* has a wide range of references among the Veddas as elsewhere, from wife through "family" to "personal kindred," until at its greatest extent it merges with *apee nayo* (our kinsmen) and the *variga* as a whole. A man's *pavula* can therefore include everyone he chooses to recognize as a kinsman, but the common usage is more restricted. When the term refers to a man's wife and children it may designate an active co-operating group, but in its more extended usage it would almost always be misleading to claim that *pavula* are groups that "act together corporately to achieve political ends," as Leach (1961a, p. 244) can do for Pul Eliya. It is true that political allies emphasize the kinship connection between them, and that a man is more likely to include in his *pavula* an ally than an enemy who is no less closely related to him, but Vedda usage favors consanguineal kin over affines and is thus closer to Leach's "ideal *pavula*" than to his "effective *pavula*" (1961a, pp. 104-25). Such collections of kin do not form active corporate groups, although they may briefly assemble on some ceremonial occasion.

Effective groups of kinsmen who are members of separate households do, however, emerge in the process of Vedda social life, particularly in the context of economic action. I shall therefore analyze their structure in the next chapter, in which I describe the organization of Vedda occupations.

4

Occupations

Whatever the former significance of hunting and food-gathering in their economy (see pp. 43-44), the Anuradha-pura Veddas today derive most of their income and subsistence from chena and paddy cultivation. These two kinds of agriculture are associated with very different forms of social organization.[1]

Unfortunately documentary sources do not permit a precise estimate of historical changes in the relative importance of chena and paddy cultivation either in the Vedda economy or in that of the region as a whole. Official production statistics are neither altogether reliable nor complete, and other reports are contradictory. For example, in his *Manual of the North Central Province*, published in 1899, Ievers states that "the staple food of the mass of the population is *kurakkan*" (1899, p. 193), *kurakkan*, or finger millet (*Elesuine coracana*) being the main chena product; but according to the Census Report of 1901, only two years later, the staple food in the North Central Province was rice (Census 1901, p. 70). One source of confusion has been the failure consistently to distinguish between the staple food and the staple product. Because rice was exported from Anuradhapura District in the nineteenth century (Leisching 1870; Ievers 1887), even some modern historians (e.g., Bastiampillai 1970, p. 10) have inferred that local

1. I hope to present elsewhere a detailed, quantified, and comprehensive account of the economy of one Vedda village (Kukulewa). For the purposes at hand it will be sufficient to indicate in somewhat general terms the relative importance of the various occupations, for my present concern is not so much with economics per se as with the social implications of the different economic activities.

consumption needs were also being amply met. But the more discerning contemporary observers were well aware that the amount of paddy being exported from the district gave little indication of how much was being consumed within it. Ievers notes in his Administrative Report for 1887 that much rice was exported from the district, but he goes on to estimate "that half the population lives entirely on chena-grown grain." The villagers were selling most of their rice to traders from Jaffna, Trincomalee, Matale, and Kurunegala, for money and for salt, salt fish, cloth, coconuts, and arecanuts.

This trade was long established. Indeed Robert Knox himself engaged in it in the seventeenth century, and actually made his escape through Nuvarakalaviya in the guise of a peddler, carrying "such wares as were vendible in those parts, as Tobacco, Pepper, Garlick, Combs, all sorts of Iron Ware, etc." (1911, p. 246). A crucial aspect of this trade was noted by Lieutenant Thomas Nagel, whose *Account of the Vanni* was written in 1793. Nagel reports that "the Jaffna Pedlers who go about with bags . . . give them [i.e., the villagers] their articles at a year's credit in order to receive in return at the next harvest paddy at the rate of eight stivers per parra" (Nagel 1948, p. 74; see also Knox 1911, pp. 239-40). In other words, the amount of paddy exported from Anuradhapura District may suggest the extent of rural indebtedness, but cannot be taken to indicate a surplus above local subsistence requirements. This state of affairs has continued into the present century and was noted, for example, in Dyson's Administration Report of 1928 (Dyson 1928).

These reports indicate that credit has been extended more on the security of paddy than of chena crops. Paddy has long been a cash crop, but with the notable exception of gingelly (*Sesamum indicum*, sesame), few chena products have been readily marketable. Freeman noted in 1915 that Anuradhapura District ought to export chena vegetables, "but the villagers, except those near the town of Anuradhapura, find transport prohibitive, and do not know of markets" (Freeman 1915). On the other hand, three years later he noted that some chena vegetables *were* being exported to Colombo and elsewhere by rail. Perhaps this was the result of Freeman's own initiative, for this remarkable man, who became the district's elected representative on the Legislative Council after he had ceased to be its government agent in Anuradhapura, was a vigorous and persistent advocate of chena cultivation. Be that as it may, the general impression is that, on the whole, the traders and creditors who traveled to the villages came away with paddy rather than chena produce. It is somewhat surprising, therefore, to find that the conditions obtaining in Pul Eliya in 1954 were almost exactly the reverse of this. One might have anticipated that the combined effect of the government's guaranteed price scheme, which is intended to stimulate rice production by offering the cultivator a high guaranteed price for his paddy, and the ration program, whereby the consumer obtains some of his rice either free or well below the market price (both programs have been instituted since the Second World War) would, if anything, have increased the proportion of paddy produced in the district that reaches the market. But this was apparently not the case in Pul Eliya, at least in 1954. Leach presents the village as a "small peasant community subsisting by the cultivation of rice in irrigated fields of fixed size and position" (1961a, p. 53). He recognizes that in years when there has been a rice crop failure the *kurakkan* grown in chenas may be a very important standby item of diet, but in general the Pul Eliya villager "looks upon this shifting cultivation as his main means of earning a cash income in contrast to his ordinary activities as a rice farmer which provide him with a subsistence living" (1961a, pp. 63-64; see also ibid., p. 289). The historical evidence to which I have referred suggests that if this is the state of affairs in Pul Eliya, then either it is a recent development or the village is exceptionally well favored for paddy cultivation.[2] But clearly one critical question to answer is how often the paddy crop does in fact fail.

RAINFALL

Successful paddy cultivation depends upon an adequate local rainfall. The village tanks of Anuradhapura District are not usually connected to any of the major irrigation systems and do not receive water from outside the district nor, indeed, from outside their own local catchment areas. The reliability of a tank is therefore a function of its location; other things being equal, a well placed tank with a large catchment area will require less rainfall than a tank with a small catchment area. Pul Eliya evidently is well placed in this respect, for Leach notes that the tank "very seldom dries up completely even in years of drought" (1961a, p. 18). Almost all the Vedda villages, by contrast, occupy the other end of the scale, having unreliable tanks with small catchment areas. These variations are offset by the use of the larger and more reliable tanks to irrigate more extensive tracts of paddy land and to support larger populations. When the rainfall is deficient, however, the fields under a small tank may be impossible to irrigate at all, while

2. Lest I be accused of misinterpreting Leach, let me hasten to acknowledge that he specifically denies any claim that Pul Eliya is a typical Nuvarakalaviya village (1961a, p. 14).

the inhabitants of a better endowed village may yet be able to cultivate a reduced proportion of their holdings, a practice institutionalized under the name of *bethma* (Leach 1961a, pp. 169-71; Pieris 1956, pp. 239-40; Farmer 1957, p. 45).

Another source of variation is the distribution of the rainfall. When the rains do come, they do not blanket the whole area but are concentrated at a particular time in particular places, so that while an inch or two of rain may fall within an hour in one village, another village a few miles away may receive no rain at all. Over a period of years such variations may be expected to cancel one another out, but it is not certain that they do so during the course of a single season.[3]

Another factor to be considered is the steady improvement in the tanks themselves, which has taken place in the hundred years since the government seriously began to address itself to the restoration and refurbishment of village irrigation works. Clearly the construction of firm bunds and the provision of adequate sluices and spills promote the more efficient use of the available water, and to that extent the irrigation of a constant extent of paddy land should require less water to be stored in the tank. In fact, as has been mentioned, the improvement of the irrigation works has been accompanied by an extension of the area under cultivation and an increase in the local population to be supported, so that the amount of rainfall required has in no sense declined.[4]

3. I do not have the necessary figures to document this assertion, which is based on casual observation. One is tempted to construct a hypothesis relating the variation in rainfall within the district in any one year to the wide dispersion of the Vedda *variga* as compared, say, to the Goyigama *variga* described by Leach (1961a). The Veddas are the poorest group within the local society and their tanks are the least reliable. In years of deficient rainfall it may be expected that some parts of Anuradhapura District will suffer more than others. The reciprocal obligations between relatively widely dispersed kinsmen may then provide a mechanism whereby subsistence goods can be channeled to those villages that are most in need from those that have suffered less. This hypothesis may have had some greater validity in an age before the government introduced relief measures in years of acute distress. Unfortunately I was not aware of this possibility during the first season of research, which was a drought year. In the second year, when the rains were plentiful, the reciprocal exchanges of food between Vedda villages would not have been sufficient to sustain a whole community for more than a few days.

4. It was officially estimated at the end of the nineteenth century that between 40,000 and 50,000 acres were under paddy cultivation in Anuradhapura District (Fisher 1885; Ievers 1899; Seymour 1921). In 1952 it was estimated that 115,670 acres were asweddumized, of which 78,860 were cultivated in the previous season (Rajendra 1952). Between 1901 and 1953 the population of the district rose from 79,100 to 229,282.

Bearing these considerations in mind, it is useful now to examine the rainfall statistics for the area in some detail.[5] Table 4.1 reports the monthly rainfall recorded at Anuradhapura between January 1871 and December 1897. I have selected this period because the government agents of the time were usually concerned to report the over-all success or failure of each season's cultivation (see Administration Reports, 1871-97). The table shows a great deal of variation in the annual rainfall recorded, ranging from 79.86 inches in 1885 to 32.58 inches in 1873, with an average of 55.16 inches. More than half the mean annual rainfall comes in October, November, and December, and it is the rain collected at this time, which is roughly the period of the northeast monsoon, that is used to irrigate the main (maha) crop. More than half of the remainder of the rain normally falls between March and May, and this sometimes permits a second cultivation season (yala). Yala rains, however, are rarely sufficient in themselves, and cultivation is often possible only if the previous maha rainfall has been abundant, and a surplus of water remains in the tank. An alternative scheme is to cultivate only a fraction of the fields in the maha season, and to conserve water for a later, yala crop (Leach 1961a, pp. 52-53). The unreliable Vedda tanks only rarely permit yala cultivation.

Yala cultivation is, then, generally subordinate to maha cultivation, and the most critical period, when rain must fall if cultivation is to be successful, is that between October and January. Water cannot be stored indefinitely in the open tanks because of what Farmer describes as an "astonishingly high" rate of evaporation in the dry season, half an inch daily (1957, pp. 25-26). Government agents reported on the success or failure of maha cultivation in eighteen of the twenty-six seasons between 1871 and 1897. In all ten of the seasons that they declared successful, the recorded rainfall between October and January (inclusive) was more than thirty-two inches. In all eight of the unsuccessful seasons the rainfall during the same period was less than twenty-five inches (table 4.2). One may infer, therefore, as a crude index, that successful cultivation requires a minimum of between twenty-five and thirty-two inches of rainfall during these four months. Fortunately for this inference the rainfall recorded between October and January in the years when the government agent failed to report on cultivation was always either more than thirty-two or less than twenty-five inches. Applying the crude rainfall index to the eight seasons omitted, the

5. For a geographer's analysis of rainfall and water supply in the Dry Zone of Sri Lanka, and particularly for a useful assessment of the zone's "effective rainfall," see Farmer 1956 and 1957, pp. 22-31.

TABLE 4.1

Monthly Rainfall at Anuradhapura, 1871-97 (in inches)

YEAR	Jan.	Feb.	Mar.	Apr.	May	June	July	Aug.	Sept.	Oct.	Nov.	Dec.	TOTAL
1871	11.29	3.71	2.87	13.24	2.14	–	–	1.82	1.82	4.81	19.15	7.29	68.14
1872	1.49	0.27	2.87	9.89	3.05	0.03	0.72	0.11	7.10	3.67	17.41	2.96	49.57
1873	0.20	2.90	1.11	4.51	3.42	0.40	0.03	4.49	–	4.53	6.12	4.87	32.58
1874	1.29	3.33	1.21	5.41	3.06	0.12	–	6.24	7.84	2.65	7.60	7.17	45.92
1875	0.69	0.02	3.42	8.45	3.96	5.27	0.03	2.01	2.82	10.60	11.27	8.27	56.81
1876	1.86	0.37	3.09	5.42	1.81	0.52	0.03	2.75	4.42	4.49	5.28	4.62	34.74
1877	0.25	–	4.61	9.01	4.52	1.03	0.05	0.44	2.89	10.69	18.35	19.97	71.81
1878	7.46	–	1.86	10.32	4.34	0.38	3.21	0.35	2.70	5.24	11.25	3.98	51.09
1879	1.72	1.10	7.41	3.73	4.53	–	7.14	3.53	2.51	8.88	15.07	7.64	63.26
1880	3.85	1.14	6.91	7.11	0.03	0.04	–	1.22	0.02	9.54	16.81	4.03	50.70
1881	5.35	0.03	1.57	6.62	2.99	0.22	0.40	0.44	4.18	3.37	12.21	12.27	49.65
1882	5.23	2.28	3.05	3.17	2.93	1.73	0.42	5.87	0.02	8.24	8.88	20.36	62.23
1883	1.94	5.58	3.01	6.81	7.02	8.53	0.72	4.54	–	12.02	16.47	8.28	74.92
1884	0.93	–	1.59	5.64	3.94	1.28	–	0.11	4.10	15.58	15.21	8.36	56.74
1885	0.74	0.37	4.73	9.45	8.79	7.29	–	0.48	4.45	15.69	16.24	11.63	79.86
1886	0.58	1.08	1.24	6.85	4.46	3.04	3.66	5.87	6.00	6.88	6.33	2.52	48.51
1887	0.86	2.72	2.21	11.45	–	0.91	–	0.29	–	15.58	6.46	26.53	67.01
1888	0.10	–	–	4.10	8.55	1.04	–	–	5.59	8.63	5.16	7.88	41.05
1889	0.86	–	1.54	10.73	3.72	0.06	4.62	1.23	5.96	8.58	9.16	3.30	49.76
1890	2.82	2.21	1.21	18.02	0.38	1.28	0.11	0.79	0.15	3.14	5.31	5.37	40.77
1891	0.50	1.14	6.41	6.44	20.33	0.53	0.28	–	0.25	19.98	7.85	10.93	74.64
1892	6.53	4.73	0.57	8.73	0.03	0.72	0.67	2.78	0.55	2.64	11.94	8.52	48.41
1893	0.72	0.64	6.41	4.71	0.49	0.58	4.40	0.03	0.08	8.79	8.12	4.88	39.85
1894	2.83	0.39	3.01	6.10	0.26	0.08	0.68	1.42	1.44	11.75	11.56	6.58	46.12
1895	3.21	–	0.99	11.38	0.06	2.33	0.04	4.39	1.16	18.90	7.83	9.50	59.79
1896	4.25	0.39	4.26	4.39	3.97	6.46	1.48	0.12	2.85	14.53	14.02	12.82	69.54
1897	6.92	1.21	0.67	7.13	1.15	3.44	0.10	1.83	6.67	4.08	8.29	18.28	59.77
Average	2.76	1.39	2.88	7.73	3.70	1.53	1.07	1.97	2.80	9.02	11.09	9.22	55.16

TABLE 4.2

RAINFALL AT ANURADHAPURA AND SUCCESS OR FAILURE OF PADDY
CULTIVATION, OCTOBER-JANUARY, 1871-72 TO 1896-97 (IN INCHES)

Season	Rainfall	Success (S) or Failure (F)	Reported (R) or Inferred (I)
1871-72	32.74	S	R
1872-73	24.24	F	I
1873-74	16.81	F	R
1874-75	18.11	F	I
1875-76	32.00	S	I
1876-77	14.64	F	R
1877-78	56.47	S	I
1878-79	22.19	F	R
1879-80	35.44	S	I
1880-81	33.73	S	R
1881-82	33.08	S	R
1882-83	39.42	S	I
1883-84	37.70	S	I
1884-85	39.89	S	R
1885-86	44.14	S	R
1886-87	16.59	F	R
1887-88	48.67	S	R
1888-89	22.53	F	I
1889-90	23.86	F	R
1890-91	14.32	F	R
1891-92	45.28	S	R
1892-93	23.82	F	R
1893-94	24.62	F	R
1894-95	33.10	S	R
1895-96	40.48	S	R
1896-97	48.29	S	R

result, for the period as a whole, is a total of fifteen successful years
and eleven years of failure. A successful crop, in other words, can be
expected in no more than three maha seasons out of five.

This is a conservative estimate, being based only on the frequency
of deficient rainfall. But the rains can also be excessive. Heavy rainfall
during a concentrated period can cause floods that breach bunds and
destroy crops. Between 1871 and 1897 this is only recorded as having
occurred on a large scale in December 1882, but it is likely that at least
some tanks were breached in other comparable months, such as December 1877 and December 1887. Moreover I have taken no account of
other hazards in the natural environment, such as crop blights or the
devastating incursions of elephants and other pests.

It seems improbable, in the light of this estimate, that more than a very few exceptionally fortunate communities, of which Pul Eliya may be one, have been regularly able to derive their subsistence from irrigated paddy cultivation. Even if yields in the successful years were startlingly high, the surpluses thus generated would hardly have been sufficient to see the villagers through an unpredictable succession of bad years. Five of the six seasons between 1888 and 1894, for example, were unsuccessful. The Veddas in particular, with their tanks of less than average reliability, cannot have depended on wet-rice cultivation for their subsistence.

The Anuradhapura District villager does not, of course, need to be told that paddy cultivation is an extremely precarious business, but observers and officials who, if not foreigners, have usually come from other parts of the island, seem to have been reluctant to learn this lesson. Agrarian policy has nearly always discouraged chena cultivation in favor of more intensive paddy cultivation. Chena crops can also suffer from a drought but are less susceptible than a paddy crop. The peasant accordingly gives priority to his chena, which he prudently sees as the least uncertain means to procure his subsistence. Officials, on the other hand, have consistently emphasized the disadvantages of chena cultivation, and the literature abounds with more or less prejudiced elaborations of the criticisms already made by Rhys Davids in 1871: "chena cultivation prevents civilized habits and enterprise; it is unwholesome and unhealthy; it is incompatible with paddy or other more remunerative cultivation because the working times clash; it destroys forest resources; and the rotation of the soil prevents any permanent improvement of the land" (1871, p. 93). Rhys Davids did also recognize, more sympathetically than some who followed him, that the villagers had good economic grounds for preferring chena cultivation, and were not simply motivated by their enjoyment of "the destruction of the forest [and] the fine blaze after it" (ibid., p. 91), or by their conservative addiction to irrational custom, but this recognition has prompted only reluctant gestures intended to soften the impact of a policy that would severely restrict chena cultivation, or even eliminate it altogether. As Leach says, "shifting cultivation . . . is a matter on which villagers and the administration hold diametrically contrasted points of view" (1961a, p. 289; see also ibid., pp. 61-64). In practice, official dogma has frequently been forced to yield to economic necessity, and chena cultivation, despite administrative harassment, has retained the villager's loyalty.

Accordingly, attempts in recent years to intensify paddy cultivation, as distinct from attempts to extend it, have made slow progress.

The government's efforts to increase rice production by intensifying cultivation are seen by the villager as an improvident invitation to gamble more of his resources than he can afford on a most uncertain outcome. It does not seem likely that the greater expenses of intensive cultivation will be willingly incurred by the villager until the government can either guarantee an adequate water supply (presumably by bringing in water from the Wet Zone) or provide an attractive and workable scheme of crop insurance, or alternatively, as an even less realistic condition, until the cultivator has accumulated sufficient capital reserves to be able to risk several successive failures before he recoups his losses.

Rhys Davids's assessment (1871, p. 85), that arable land in Nuvarakalaviya is cultivated on average in two years out of five, not only gives some support to my own estimate but also draws attention to another expression of the cultivator's prudence. Unsuccessful seasons are often marked not so much by crop failure as by the failure to cultivate at all. Here again the government and the cultivator have frequently clashed, and for the same reasons that I have just adduced. Farmer supplies an authoritative defense of peasant practice in this respect:

The peasant is . . . often criticized for waiting until his tank is full before starting *Maha* (north-east monsoon) cultivation, thus wasting the direct effect of early rains which occur often enough to permit preliminary cultivation without irrigation. But this practice is, in reality, like so many apparently ill-based indigenous customs, a sensible reaction to local circumstances; for if, encouraged by early rains, the peasant cultivates before his tank is full, he stands to lose both effort and seed if later rains fail. [1957, p. 45]

The villager is in any case busy at this time with the chena on which his subsistence more fundamentally depends.

CHENA CULTIVATION

The Veddas begin to clear their chenas in August, in order to have them fired before the rains come and ready for sowing when they do come. The crops are sown piecemeal, which spreads out the work, more importantly at harvest than at sowing, and ensures that not all perishable vegetables ripen at once. *Kurakkan* is the main crop and alongside it maize, tomatoes, chilies, manioc, and a variety of squashes are commonly grown. If the chena contains a slight depression, which will attract more moisture than the rest, a little paddy may also be cultivated. This maha chena is intended for subsistence. There is a small market for the products mentioned, and the cultivator may, for example, trade a little of his *kurakkan* for some other items of consumption, such as coconuts or kerosene, but the bulk of his chena produce is consumed within his own household. He may then attempt a second cultivation during the yala season, in which case he usually plants gingelly, a cash crop. This is a risky enterprise, as the rainfall is frequently ineffective, but the rewards for success are considerable. It is attempted only by the most prosperous and ambitious Vedda villagers. Mustard and chilies offer other opportunities for a cash crop, and there is evidence that a few Veddas grow small quantities of marijuana in well hidden chenas.

The entire household cultivates the chena. The initial heavy work is done by men, who also usually sow, while women do most of the harvesting. This is not, however, a rigid division of labor, and men, women, and children may all participate at each stage of the process. A widow or divorcée may even cultivate her own chena, if she can persuade a brother or an adult son to clear a plot for her, or allow her the use of a plot that was cultivated the previous year. She will, however, require the assistance of at least a child, for when the crops are ripening they must be guarded day and night against the perils of the jungle. The normal practice is to assign a youth or child to watch the chena during the day, to drive off the monkeys and birds that would otherwise plunder it, while the man of the household spends his nights in the watch-hut he has built. There, armed with an antique gun or firecrackers and a hoard of magic, he attempts to discourage the appetite of elephants. The availability of children who will watch the crops by day is important in determining whether or not to grow a chena. The overwhelming majority of Vedda households do cultivate their own chenas, but those who do not are nearly always young men whose children are not yet old enough to undertake this responsibility. Young married men find it more profitable to go outside the village for wage labor, or alternatively, because they are often still closely associated with their parental households, they may work a common chena with their father or father-in-law. Such cases are virtually the only exceptions to the rule that each household cultivates its own chena. If the two households are separate, however, it is more common that the chena will also be divided. A single wood and brush fence will then enclose the chena, a certain portion of which will be allotted to the younger couple. This reduces the amount of fencing required and also lightens the burden of watching. The parents' younger children will guard the chena by day, and nocturnal duties will be shared by the adult men.

This procedure also recommends itself to other kinsmen, neighbors, and friends. Chenas are worked independently, but adjacent sites reduce the burden of fencing and protecting. Some men prefer to work their chenas in isolation, but it is common to find a cluster of several plots adjoining one another.[6] Men who cooperate in this way are usually political allies, but their alliance can be jeopardized by the failure of one party to build adequate fences or to take his turn at watching.

Most chenas comprise between one and three acres. They are usually cultivated for two years and then abandoned. It is difficult to determine the average length of time that is then allowed for the jungle to regenerate, nor the extent of erosion. Farmer notes that the peasant "is aware of the insufficiency of the short period of regeneration (e.g. seven years) enforced by a growing population" (1957, p. 48), and Veddas concur that this period is now both common and insufficient. But Farmer also refers to the work of Joachim and Kandiah (1948), which shows "that under the system practised in these regions chena cultivation depends almost entirely on nitrogen and nutrients made available by the burning of the jungle, soil reserves remaining largely untapped and in any case being readily restored after five to ten years of regeneration" (Farmer 1957, p. 48; cf. Conklin 1961). Farmer considers that "under the physiographic and demographic conditions which have prevailed since [ancient times] in most parts of Nuwaraka-laviya and the Wanni it [i.e., chena cultivation] has enabled high land to be used for very many centuries without impairing the soil" (1957, p. 48). The maintenance of this regime has up to now been threatened less by population growth than by the official policy that was intended to protect it. Leach comments on the government regulation, designed to conserve forest resources, which requires that "where land is cleared for shifting cultivation it must be jungle which is 'not more than ten years old'! This implies that the fertility of this cleared ground shall be as low as possible and it also, incidentally, makes it certain that the resulting erosion shall be the maximum possible" (1961a, p. 62). With regard to population, Farmer cautiously estimates that the critical density in Nuwarakalaviya, where the villager also undertakes paddy cultivation, is about two hundred to two hundred fifty per square mile (1957, p. 49). Even if this estimate proves optimistic it is still four times the population density recorded in 1953 (Abhayaratne and Jayewardene 1967, p. 45).

Of course the population is not evenly distributed within the district, and chena land is therefore not equally available everywhere. In this respect, as will be discussed again later, some Vedda villages have

6. The Veddas of Kukulewa are familiar with the idea of a "wheel chena," the traditional form of cultivation described by Leach (1961a, p. 291-95), and they claim that in former times they too used to organize chena cultivation in this fashion, but they do not do so today.

felt the impact of population growth more than others. In particular those villages such as Dambagahaulpota (37)[7] and Migahapattiya (36), which have been displaced by major colonization schemes, and others such as Rotawewa (42) that are immediately adjacent to colonies, have suffered a serious reduction of their chena lands. On the other hand the small Vedda villages in Willachchiya, northwest of Anuradhapura (1-20), which remains an area of sparse population, are still surrounded by relatively extensive tracts of jungle.

But while the prospects for chena cultivation vary somewhat among the villages, within any one village all inhabitants enjoy equal access to the surrounding jungle. As I noted in chapter 3, chenas are grown on crown land that, with very few exceptions, has not become alienated to individuals. It is recognized that a man who has cleared a particular plot has the right to work it again in the following year, but the individual possession of jungle plots does not extend beyond this. At various times the government has attempted to restrict chena cultivation to the poorest class of villagers, but to the limited extent that this policy has ever been effective, it has discriminated little among the Veddas, virtually all of whom are, even by local standards, extremely poor. It is possible that regulations restricting the permissible size of chenas have been more successful, but if so, this is probably only partly due to the regulations themselves. Rather, it has been the steadily increasing availability of wage labor outside their own villages, and, since at least as early as the 1870s, the provision of relief in years of acute distress that have somewhat diversified the Veddas' defenses against famine. If the Veddas formerly grew larger chenas than they needed in normal years so that sufficient crops would survive in years of drought, it may be that they have now come to rely on wage labor and relief measures to see them through the bad years. But this is speculation; it may equally be that they grew smaller chenas in an age when game was more plentiful.

In summary, chena cultivation is egalitarian. It is undertaken by the smallest continuously cooperating economic unit, the household, on land that is not individually owned and is equally accessible to all. The capital requirements are minimal, an ax, a *mamoty* (hoe), and a sickle being the only necessary tools. Official regulations aside, it is restricted only by the amount of manpower that the individual household can muster. It is largely geared to subsistence—very few Veddas have been in a position to undertake the large-scale cultivation of chena products for the market. It thus provides few opportunities either for monetary

7. Numbers in parentheses after the names of villages refer to map 2.1.

profit or for the elevation of one villager above his fellows. In all these respects it differs from paddy cultivation.

PADDY CULTIVATION

The uncertainty of paddy cultivation does not make it unprofitable. On the contrary, a successful harvest brings great rewards, while the risks of failure can be minimized. I have already mentioned the main precaution the villagers take, that of waiting until the tank is full before beginning to cultivate. This does not insure success but it does limit losses. Nevertheless, although the Veddas do not practice intensive cultivation, their paddy crop still requires a greater capital investment, quite apart from the permanent investment in the irrigation works, than does chena cultivation. The return from seed is about half that of *kurakkan*, and seed is more expensive. The necessary agricultural tools are also more expensive, as well as more numerous. If buffaloes are not owned they must be hired for certain operations, and it is commonly the case that at certain times a greater concentration of labor is required than can be mobilized within a single household. Cultivators in different households therefore enter into a variety of relationships with one another whereby labor is exchanged either for payment in kind, or for wages, or for an equivalent return of labor at some other time. In addition the private tenure of paddy land gives rise to a complex system of relations among those who have an interest in a particular plot of land, between owner and tenant, mortgager and mortgagee, employer and employee. In contrast to the independent household organization of chena cultivation, paddy supports a dense network of social relations among members of different households. These relations reinforce the conditions fundamentally laid down by common interest in the village irrigation system, which requires close cooperation among the cultivators while providing ample opportunity for conflict.

Since different cultivators are dependent on the same irrigation system, their activities must be closely coordinated. The necessity of cooperation is institutionalized through the formal meeting of cultivators, held just prior to the agricultural season, which fixes the dates by which the various operations must be concluded (see pp. 50-52). Since paddy cultivation requires different quantities of water at different times, it is evident that all the plots in a field must be in approximately the same stage of cultivation at the same time, if one man's requirements are not to clash with another's, and if the fullest use is to be made of the limited water available. Conversely, when one man fails to fulfill his common obligations, it is not only he himself who suffers but also his fellows. If he fails to maintain his section of the irrigation channel, all the plots below his own will suffer. When cattle enter a paddy field through a poorly built section of the fence they do not consume only the offender's crop. The combination of private ownership and mutual dependence in the process of production is a constant source of conflict.

Private ownership also combines with the limited possibilities of paddy cultivation to make control of paddy land a major focus of political action within the village and the means whereby village leaders come to dominate their fellows. For if a man chooses to grow twice as big a chena as usual, he does so at the expense, perhaps, of the jungle, or even of the crown, but not of his fellow villagers. But at any one time the amount of privately held paddy land is close to the limits imposed by the condition of the irrigation works and the available water supply. If a man is to increase his holding of paddy land, then, he can often only do so at the expense of others. At the same time, as I observed earlier, the last hundred years have been marked by a considerable expansion of the total area under paddy cultivation. In examining the distribution of landholdings it is therefore necessary to consider the ways in which new lands are acquired, as well as those by which existing holdings are transferred.

Between about 1900[8] and 1935, when the Land Development Ordinance (L.D.O.) was promulgated, an enterprising villager could purchase land[9] from the crown, which he could then convert into paddy fields. Such grants were *sinakkera* (freehold) and, although the ownership of *sinakkera* lands is less prestigious than that of *paraveni* (ancestral) holdings, the proprietor's rights are virtually equivalent. In particular, there are no restrictions on how he disposes of his property. Thirty-three of the forty acres of *sinakkera* land obtained by Kukulewa villagers during this period have been asweddumized, that is, converted into paddy fields, and are cultivated as regularly as the *paraveni* fields. In most cases several villagers came together to buy a block of *sinakkera* land, which they immediately divided among themselves proportionately to the amount of their contribution to the purchase price. Only rarely did a single individual have access to sufficient cash to purchase more than one acre of *sinakkera* land. Very few of the original purchasers still survive, and because most acquisitions have been further subdivided in the course of inheritance, there are now no plots of *sinakkera* land in Kukulewa larger than one acre.

8. The first recorded purchases in Kukulewa took place in 1909.

9. In this section, when I refer to land, it may be taken that I am referring specifically to *mada idam* (mud land) that either is already paddy land or is intended to be developed into permanent irrigated fields.

Since the passage of the Land Development Ordinance the government has granted land only on *badu* (lease) and subject to the conditions noted in chapter 3. The conditions that are most relevant here are the requirement that a *badu* holding be transmitted to a single, specified heir, and the restrictions imposed on mortgaging a holding. In practice most *badu* lands have been acquired during the last ten or fifteen years and have not yet been subject to inheritance, while their private and illicit mortgage is frequent.

Prior to 1935 the acquisition and development of new paddy lands were left largely to the initiative of individual villagers. Since the Land Development Ordinance, however, not only has the state increasingly endeavored to extend paddy cultivation and stimulate production, but administrators and politicians have also been much concerned with landlessness among poor peasants. Where the government has undertaken to repair and improve existing village irrigation works, or to construct new ones, its policy has been to distribute equably the lands thus newly made accessible to irrigation, and, in particular, to ensure the provision of at least a little land to all landless householders. Most of the ninety-eight acres of *badu* paddy land in Kukulewa were given out between 1955 and 1965, and as a result of this policy virtually all men who were heads of households at the time were granted at least one acre. More than half of the twenty-five households (out of a total of ninety households in the village) whose members today hold no *badu* land are households that have been established since 1965. Of the remaining heads of households that lack *badu* land several are old widows, one is an outsider who works in Anuradhapura and does not cultivate, another is an epileptic cripple and two were granted land in one of the major colonization projects.[10]

Those who have obtained *badu* lands have not, however, all received equal amounts, nor are their holdings of equal value. The village of Kukulewa contains two small and long-abandoned tanks, called Palugaswewa and Nithulgaswewa, which the government helped restore in the early 1960s and under which it has since distributed fifty-four acres in one-acre plots. Previous to the government's intervention, however, three villagers had privately undertaken some minor repairs to these tanks, sufficient to bring several acres under cultivation. Although this was strictly speaking an illegal encroachment on crown land, it was decided to recognize the men's efforts and enterprise, and accordingly they were not only granted the choicest plots but, by an administrative nicety, were given larger extents than their fellows. Whereas the general

10. A total of four Kukulewa householders have received allotments in one of colonies.

policy was to grant a single plot of one acre to each householder who was a cultivator, these three men were also given plots adjacent to their own in the names of their wives and eldest children. Furthermore, although the tanks have been partially restored and the land granted, no adequate system of sluices and irrigation channels has yet been constructed, with the result that half of the fifty-four acres distributed under Palugaswewa and Nithulgaswewa have not yet been asweddumized. Indeed it would seem that in this case official expectations have been excessive and that even if the sluices and channels were built there would very rarely, if ever, be a sufficient supply of water to irrigate all fifty-four acres. This case is not unique, and it has thus come about not only that *badu* land is unequally distributed among the villagers but also that more than half the households in Kukulewa either hold no *badu* land at all or hold plots that are not at present asweddumized (table 4.3).

TABLE 4.3

HOLDINGS OF *BADU* LAND IN KUKULEWA BY HOUSEHOLD

Badu Land	Holdings (in acres)					
	0	0-1/2	1/2-1	1-2	2-3	3+
All	25	0	42	8	12	2
Asweddumized	49	0	23	13	3	2

Nevertheless the acquisition of *badu* land has gone some way toward effecting a more general distribution of paddy land than would otherwise be the case. Table 4.4 shows that twenty-six households possess no *paraveni* or *sinakkera* land. Eleven of these are headed by men who also hold no *badu* land, but almost without exception they are recently married men, and most of them can eventually expect to inherit something either from their own or their wife's parents. Several others, who hold *badu* but not *paraveni* or *sinakkera* land, also have a living parent or parent-in-law who holds paddy land, but there are eight or nine households, or about 10 percent of the total, which would be without either land or prospects were it not for their *badu* holdings.

TABLE 4.4

HOLDINGS OF *PARAVENI* (ANCESTRAL) AND *SINAKKERA* (FREEHOLD) LAND IN KUKULEWA BY HOUSEHOLD

Paraveni and *Sinakkera* Lands	Holdings (in acres)					
	0	0-1/2	1/2-1	1-2	2-3	3+
All	26	33	14	9	4	4
Asweddumized	27	36	14	7	3	3

When we turn from *badu* to *sinakkera* and *paraveni* land we move
also from the ways in which new land is acquired from the government
to consider how property is transmitted between individuals. Very little
sinakkera land is still held by its original purchasers, while *paraveni*
land has, of course, changed hands many times.

The only fully approved mode of transferring possession of paddy
land is by inheritance, which normally takes place between parents and
their children. The rule of inheritance is bilateral, sons and daughters
having equal rights to receive property from both their parents. It is
also generally agreed that all children should inherit equal proportions
of the parental property, although if, as is sometimes stated to be the
ideal, the youngest child remains in the parental household to care for
his mother and father in their old age, there is some feeling that he
should inherit a little more than his siblings.

Paddy land is almost always physically divided among the heirs. The
Veddas generally lack other forms of valuable property that could be
transmitted to certain heirs instead of land, such as the cash dowries
given to daughters in other parts of Sri Lanka (Leach 1961a, pp. 135-
36; Obeyesekere 1967, pp. 43-44; Yalman 1967, pp. 172-76, 291-93).
Thus the physical division of land in each generation could, in principle,
lead to such fragmentation of holdings that they would be economically unworkable. But the Veddas are not so irrational. In practice most
villagers enjoy several holdings in different parts of the fields, and these
can often be distributed among the heirs without requiring any one of
them to be itself divided. If, however, there are several heirs to a small
plot that it is not feasible to divide physically, there is the institution
of *tattumaru*, whereby each heir in turn works the whole property (Obeyesekere, 1967, pp. 18-21, 35-36; Sarkar and Tambiah, 1957, pp. 74-
75). Recourse to *tattumaru* is uncommon in Kukulewa. There are at present only three or four plots that are worked in this way, and none of
them is more than a quarter of an acre in extent.

But the main limit to the fragmentation of holdings is that in
practice not all heirs do inherit equally, and some do not effectively
inherit at all. Such deviations from the ideal rule are explicable in terms
of the size of the estate, the residence of the potential heirs, and the
age at which the proprietor dies.

In most cases effective possession of landed property passes only to
those heirs who continue to live in the village in which the property is
located, for most villages are too widely separated for a man to be
able conveniently to live in one village and work land in another. And
most inheritances are too small for a nonresident proprietor to find it
worthwhile to supervise cultivation by a tenant and to ensure that the

rajakariya duties, which remain with the proprietor, are properly performed.

A virilocally resident man will sooner or later receive land from either or both of his parents' estates. If he has found his wife in his own village, he will also be able to claim her share of her parents' estates, although in this case he will never acquire full ownership. He will only manage the property on behalf of his wife and her children, to whom it will eventually pass. If the wife dies without issue, the land will revert to her parents or pass to her siblings. If she leaves small children when she dies, her widower may continue to enjoy possession on their behalf.

When a man marries a woman from a different village than his own, however, he will probably only be able to exercise effective claims to productive property in the village in which he lives. Uxorilocal husbands and virilocal wives do claim a share of their parents' property in their native villages, but the benefits they enjoy are largely symbolic (see pp. 82-83). However, their prospects can be improved in several sets of circumstances:

1. The couple can shift its residence and revive its claims in the village to which it moves. This is most likely to be effective if the parents are still living and have retained control of their property, so such a strategy is more attractive to young couples than to older ones. Its disadvantage is that it involves a relaxation of claims in the village of previous residence.

2. A man may settle uxorilocally in the native village of his virilocal mother or uxorilocal father, and he may then be able to resurrect the inheritance rights of his parent. This strategy is most likely to be successful if he marries his first cross-cousin. A similar opportunity exists to claim an inheritance on behalf of a virilocal wife who settles in a village of which one of her parents was a native.

3. Although Vedda villages are usually too widely scattered for a man to be able conveniently to live in one village and work land in another, especially because cultivation involves both cooperation with others and the fulfillment of *rajakariya* obligations at specific times, in a few cases two villages are no more than two or three miles apart, and a man may then be able to work land in both.

4. I also noted that most inheritances are too small for a nonresident proprietor to find it worthwhile to supervise its cultivation by a tenant and to ensure that the *rajakariya* duties, which remain with the proprietor, are performed. In a few cases, however, this is not so, and the nonresident heir accordingly retains possession.

The general effect of inheritance practices is thus to ensure that most landed property remains in the hands of village residents. One other circumstance that threatens to introduce further deviations from this pattern occurs when a proprietor dies before his children have grown up. In such cases his property is usually divided among them all, although some will probably later marry away from their native village. But again almost all proprietors who emigrate from the village in which their property lies either sell it or mortgage it or, if their holding is very small, simply allow their claim to lapse and let the land pass to their siblings who remain in residence. If a nonresident owner sells or mortgages his inheritance it is considered proper for him to offer it first to his close kinsmen, and this convention seems to have been particularly closely followed with respect to *paraveni* property.

At the present time there are twenty-five plots of paddy land in Kukulewa, totaling twelve and one-half acres, or slightly less than 10 percent of the whole, that are held by nonresidents. All these non-resident proprietors were themselves born and raised in Kukulewa, but only one of their holdings is now cultivated by the owner. Twenty are mortgaged, two are given on *ande* (share-cropping tenancy) to Kukulewa residents and two are worked without payment by close kinsmen in the village. In one of these latter cases the cultivator is the owner's son-in-law, in the other he is the owner's young brother. Ten of the twenty mortgages involve *paraveni* property, and in the majority of these cases the mortgagees are close kinsmen of the mortgagers, including a daughter's husband, a mother's sister's son, a brother, and a wife's brother. Kinship between the mortgagers and mortgagees of *sinakkera* and *badu* property is frequently more distant, and in three cases the mortgagee is not a Vedda at all, but is a shopkeeper in the neighboring Goyigama village of Mekichchawa.

Because there is a statistical preference for virilocal over uxorilocal residence (see pp. 81-84), one may anticipate that a larger proportion of landholders will be men than women; roughly two-thirds of *paraveni* and *sinakkera* property is at present in male hands.[11] This, however, is only partly a consequence of the residential preference; approximately one-third of the *paraveni* and *sinakkera* land has been acquired by its present owners not by inheritance but by purchase. In almost all cases those who have bought land have been men, while half the sellers have been women. Sellers of paddy land may be divided into two classes: one is comprised of emigrées from the village; the other, less willing,

11. I exclude *badu* land from this calculation on the grounds that a. it has been largely granted to men rather than women, under the circumstances described earlier, and that b. it has been recently acquired and not yet inherited.

sellers are men and women who have fallen upon hard times, who need to raise cash, and whose credit is exhausted. The sale of paddy land is an unhappy, desperate, and all too often temporary solution to such problems, but it is not only the improvident who have recourse to it. Others may simply be unlucky, afflicted, for example, by chronic sickness in their households.

Mortgage (*ukas*) provides a somewhat less extreme remedy; the proprietor retains at least nominal title to his land, but it is still considered shameful and most villagers are reluctant to admit the extent to which their lands are mortgaged. A mortgage is also more attractive to the owner because it can establish an enduring and rewarding relationship, in contrast to that involved in outright transfer, which is terminated by the sale itself. The usual mortgage is for the owner to offer his property as security for a cash loan, and for the mortgagee to acquire right of possession in lieu of interest. When the owner is a village resident it is very common for the mortgage to be combined with an *ande* (share-cropping) tenancy. It is agreed at the time of the mortgage, which is itself rarely formally documented, that the mortgagee will hand the land back to the owner for the latter to work on *ande*. There is a good deal of variation in the details of *ande* tenancies, but it is normal for the landlord (in this case the mortgagee) to provide seed, buffaloes, and plows, and for the crop to be divided more or less equally between the parties.[12] This arrangement has advantages for both mortgager and mortgagee. The former acquires a creditor who will bear the heavy costs of cultivation, which occur at the time of the year when his own resources are most extended, while the latter not only obtains a high rate of interest on his loan but also gains a client who can be expected to be his political supporter.

Because owners who have mortgaged their property are disinclined to say so, it is difficult to assess the extent of the practice. When an owner is working his mortgaged land on *ande* there is no direct evidence of the fact until the mortgagee arrives at the threshing floor to collect his share of the crop. Unfortunately my field work ended with the first successful harvest in two years, and the threshing of many crops was then postponed as the villagers hurriedly prepared their fields for a second, yala, cultivation. It is highly probable, therefore, that my account underestimates the extent of mortgaging, perhaps seriously so, since it includes only those cases that were admitted to me.

12. For an analysis of the variable details of *ande* arrangements, see Leach 1961a, pp. 266-70. Vedda practice is similar to that which Leach describes for Pul Eliya.

A number of instances were revealed to me by villagers who were not directly involved and, armed with apparently confident knowledge, I could sometimes extract an unwilling confession. It is possible that a high proportion of mortgages inside Kukulewa were eventually revealed to me. But it is also likely that the amount of land mortgaged to outsiders, particularly the shopkeepers in Mekichchawa to whom many villagers are more or less constantly in debt, is much greater than is recorded in my notebooks. Such mortgages could be arranged quite privately, indeed secretly, and would normally be accompanied by *ande* tenancy by the original owner.

My information is that approximately forty-one acres of cultivable paddy land (32 percent of the total) are currently mortgaged. This figure comprises fourteen acres of *paraveni* land (42 percent of all *paraveni* land), seven acres of *sinakkera* (21 percent) and twenty acres of *badu* land (31 percent). Twenty-six acres are mortgaged to village residents, the remainder being almost entirely held by Goyigama creditors in Mekichchawa.

The few Kukulewa villagers who are in a position to act as creditors to their fellows are, by and large, the same individuals who bought land outright, and although it is certainly possible for a man's fortune to rise and fall sufficiently rapidly for him to be obliged to sell or mortgage land that he himself has previously bought, it is more common for an inheritance to intervene. Only two and three-quarter acres of currently mortgaged land were obtained by its present owners by purchase. Sale and mortgage are largely complementary means of transferring control of property, although since the final outcome of a mortgage can be the outright transfer of the property to the mortgagee, they may also be sequential. I have already mentioned that one-third (twenty-two acres) of all *paraveni* and *sinakkera* land was acquired by its present owners by purchase. When this figure is added to that of the currently mortgaged land, and the small amount of land that was bought but is now mortgaged is subtracted, the result is sixty acres, or 46 percent of the total. If the recently acquired *badu* land is removed from consideration, the figure is forty acres out of sixty-six, or 61 percent. This indicates the extent to which the effective control of land has been transferred among living individuals. But to what extent do these exchanges lead to the concentration of landed property in the hands of a few?

The top row of table 4.5 shows how the ownership of paddy land in Kukulewa, whether asweddumized or not, is distributed among the ninety households. Only eleven households are entirely landless, and no one owns more than eight acres. When only asweddumized land is considered (row 2) there are nearly twice as many landless households,

TABLE 4.5

DISTRIBUTION OF PADDY LAND HOLDINGS IN KUKULEWA BY HOUSEHOLDS

							Holdings (in acres)						
	0	0-1	1-2	2-3	3-4	4-5	5-6	6-7	7-8	8-9	9-10	10-11	11-12
Nominal Ownership, All Paddy Land	11	26	22	13	9	3	3	1	2	—	—	—	—
Nominal Ownership, Asweddumized Land	21	26	20	13	4	4	1	1	—	—	—	—	—
Effective Control, Asweddumized Land	32	25	14	9	3	2	2	—	1	—	—	1	1

and the largest holding is less than seven acres. When account is taken of mortgages (row 3), the number of landless households rises to thirty-two, while a further twenty-five have no more than one acre; that is to say, almost two-thirds of the households control one acre or less of paddy land. At the other end of the scale there are now two households that, by virtue of the mortgages they have acquired, control more than ten acres each.

A simple classification of owners and mortgagees by household affiliation, however, does not elucidate the extent to which productive property becomes concentrated in a few hands. In the first place it is an unsuitably static measure for a dynamic process. In the second place, with respect to paddy cultivation, the household is a unit of consumption rather than of production, and while members of the same household do cooperate in production, a classification into household units does not adequately describe the groups that combine in productive activities and that share access to the means of production. This is made clear by recalling that inheritance is a gradual process that may extend over many years. Thus at any time it may be unwarrantably arbitrary to assign "ownership" of a plot of land between the independent households of a man and his son or daughter. Some land held in the name of married children in independent households is still controlled by their parents, while other land that is worked by independent sons is still nominally owned by their parents.

When fathers and their married sons are both active cultivators there is usually, but not invariably, close cooperation between them, even if they maintain separate households. The same is true, to a lesser extent, of fathers-in-law and their sons-in-law. It will be useful, then, for purposes of exposition, to distinguish three relationships that obtain between those who assist one another in cultivation. Using this classification to identify and analyze the composition of those groups in Kukulewa, larger than the individual household, that control most of the paddy land and direct its cultivation, it will be possible to illuminate the process of inheritance in greater detail, and also to generate a model of the developmental cycle of productive groups. This model can then be articulated with the process of household development that I have already examined. This analysis will further indicate some of the dynamics of village society and the strategies that are available to those who are ambitious to become village leaders.

The first, and most intimate, class of productive relationships is that of the *generalized reciprocity* that obtains between members of the same household, but which is also maintained, with respect to paddy cultivation, between some independent households. Here labor and other resources, most notably tools, seed paddy, and buffaloes, are freely exchanged or loaned without specific compensation. Since the occasional and casual offer of labor and tools is not unknown in other contexts, the free loan or gift of seed and buffaloes provides better criteria for identifying the groups of intimately associated households cooperating in this way.[13] The groups themselves, which may be called *basic cultivating groups* or *basic productive units,* are nearly always dominated by a single leader who is the father or father-in-law of the heads of the other associated households.

The second class of relationships connects the leader of a basic cultivating group with associates, supporters, and assistants on terms that are also *privileged* but that require some formal payment, more frequently in kind than in cash, for the loan of seed and buffaloes. Groups formed by such alliances between members of separate basic cultivating groups may be called *secondary cultivating groups.*

The third class is that of "normal" contractual relations. Laborers are paid, seed sold, and buffaloes hired at the prevailing regional rate. Payment may still be in kind, but today a money transaction is more frequently involved. This class of relationships also includes the standard *ande* tenancy under which the owner or mortgagee advances seed, buffaloes, and tools, and then recovers his expenses and half the crop at harvest.

---

13. Institutionalized forms of labor exchange deserve a brief mention. The term *attan,* designating a formal relationship whereby one man works in another's field and receives an equivalent return of labor on a subsequent occasion, is not commonly used in Kukulewa. Villagers do use the term *udowwe* (help) in a similar context, which appears, however, to be somewhat less formal than that described elsewhere (Robinson 1968; Obeyesekere 1967, p. 8).

Vedda cultivators also sometimes organize a *kaiya* (labor team). Under this arrangement a number of men will work in the cultivator's field for a day in return for a full complement of meals. Today it is also often necessary for the *kaiya* organizer to supply liberal quantities of alcohol. It is the normal expectation that the organizer of a *kaiya* will return an equivalent amount of labor on a similar occasion, but this expectation is not always realized. A *kaiya* is most commonly organized by a man who is behind in his cultivation or by one who has no access to buffaloes and needs a concentration of labor to turn the ground in his field (cf. Leach 1961a, pp. 264-66, 271-83; Obeyesekere 1967, p. 8).

As Leach demonstrates, the membership of a *kaiya* can provide an important index of social groupings, but this form of labor organization is infrequent in Kukulewa and is anyway not critical to my present theme. Since Kukulewa and Pul Eliya are different "societies" it is difficult to assess precisely the extent to which the lower frequency of *kaiya* organization in the former community is a direct consequence of the expansion of the cash sector of the economy since 1954.

It must be acknowledged that a classification of cultivating groups based on the distinction between the three classes of relationships is not simple, because two householders may establish different relationships with each other at different times or with respect to different plots of land. For example, a man may be a member of his father-in-law's basic cultivating group when he is working the latter's land, but may enjoy only a privileged relationship (the second class) when he is working land he has inherited or acquired himself.

It is worth noting specifically, then, that although membership of basic cultivating groups in Kukulewa proves not to overlap, a man who is a member of one group may enjoy a privileged relationship with the leader of a second group. In such cases the leaders of the two basic groups are almost always closely allied.

Kukulewa contains nine basic cultivating groups that each control at least five acres of paddy land. As an introduction to their description, some preliminary observations may be drawn from table 4.6, which shows how they acquired the land they now control. It will be noted that the nine groups, comprising nineteen households, hold almost all the land (93 percent) that is mortgaged within the village. Inheritance has been the most important mode of acquisition in only one case, and accounts for no more than one-sixth of the land collectively held by the nine groups. Purchase has been the chief source of acquisition in two cases, and crown leases (*badu*) in four. Two of the enterprising cultivators who opened up the land under Palugaswewa and Nithulgaswewa and were granted unusually large allocations are represented here. Now let us look at each group in turn.

Group A: K. Wannihamy

Wannihamy is a native of Kukulewa who inherited very little from his parents. After some time away from the village he returned with sufficient capital to open a shop that has now flourished for ten or fifteen years. His was the only shop in the village that stayed in business throughout the period of my research. More than half the villagers trade with him and many are in his debt. His business activities also bring him into contact with a number of more powerful traders (*mudalalis*) outside the village, but it is difficult to determine to what extent he, in turn, is indebted to them. His prosperity has been built on his shopkeeping activities and on the mortgages he has been able to obtain from his fellow villagers.

His closest supporters are his sons and sons-in-law. His eldest son and daughter are married to two children of A. Dingiribanda (Group H), and the two groups are firmly allied. Wannihamy's own closest kin is

TABLE 4.6

Mode of Acquisition of Paddy Land Controlled
by the Nine Leading Basic Cultivating Groups in Kukulewa

Group	Leader	Number of Households	Buffalo Team Owner	Inheritance	Private Sale	Crown Sale	Crown Lease	Mortgage	Total
						(in acres)			
A	K. Wannihamy	2	yes	0.50	1.375	-	1.00	*9.50*	12.375
B	K. Seerala	2	yes	1.25	1.50	1.00	*4.00*	3.75	11.50
C	W. Herathamy	1	no	0.50	-	-	*5.00*	5.25	10.75
D	H. V. Bandathe	3	no	1.25	*4.375*	0.50	2.00	0.25	8.375
E	P. Tikiriappu/ A. Kapuruhamy	4	yes	0.8125	-	-	*5.00*	0.50	6.3125
F	W. Appurala	2	yes	0.875	-	-	*4.00*	1.125	6.00
G	B. Punchirala	2	no	0.125	*3.25*	-	-	2.50	5.875
H	A. Dingiribanda	2	no	1.25	0.25	-	*3.00*	1.375	5.875
J	B. V. Malhamy	1	no	*5.625*	-	-	-	-	5.625
9		19		12.1875	10.75	1.50	24.00	24.25	72.6875

NOTE: The chief mode of acquisition for each group is italicized.

his widowed sister, who lives next door to him and to whose son another of his daughters is married. Shortly after field work ended I learned that Wannihamy's second son has also married a child of the widowed sister. Wannihamy's children's marriages have thus been restricted within a narrow range, and this has material advantages for a shopkeeper whose kinship obligations might otherwise force him to extend credit beyond the limits of financial prudence (cf. Leach 1961a, p. 131).

Apart from the land he controls in Kukulewa, Wannihamy also holds three acres of his own in the colony at Maha Kanadarawa and another three acres that are mortgaged to him in the same place. In the 1969-70 cultivation season his second son was delegated to work Wannihamy's own land in Maha Kanadarawa. Since this son was not married at that time and was a member of his father's household there was no need to divide the crop between them. The land mortgaged to Wannihamy in Maha Kanadarawa was given to his two sons-in-law to work in partnership on *ande*. Wannihamy financed the operation and the produce was divided among them. Wannihamy's expenses were first deducted and then he received half of the remainder. The other half was divided between the two sons-in-law.

Some of the land mortgaged to Wannihamy in Kukulewa was given back on *ande* to the owners. The rest, and all the land directly owned by him, was worked either by himself or by his eldest son. His other adult son and his sons-in-law contributed occasional labor without direct reward. The eldest son's operations were also financed by his father, but in this case, even though the son maintains an independent household, it was stated that Wannihamy would not receive the half share of the produce to which, under the normal terms of *ande* tenancies, he would be entitled. Only the amount of seed paddy he had provided would be repaid. The use of his buffaloes and agricultural tools was given free.

The scope of Wannihamy's activities requires more labor than his sons and sons-in-law alone can provide. Apart from paddy cultivation and trading he owns a considerable number of cattle, and he was the only villager to grow a chena cash crop on any scale between 1968 and 1970. At various times, in this as in his paddy cultivation, he is able to offer wage labor to his fellow villagers. Moreover his extensive contacts beyond the village enable him to act as a labor contractor for outside interests. Potential employers advise him that they require a certain amount of labor and he undertakes to provide it. His powers of patronage and employment combine with his trading, cultivating, banking, and proprietorial interests to make him the most influential, as well as the wealthiest, man in the village. In addition he is treasurer of the local cultivation committee, of which one of his sons-in-law is also a member.

He is not, of course, without his enemies, but the predominant opinion seems to be that although he is a hard man, he is also honest and direct. Certainly he received overwhelming support in his re-election to the cultivation committee. On the other hand, when he was held in jail for six months in 1969 on suspicion of murder, apparently on the basis of one or two malicious statements and anonymous "petitions" to the authorities, one seemed to detect an undercurrent of satisfaction that now "ambition's debt is paid."

Group B: K. Seerala

Seerala's cultivating group consists of himself, his son and a son-in-law who is also his sister's son. His sister and her husband are both dead. The son is a recently married man who has not yet established an independent household. The son-in-law, who is older and has several children, lives separately. The group's paddy land derives from several sources. Seerala holds several small mortgages, while the son-in-law is one of the men who opened up the land under Palugaswewa and Nithulgaswewa. The rest of the son-in-law's land is inherited from his mother and lies adjacent to land held by Seerala. Both households own buffaloes, which they borrow freely back and forth. They are also often to be seen working in each other's fields.

Seerala himself is an old man who is on the verge of retirement from active cultivation. His daughter has not yet inherited from him, and it is possible that when he does retire he will divide his property and the group will cease to function as such. But the proximity of their holdings and the convenience of sharing the use of each other's buffaloes may keep the two younger men together for a while.

This group also has more land than it can work entirely by itself, even though most of that held on mortgage is given back on *ande* to the owners. The group therefore hires wage laborers as necessary, and also, in the 1969-70 season, after Seerala became sick, it gave out some unmortgaged land on *ande*. However, it has more than enough buffaloes, and as well as working all its own fields, its animals were hired out to other cultivators.

Seerala was formerly an officer of the *variga* court but is no longer politically active.

Group C: W. Herathamy

One of the bases of Herathamy's success is a strategic marriage. Although a native of the village he inherited no land at all, but his wife is the adopted child of a deceased couple whose siblings and other children now live in other villages. In addition to the half acre that has devolved upon his wife, Herathamy has been able to acquire mortgages on another two acres owned by his nonresident affines, which he works himself. His other holdings are mainly under Palugaswewa and Nithulgaswewa, which he helped develop. As well as his own grant he holds mortgages on several plots, giving him effective control of six acres in that area.

Herathamy has two grown sons, still unmarried, who help him cultivate. His one son-in-law, who is also a native of the village, does not cooperate with him but assists his father. Herathamy occasionally employs other villagers to work in his fields but works most of his land with the resources available within his own household. Although he holds mortgages on more land than anyone else except Wannihamy, he has not built up a network of clients. He himself works not only the land owned by his wife's kinsmen but also most of the land mortgaged to him by village residents. Nor does he own buffaloes that could be hired out to other cultivators. Instead he rents what he needs from Mekichchawa. Thus although he is recognized as an industrious man he exerts less personal influence than the extent of his holdings might suggest.

Group D: H. V. Bandathe

Bandathe is the former Vel Vidane, and it was during his tenure of office that he acquired, by purchase, most of the land that his group now controls. Half of this land has now been formally transferred to his eldest son, the only child of his first marriage,[14] who supports a large independent household and who is regularly employed as a laborer by the village committee. One son of Bandathe's second marriage is also married, and he too maintains an independent household. There are two other, unmarried sons who are old enough to do substantial work in the fields.

Bandathe himself does very little work on the land. The cultivation of his group's holdings is largely organized and financed by his eldest son, who takes a number of days off work during the season in order to supervise it. The son is now assuming leadership of the group, thus providing one of the few instances of a man achieving prominence on the basis of inherited property. The cultivation of both his own and his

14. This apparent divergence from the rule of equal inheritance by all children is justified by the theory that whereas inherited property should be equally divided among all the children, additional property acquired during the course of a marriage should pass only to the children of that marriage.

father's fields is mostly done by his younger half-brothers, but my most diligent inquiries were unable to discover precisely how the produce of this group's land was allocated.

When Bandathe was Vel Vidane he became adept at stalking the labyrinthine corridors of local bureaucratic power, and he established a number of enduring relationships that enable him still to present himself as the leader of the village. Although he now lacks formal authority, the access to officialdom that he enjoys allows him some vestigial influence and prestige in certain quarters of the village. But most Kukulewa villagers are agreed that his tenure of office was arrogant and autocratic, and few now accord him the respect to which he considers himself entitled.

Group E: P. Tikiriappu and A. Kapuruhamy

This group is exceptional in that it is formed by an alliance between two men who are "cross-cousins," a son of each being married to a daughter of the other. One man's son is still a member of his father's household; the other lives independently. A fourth household, that of another married son of A. Kapuruhamy, is also included within the group.

The members of this group are not exceptionally wealthy. Indeed their average holding per household is only slightly above that of the villagers as a whole. They also operate independently in most stages of cultivation and only qualify here as a unified cultivating group by virtue of their cooperation in one aspect of the production process. At least one member of each household owns one or more buffaloes, but no household can itself muster enough to provide a full team, which normally consists of four animals. They therefore regularly combine their resources to form a team that is employed in the fields of all the four households, without specific payment being made on each occasion. In other respects they are typical of the middle range of independent cultivators and none is a leading political figure.

Group F: W. Appurala

Appurala is a uxorilocally married man who acquired a modest inheritance through his wife and who has worked hard to bring new land under cultivation. He has a married son who lives adjacent to him in a separate household. The son has an acre of *badu* land in his own name, which he works independently, though he uses his father's buffaloes without charge.

Appurala also hires out his buffaloes to other cultivators, and has taken on several small mortgages. He is an ambitious and industrious man but inclined, perhaps, to overextend his resources. He tries to run a shop, but finds difficulty in sustaining it. More than once during the period of research he was obliged to close it down for two or three months. His stock was never more than paltry in comparison to Wanni-hamy's prosperous establishment, but he could count on a little regular custom from his allies, affines, and neighbors, and from those who refused to trade with Wannihamy.

Group G: B. Punchirala

Punchirala's group contains himself and two married sons, one of whom is still a member of his own household. Some of the group's land is held in the name of the elder son, but Punchirala directs and finances all the cultivation. Most of the land is either held on mortgage or was bought. As in the case of W. Herathamy (Group C), Punchirala's marriage has been helpful in this respect. His wife comes from Kiri-metiyawa, a small village that was founded from Kukulewa a generation or so ago. The founders of Kirimetiyawa retained land in Kukulewa that Punchirala, after his marriage, persuaded them to sell to him. Apart from the holdings shown in table 4.6, Punchirala also owns another two and one-half acres he has mortgaged to a shopkeeper in Mekichchawa and that he works on *ande.*

Punchirala and his sons work all their land themselves without hiring additional labor. When they are available he uses the buffaloes belonging to his elder brother, B. Undiyarala, for which he pays an amount of paddy equivalent to the sowing extent of the plot being worked, a common arrangement between close kin.

Group H: A. Dingiribanda

As noted earlier, Dingiribanda has a son and daughter married to children of K. Wannihamy (Group A), to whom he is closely allied. This is the same relationship as that connecting the leaders of Group E, but in the present case the various parties have not merged into a single cultivating group. The basis of cooperation in Group E is the members' mutual dependence in forming a working team of buffaloes. The greater resources of Wannihamy and Dingiribanda enable them to operate independently. It is true that Dingiribanda's son works for Wannihamy, but when he is working his own parental lands he receives no assistance from his father-in-law.

Group J: B. V. Malhamy

Malhamy's group consists of a single household containing himself and his wife, his widowed mother, who died in April 1970, and his younger brother and sister, who are both unmarried. This is the only one of the nine groups that has acquired most of its property by inheritance. It is highly probable, if precedent is any basis for prediction, that when Malhamy's brother and sister get married the property will be divided and the group will split up. At present Malhamy directs the cultivation, although his brother is old enough to assist him in the field. These two young men cultivate their land themselves, using the team of buffaloes owned by B. Undiyarala, who is Malhamy's father-in-law.

Undiyarala himself does not control sufficient land to be included here, but his activities, and those of the owners of the only other team of buffaloes not already discussed, are worth a brief mention. Undiyarala is the third Kukulewa member of the cultivation committee and is the agent for the *paraveni* lands. He is frequently referred to as the Vel Vidane, although, as we have seen, the office is now abolished. He also owns a part of the *gamwasama* holding in the *paraveni* field, and by virtue of this is entitled to be known as the Gamarala (see chapter 2). He is a man of great dignity and authority, whose advice is solicited by many villagers and who is widely called upon to adjudicate domestic disputes. He lacks the outside connections developed, for example, by Wannihamy (Group A) or Bandathe (Group D), but along with his younger brother B. Punchirala (Group G) he is universally respected by those who value traditional behavior. His economic standing is above average, but he is not among the wealthiest villagers. He owns about three acres, which are worked by himself, his two unmarried sons, and his three sons-in-law. One of his sons-in-law is B. V. Malhamy (Group J), who has little time to work any land other than his own. A second son-in-law, who is also his sister's son, has no land of his own. The third has less than half an acre.

Most of Undiyarala's land is worked by himself and his sons, who are members of his own household. Portions of it, however, are given out to the two sons-in-law who have little or no land of their own. In these circumstances Undiyarala provides seed paddy and lends his buffaloes free of charge. But when his sons-in-law use his buffaloes to work land that does not belong to Undiyarala himself, as in the case of Malhamy's inherited lands, they rent them on the same terms that obtain between Undiyarala and his brother Punchirala; that is, the owner of the buffaloes receives at harvest an amount of paddy equivalent to the sowing extent of the plot in which the buffaloes are used. Undiyarala, like other owners, also hires out his buffaloes for cash to villagers who are more distantly related to him.

The ownership and use of the only other team of buffaloes not yet discussed presents another variation. As in the case of Group E, this team is composed of animals owned by members of separate households, but here the owners are adult brothers who have divided their inherited property, but who bring together their buffaloes into a single team, which is freely employed in the otherwise separately worked property of each.

The various arrangements I have described indicate the hazards of drawing summary conclusions concerning the organization of paddy cultivation. One may safely assert, however, that the kinship connection involved is a significant indicator of the terms under which cultivators cooperate. Sons receive generous treatment from their fathers, even when they have established independent households. Indeed the terms under which they work parental property are frequently more favorable than if the land had already passed to them, because the costs of cultivation are often met by the parent. Men who are working land belonging to their fathers-in-law may enjoy similar privileges. The exchange of goods and services within basic cultivating groups may be seen as a system of generalized reciprocity operating between the closely related households forming such a group. When sons-in-law are working land derived from their own parents, or obtained by themselves, they may still be given seed paddy or the use of buffaloes on favored terms, but it is likely that some formal payment will be required. Almost always such payments are made in kind. The kinship distance at which such special relationships cease to obtain is impossible to specify precisely, since it is subject to much variation. There is in fact an area of kinship wherein cooperation in cultivation is uncommon, perhaps precisely because there is too much room for disagreement and conflict over the conditions that should govern the relationship. This area includes brothers whose parental property is divided and other collateral kinsmen within the range of first cousins. Beyond the latter range the terms are those of standard contractual arrangements, and cash transactions are more frequent.

The organization of paddy cultivation must be further examined within a developmental framework, one that will articulate with the cyclical process of household formation described in the previous chapter. The most appropriate focus for this endeavor is that provided by the transmission of property from parents to their children.

While a young man is unmarried he normally works as a subordinate member of his father's productive unit. Instances of an unmarried man being allocated land to work independently by his father, for example, K. Wannihamy's (group A) allocation to his second son, are very rare, and even here it is only the cultivation that is conducted separately, the produce itself being aggregated with that of the parent's other fields. On the other hand, some young children whose parents are still living are already the nominal owners of paddy land. This too is a device that is restricted to the wealthier proprietors, some of whom have transferred formal possession of enough of their holdings in this way to be able to present themselves as sufficiently poor to qualify for the allocation of lease lands by the government. But this is uncommon. It is much more usual for formal title to remain with a proprietor until his death, even though effective possession may have passed to his children many years earlier. Indeed a good deal of property is still officially recorded as being held by men and women who have been dead for some years.

When a young man marries he begins to look for some more or less permanent allocation from his parent's property. At this stage, however, as I have noted, the productive activities of father and son usually remain closely linked. The virilocally resident son does not often receive a plot of land to work on his own until he has also established an independent household, and even thereafter he may remain a member of his father's basic cultivating group, with the father providing seed and the use of his tools and buffaloes to the son, and the latter returning labor. Similar relations obtain between a uxorilocal husband and his wife's father. The son-in-law does not expect immediately to prize loose his wife's potential inheritance, certainly not before he has set up his own household, although he may hope to receive land from his own parents if the latter live sufficiently close for him to be able to work it.

The allocations that proprietors make to their recently married sons and daughters are not necessarily permanent or immutable. When a marriage is dissolved and the husband and wife rejoin their parental households, any paddy land that they have been allocated is also likely to revert to their parents' control. But in most cases the land a young man is given to work is property that all concerned anticipate will eventually pass fully to him or, in the case of a grant from his wife's parents, to his wife's children. And the more years a young man has regularly worked a particular plot the more difficult it will be to dislodge him from it, even though nominal ownership may remain with the parent until his death.

Thus the inheritance of productive property in land is to be seen as a gradual and somewhat variable process rather than as a single, uniform act. But despite these variations it is possible to augment the finding that connects the residential separation of parents and their married children with the number of children born to the younger couple, by making the further assertion that this residential separation is also correlated with the economic independence of the younger couple as a producing no less than as a consuming unit, and, more specifically, that it is also correlated with the degree of their mutually independent access to the means of paddy production.

This conclusion, however, demands an important amplification that will take account of variations in wealth within the community and will thereby clarify the means of advancement in Vedda society. I have stated that young couples seek to establish themselves independently, but that their parents want them to remain close at hand. This is a matter of economics as much as of sentiment. Young couples do indeed seek independence, but they like to take with them as much of their potential inheritance as possible. Parents, for their part, expect to allot land to those of their married children who have left their household, but they do not feel obliged to transfer all their rights. Under these conditions the more substantial parents can hold their married children by giving the latter less to cultivate than they eventually expect to inherit. Sons and sons-in-law are thus encouraged to give their parents the continued benefit of their labor. Poorer villagers, by contrast, have less use for their children's labor, and their sons may lose little by living independently from shifting cultivation and wage labor. The ability to retain the active support of sons and sons-in-law by holding out the prospect of further benefits to come is enhanced when the parent is growing wealthier. If he is acquiring land by sale and mortgage he is better able to persuade his sons and sons-in-law that they will gain by staying with him and continuing to work under his direction. And if he does continue to direct and enjoy their labor, he *is* better able to expand his operations. His sons and sons-in-law invest their labor in his enterprise in the confidence that they will receive a subsequent return in the form of a greater inheritance.

Thus the rising and successful men are those whose married children continue to cluster around them. The wealthiest and most prominent figures in Kukulewa are middle-aged men closely supported by their married children and their spouses. Such groups, of course, are bound to the individual life cycle, and they start to disintegrate as the parent passes beyond middle age and disengages himself from the active direction of cultivation. While their father is still providing active leadership a group of siblings is united in exploiting and extending the family estate. But this solidarity of siblings and siblings-in-law requires the integrating authority of the father. When the father dies or withdraws from active life, the divergent and, indeed, conflicting interests of the children come increasingly to the fore. Siblings are now competing with one another over the division of their parents' property. For brothers this is a final separation. Formerly allied under their father's leadership, as independent proprietors their interests now necessarily diverge and may even conflict. Particularly in the smaller villages, the ambitious man may only be able to increase his holdings at the expense of his brothers. Between a son and a daughter's husband, however, that is, between brothers-in-law, another possibility obtains, since their fortunes can be reunited by a marriage between their children.

WAGE LABOR AND THE CASH ECONOMY

I have mentioned that several of the wealthiest men in Kukulewa find it necessary to hire labor in order to cultivate their fields. The laborers they engage are always their fellow villagers. Opportunities for employment, however, are strictly limited in a village with only 130 acres of cultivable land and a population of 552. Since his holdings, like those of others, are distributed in several different blocks, which can be cultivated according to slightly different schedules, even K. Wannihamy can muster most of the labor he requires from among his sons and sons-in-law. Only at harvest does the demand for labor regularly exceed the resources of the basic cultivating groups and their privileged associates.

Nevertheless wage labor provides the main source of cash income for a majority of Veddas, but they must go outside their own villages to obtain it. Thus, while wage labor is certainly important in the Vedda economy as a whole, I afford it relatively little space here, since my primary concern is with the social relations that exist among the Veddas themselves. Wage labor establishes the Veddas as a class of employees with respect to other groups, but it does not generally inform the system of relations established among themselves. With the possible exception of Wannihamy, no Kukulewa villager can sustain a following on the basis of the employment he can offer.

Most of the available employment is in the fields of other, more prosperous villages. Vedda communities that are close to one or other of the major colonization schemes also often supply labor in the colonists' fields. Commercial chena cultivation is another source of employment, and there are occasional opportunities to work in nonagricultural jobs such as house construction. Mention should also be made of the relief work, mainly in the form of tank restoration and repair but occasionally including such activities as road building, which the government sponsors in years of acute shortage.

Wage labor is mainly performed by men, but women are also in demand at harvest, the only stage in the process of paddy cultivation in

which they normally participate. Some young men will travel twenty
or thirty miles for wage labor, and there is a fine network of communications among the scattered Vedda villages that enables labor to be
concentrated wherever work is available. When traveling so far to find
work, the young men will often make up informally organized work
parties with their friends and will remain away from their home village
for a week or two at a time.

Some of the older men consider wage labor demeaning, but few
can afford to match their disdain with abstention. Young men, who
frequently like to visit the cinema and enjoy other urban entertain-
ments, and who aspire to own bicycles, wrist watches, flashlights, and
nylon shirts, no longer admit to such sentiments.

The widespread practice of wage labor is undoubtedly a recent
development. Leach, who is writing of conditions in 1954, describes
how the Veddas of Tulaveliya (27) were at that time still working in the
Pul Eliya fields in return for a traditional payment in kind (1961a,
pp. 251-52). Most such relationships between Vedda villages and neighboring Goyigama communities are now transacted on a cash basis. One
Kukulewa villager regularly works six acres on *ande* from a man in
Mekichchawa, and in the 1969-70 season two other men acquired
ande tenancies from an owner in the nearby village of Kuda Kapiri-
gama, but such cases are exceptional. Many other Kukulewa villagers
frequently worked in these and other villages, but in all cases, in so far
as I could discover, they were paid in cash.

This transformation has been accompanied by related changes in
the pattern of trade and shopkeeping. Leach shows that up until 1954
the traders and shopkeepers in Pul Eliya were "very frequently outsiders from some other *variga;* often they [were] Moslems or Tamils"
(1961a, p. 131). Although the two shopkeepers in the village at the
time of his research were members of the Pul Eliya *variga*, he is somewhat skeptical of their ability to survive. The pressures of kinship
constantly impel them "to give terms of credit which must ultimately
lead to bankruptcy" (ibid.).

Similar conditions prevailed in the Vedda villages, where it appears
that up until about fifteen years ago all the successful shopkeepers were
outsiders. Many villages were too small to support a shop of any kind,
but even in the larger villages most of the Veddas who tried their hand
at the business were doomed to an early failure. Since that time, however, conditions have altered sufficiently for at least the shrewder
Vedda entrepreneurs to sustain quite flourishing businesses. K. Wannihamy's success in Kukulewa is replicated elsewhere. Just as the expansion of the market economy has changed the basis on which Vedda
labor in the fields of other villages, so the greater tolerance of directly

financial transactions among kinsmen has surely strengthened the viability of locally owned shops.

The themes of wage labor and shopkeeping also converge in the observation that although the Veddas often work in the fields of ordinary cultivators in neighboring villages, much of their labor is either done directly for traders and shopkeepers, or is organized by them. It is beyond the scope of the present work to attempt a full assessment of the part played by this class of rural entrepreneurs (the *mudalalis*) in the economy of the area, but it may be noted, for example, that wages earned from them are commonly required to be spent in their shops, and that most Vedda villagers are chronically in debt.[15]

15. A comprehensive analysis of the role of the *mudalali*, which has not to my knowledge been attempted, would fill a serious gap in our understanding of the dynamics of rural Sri Lankan society. We must be all the more grateful, in the meanwhile, for the brief but insightful observations of Amunugama (1964, 1965), Tambiah (1963), and Yalman (1967, pp. 49-54). Amunugama's analysis is particularly useful in the present context, although it is based on research in a colonization project in the south of Sri Lanka where *mudalalis* appear to operate on a larger scale than do those who intrude directly into the Vedda villages. A study of the network of relations connecting the small *mudalalis* in the village, represented, for example, by K. Wannihamy in Kukulewa, through various intermediaries to the large-scale *mudalalis* or *bisnis kariyo* (businessmen) in the cities and towns would be particularly fascinating and illuminating.

Mudalalis receive a generally bad press and are often presented as a class of devious and rapacious middlemen who flourish at the expense of the poor and innocent peasants. They appear to be especially irksome to the urbanized and Westernized middle class, which yet retains links with the villages but whose image of village life is one of bucolic harmony, undisturbed by the profit motive. (An investigation of urban middle-class images of village life would make another absorbing study.)

A good deal of recent legislation has been intended to reduce the power of the *mudalalis*. For example, the government now directly involves itself in the provision of rural credit by sponsoring, through the Department of Agrarian Services, a series of "cultivation loans" administered by the People's Bank and the local cooperative societies. It would seem, however, that these loans, which are welcomed by the villagers, have simply increased the burden of their indebtedness and have not to any significant extent dissuaded them from accepting the credit also offered by the *mudalalis*. Good communications, a high literacy rate, and, not least, the promises of politicians have stimulated a level of aspiration and expectation, even in the peasant sector, that is far beyond the present capacity of the nation to realize. It may be noted parenthetically that this has not escaped the notice of foreign journalists covering the 1971 insurgency in Sri Lanka (see, e.g., *The Daily Telegraph* of London, March 30, 1971). In these circumstances villagers have been ready to accept all the credit they can get and have not abandoned one source simply because another is also made available.

Amunugama notes the advantages the *mudalali*, as creditor, enjoys over the

OTHER OCCUPATIONS

Regular employment, as distinct from the casual labor previously discussed, is highly valued but scarcely obtainable. Two men in Kukulewa are full-time employees of the local village committee and work as laborers to maintain the minor roads and tracks for which the committee is responsible. But the majority of Vedda villages contain no men who are employed on a full-time basis. Nor have most villages produced

---

bureaucrat—his easy accessibility and intimate knowledge of the local situation, the absence of red tape, the flexibility of his operations, and so on. It must also be acknowledged that at least the lower levels of the local bureaucracy are not merely inefficient but frequently corrupt. I would add that the *mudalali*'s aggressive loyalty to the rural idiom, expressed in his dress, language, and behavior, does not establish that social distance between him and his clients that seems to impede communication between the villager and the trousered, English-speaking official. On the contrary, the flamboyant elaborations of native style and the visible signs of toughness and prosperity that many *mudalalis* display—the large and arrogantly worn money belt, the wad of banknotes, the close circle of henchmen—inspire admiration and respect. No doubt they also encourage the settlement of debts.

Amunugama also draws attention to the latent functions performed by the *mudalali* system, which indeed he directly compares with the bossism discussed by Merton in his original analysis of manifest and latent functions (Merton 1951). The *mudalali* acts on behalf of the villagers in encounters with politicians and government officials, and undertakes to deliver votes at election time. He can offer assistance in emergencies and he makes large contributions to communal festivals. Against these services must be set his high rates of interest.

The emergence of the *mudalalis* is often presented as a new phenomenon (see e.g., Amunugama 1965, p. 149). Doubtless the rapid expansion of the market economy in the rural sector has pitched the operations of traders, creditors, and middlemen onto a new level, extending their scope and opening up new kinds of opportunities that may be particularly remarkable in the unprecedented conditions of the colonies. But I have already noted the activities of traders and creditors in Nuvarakalaviya as early as the eighteenth century, and the historical roots of the *mudalali* system may be much deeper (see Knox 1911, pp. 239-40).

Let me summarize the aspects of this digression that are most relevant to the present work. The emergence of a class of small, Vedda *mudalalis*, represented by K. Wannihamy in Kukulewa, is a recent development. Their activities are as yet strictly localized and do not challenge the hegemony of those more powerful *mudalalis*, the scope of whose operations it is difficult precisely to assess, but who undoubtedly play a key role in the economy of the region. Despite their lesser power the Vedda *mudalalis* are nevertheless able to perform at least some of the functions described by Amunugama. Their appearance represents a dilution of kinship rules operating in the economic sphere that parallels the retreat in political affairs I described in chapter 2.

Finally, these comments may serve to emphasize again a situation that the restricted focus of this work might otherwise dissemble, namely, that the Vedda villages do not now constitute "a number of small agricultural republics" but form an integral part of the regional, and indeed national, society.

men or women who have permanently left home to seek employment elsewhere and whose remittances might help sustain the village economy. One or two villages, however, have established channels whereby a few young girls have been taken into urban homes to work as domestics. These girls sometimes send part of their wages back to their families, but they themselves rarely return to settle down in their native villages.

Stock raising is widespread but is important to relatively few Vedda households. The discussion of paddy cultivation has already indicated that the ownership of buffaloes is restricted, and with regard to these animals it is only necessary to add that they are not systematically milked.

The basis of cattle ownership is somewhat broader, and perhaps as many as a quarter of all Vedda households own at least one or two animals. But very few household herds are larger than twenty. Like other forms of property cattle are individually owned, and in this case the property is to a large extent nominally held by children, for it is the common practice to brand the animals that are acquired in the names of successive children (cf. Leach 1961a, p. 144). Most cattle are not closely herded but are allowed to forage more or less freely in the jungle. Sometimes an adolescent boy is delegated to watch them. A few bullocks are trained to pull carts, of which there are four or five in Kukulewa, and these more valuable animals are closely tended. Those who own carts and bullocks are usually also the owners of the largest herds and are the same men who are relatively wealthy in other respects. Only one man in Kukulewa owns a sizable herd of cattle but is not a major paddy cultivator. Unlike paddy cultivation, stock raising does not normally involve the householder in relations with his fellows.

Apart from the cart bulls, most cattle are eventually sold to the Moslem traders who supply the urban meat markets. Herds are much reduced in years of agricultural shortage, not because the hardy cattle cannot themselves survive, although there is always a risk of disease, but because they are then gradually sold off to meet their owners' ongoing household expenses. In this sense possession of cattle provides a reserve fund in case of emergencies. Their cash value and the prestige of ownership are the chief attractions of cattle raising. The animals are allowed to graze in the paddy fields after harvest, but otherwise little use is made of their dung as fertilizer and none at all as fuel. Nor do they provide a source of protein in the Vedda diet. The Veddas do not share the total aversion to meat that some Sinhalese people profess, but none would consume his own cattle.

Some few Veddas also keep goats, whose popularity appears to be rising, but a number of villages lack them entirely. Again they are often given into the charge of a juvenile member of the household and are eventually sold to Moslem traders. Many households also keep a chicken or two whose eggs are also sold.

Domestic meat, then, is absent from the Vedda diet. Game, on the other hand, is much appreciated, but it has become extremely scarce, especially in some areas. The Veddas of Willachchiya, to the northwest of Anuradhapura, seem able to pursue it more successfully than those elsewhere, but nowhere does it provide a major source of food. There are two men in Kukulewa who are recognized as skillful hunters and who spend much time at it, but neither is a full-time specialist. Both also cultivate chenas, but they prefer to neglect paddy cultivation in favor of hunting. Because game is scarce, those who do make something of a profession of hunting are often among the poorest men in the village and do not own their own guns. But if they enjoy a good reputation as hunters, they can obtain the use of more prosperous villagers' guns on *ande*, the terms being similar to those in paddy cultivation. The return of a successful hunter with the carcass of a wild pig or a deer is an occasion of some excitement in the village. It is probable that the flesh will be divided up and sold, and many households will then enjoy the rare pleasure of a meat curry. But the very rarity of it adequately indicates its place in the over-all economy.

There are a few ritual skills that supplement some Vedda incomes. Although it has been suggested that the traditional caste profession of the Veddas was that of priest-medium or *kapurala*, the provision of such services does not now make a substantial contribution to the Vedda economy. It may, however, be important in individual cases. The Veddas who have become *kapuralayas* in the temples (devales) at Padaviya and Huruluwewa colonies enjoy a useful income and considerable prestige. Those practitioners whose direct concern is with health, either in the tradition of *ayurvedic* medicine (the *vedarala*) or in that of magic (the *anumetirala*) can also develop a profitable clientele, but they have had to face the competition of steadily improving medical facilities provided by the state. In the present day the most successful Vedda *vedaralas* seem to be specialists either in the treatment of snake bites or of children's diseases, while the perils of childbirth bring most of their clients to the *anumetiralas*. Kukulewa has one *vedarala* whose reputation attracts patients from other villages, but the one *anumetirala* in the village performs no more than two or three times a year. Lesser practitioners, known as *dehi vedaralas*, who, unlike the *anumetiralas*, do not become possessed, are more frequently called upon, but payment for their services is less. The Vedda village of Elapatwewa (32) does, however, contain a *kapurala-anumetirala* who enjoys an extensive reputation enabling him to be almost a full-time practitioner of his art. He is certainly the wealthiest and most powerful man in the village.

SUMMARY

The Veddas derive their livelihood mainly from chena cultivation, paddy cultivation, and wage labor. To the extent that wage labor is largely performed for outsiders it establishes the Veddas as a class with respect to their employers but is less important in the system of relations established among themselves. Chenas are geared to subsistence and are cultivated by independent household units on land to which all have equal access. Capital requirements are minimal and no more labor is needed than the average household can itself muster. Paddy cultivation requires greater inputs of both capital and labor, which inform a denser network of relations among different households. Moreover, paddy land is privately held, and its transmission, which is normatively regulated by bilateral inheritance, is accelerated and diverted by sales and mortgages. This permits a concentration of land in relatively few hands.

Those who emerge in control of the largest amounts of land are generally middle-aged men closely supported by their sons and sons-in-law. Such men are the leaders of cultivating units that may also form the core of political factions. Because both are tied to the life cycle of the individual, the cyclical process through which cultivating units develop corresponds closely to that of the domestic groups previously described.

Analysis of this process has indicated the various means by which ambitious and enterprising men can gain control of paddy land, the major scarce resource, and thereby achieve a position of political strength. Inheritance, financial skill, a strategic marriage, industry, and other, more idiosyncratic, qualities may all be important. The point is that the means *are* available and that, although the idiom of kinship is pervasive, a man is not the passive plaything of a fate mechanically regulated by the automatic operations of the kinship system. Nevertheless it is clear that the most solidary groups that do emerge are defined in terms of kinship. A man's ability to acquire a following of supporters and dependents more extensive than that provided by his sons and sons-in-law is largely based on the manner in which he deploys his further resources, that is, on the skill with which he uses the patronage, employment, and credit he can offer to bind others into his operations.

These findings have been largely derived from the Kukulewa data.

But having established them it becomes possible to broaden the perspective and examine all the Vedda villages over a considerable period of time.

K. Seerala (see chapter 4), former Kukulewa member of the Vedda *variga* court, with his official hat and staff.

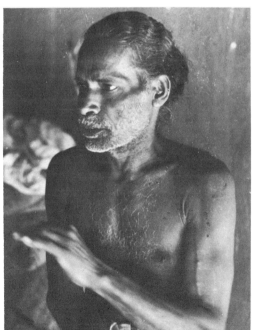

B. Undiyarala (see chapter 4), Kukulewa village elder and member of the Mekichchawa Cultivation Committee, in conversation on his verandah.

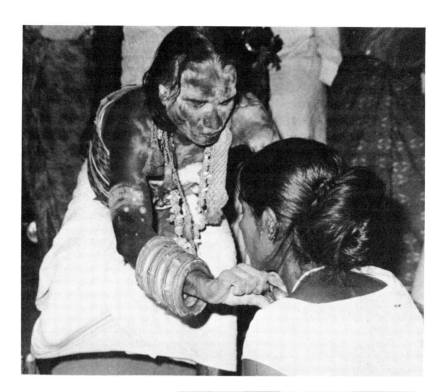

Above, The Kukulewa *anu-metirala* (see p. 132) perform-ing a ceremony to ensure a safe delivery for T. Meni-khamy, who had suffered several previous miscarriages; *right*, T. Menikhamy, several months later, with her young daughter.

Kukulewa women weave mats for domestic use, and some also sell them in nearby markets.

A girl's puberty ceremony in Kukulewa. M. Kandathe's daughter, after being ritually bathed, contemplates the sacred objects prepared by the Washerman caste man who is in charge of the ceremony.

Above, Kukulewa villagers often meet at K. Wannihamy's shop for relaxed discussion of the day's news; *right*, Kukulewa women cook on their verandahs. Dogs are constantly on the lookout for scraps.

B. Undiyarala (see chapter 4) about to pour water to cool the anger of a valued cart bull that has just been castrated and branded.

The *kiribat* (milk-rice) consumed at a village ceremony is cooked by men, but women help in preparing it, by hauling fuel and water, and are here about to serve it.

Right, H. V. Bandathe, the former Vel Vidane of Kukulewa (see chapters 2, 4, 7), using an axe to clear his chena. *Below*, All the members of a Vedda household participate in chena cultivation. The Kukulewa man here is holding a *mammoty*, a kind of hoe that is also much used in paddy cultivation.

B. Kandathe and members of his family reaping their paddy crop in Kukulewa. This is the only stage of paddy cultivation in which women commonly participate.

W. Herathamy of Kukulewa (see chapter 4) bundling sheaves of reaped paddy.

Above, W. Kiribanda, son of
K. Wannihamy, the Kukulewa
shopkeeper, threshing paddy,
helped by his wife's young
brother; *right*, W. Kiribanda
winnowing paddy.

5

Willachchiya: Marriage and Migration

A Vedda community, like any other, acquires new members either by birth or by immigration. Likewise it loses members either by death or emigration. Among the Veddas migration most commonly takes place at marriage, which also, however informally celebrated, usually precedes a birth. The questions of whom to marry and where to live are therefore crucial, if not necessarily for the happiness of the individuals involved, then certainly and cumulatively for the continuity of the several communities. Accordingly marriage, migration, and residence present themselves as the central themes in the following analysis of the structural history of the Vedda villages.[1]

Migration occurs more dramatically and on a larger scale when an established village is abandoned or when a new one is founded. Such events, however, have been rare, except in the area northwest of Anuradhapura, called Willachchiya. Because a comprehensive account of an

1. I use the term *village* to refer both to a distinct parcel of land and to the people who live on it. The parcel of land usually contains at least one tank and the paddy fields irrigated by it, a cluster of dwellings, and a surrounding extent of jungle (see chap. 2). For stylistic reasons I also sometimes refer to the people who live in a particular village as a "community," and I describe the place where they reside as a "settlement." But I also use "community" to refer to all the members of a particular *variga*, although they are almost invariably dispersed among a number of villages. For example, I write of "the Vedda community," or "the Moslem community," or, when I want to refer to all the Veddas within Willachchiya, of "the Willachchiya Vedda community." The context will make clear which reference is intended.

historical process should deal fully with the emergence and dissolution of the phenomenon in question, I shall give disproportionate attention to the Willachchiya villages. These villages are also generally smaller than those elsewhere and it is therefore possible not only to observe quite clearly, and at the level of the whole community, the operation of those processes of group formation that have been discussed, but also to make some inferences concerning the former condition of the larger villages, whose average population eighty years ago was approximately that of the Willachchiya villages today.

INTRODUCTION TO THE VEDDA VILLAGE OF WILLACHCHIYA

Willachchiya is taken here as a convenient term to designate the former Willachchiya and Galkadawala *tulanas*, now Gramasevaka's divisions numbers one and fifteen in Anuradhapura District (map 5.1), one of the most sparsely inhabited parts of the district. Population density declines steadily with distance from Anuradhapura, approaching zero at the boundaries of Wilpattu National Park.

Smaller and less stable than villages elsewhere, only four of the present twenty-one Vedda villages in the area are recorded as being inhabited in the census of 1891. During the same period at least five villages have been abandoned. The increase in the total number of villages has been accompanied by an even more rapid growth of population (table 5.1). Six Vedda villages were reported in the census of 1891 and together they contained a population of 94 (average population: 15.7). By the time of the 1931 census there were nine villages with a total population of 224 (average: 24.9). By 1970 the population had reached 813, distributed among twenty-one villages (average: 38.7).[2] This startling rate of growth, which substantially exceeds that of Sri Lanka as a whole, is attributable to migration differences as well as to natural increase.

A single macadamized road leads out from Anuradhapura to the northwest. After ten miles it becomes a dirt road, but for the last fifteen years it has been sufficiently maintained to allow the ubiquitous buses of the Sri Lanka Transportation Board to service the colonization scheme at Maha Willachchiya. These are a number of villages to the

2. Population figures for 1970 are derived from my own research. All earlier figures are from the official census reports of the government of Sri Lanka. Note that my own criteria for distinguishing an independent village differ from those employed administratively (see chap. 3). In the present case the number of villages existing in 1970 by administrative reckoning might be no more than fifteen. Published reports of recent censuses (1946, 1953) have not provided population figures for individual villages.

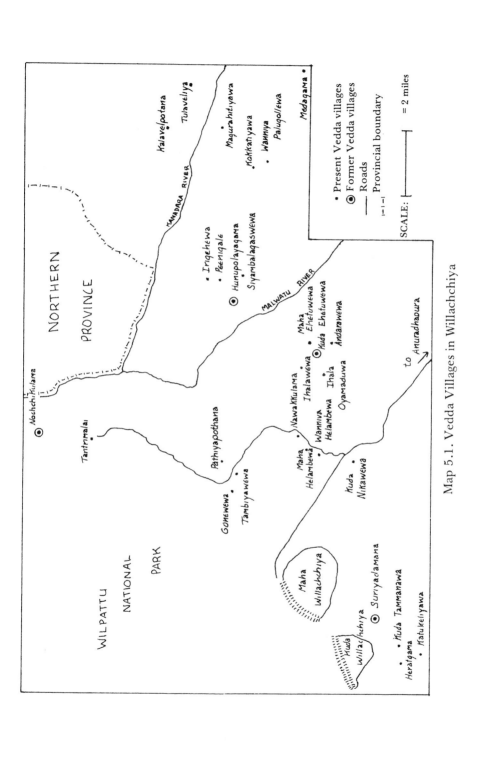

Map 5.1. Vedda Villages in Willachchiya

TABLE 5.1

POPULATION OF VEDDA VILLAGES IN WILLACHCHIYA, 1891-1970

	1891	1901	1911	1921	1931	1970
Wanniya Helambewa	8	28	16	13	17	136
Maha Helambewa	—	—	—	—	—	10
Maha Ehetuwewa	—	20	41	51	50	76
Nawakkulama	—	—	—	—	—	89
Ihala Oyamaduwa	—	—	—	—	—	25
Andarawewa	—	—	—	—	—	10
Kuda Ehetuwewa	—	—	13	17	38	—
Tambiyawewa	—	—	—	—	—	110
Ihalawewa	—	—	—	—	—	16
Pathiyapothana	—	—	—	—	—	8
Gonewewa	—	—	—	—	—	17
Nochchikulama	—	—	—	6	27	—
Kongarayankulam	—	—	—	—	—	—
Tantrimalai	—	—	—	—	—	26
Kuda Nikawewa	6	13	7	6	10	13
Suriyadamana	—	—	54	21	29	—
Kuda Tammanawa	—	—	—	—	—	65
Heratgama	—	—	—	—	—	9
Katukeliyawa	—	—	—	—	—	10
Hunupolayagama	19	15	14	21	18	—
Siyambalagaswewa (B)	—	—	—	—	—	26
Irigehewa	—	—	—	—	—	12
Peenigale	—	—	—	—	—	12
Wanniya Palugollewa	48	17	21	23	22	68
Kokkatiyawa	—	—	—	—	—	46
Magurahitiyawa	13	14	15	38	13	29
Total	94	107	181	196	224	813

SOURCES: 1891-1931, official censuses; 1970, author's census.

NOTE: Kongarayankulam was founded after 1931 and was already abandoned by 1970.

south of this road but only four of them are Vedda communities—Kuda Nikawewa, Kuda Tammanawa, and two small villages recently settled from the latter, Heratgama and Katukeliyawa. Kuda Tammanawa was itself founded about twenty years ago when the Veddas abandoned their former village at Suriyadamana, two miles away. North of the road the general population is much more thinly spread, but it contains a number of Vedda communities.

At Nikawewa, twelve miles along the road from Anuradhapura, a jungle track leads off to the north. The area to the west of this track, stretching to Wilpattu National Park, is uncleared jungle, completely uninhabited by man. But along the track itself are several villages, all

of which are Vedda communities. Within a few hundred yards of the
junction at Nikawewa is the village of Wanniya Helambewa, one of the
four villages in Willachchiya that have been continuously occupied by
Veddas since 1891 and now the most populous Vedda community in
the area. A daughter village nearby at Maha Helambewa, containing
only two households, was founded about ten years ago. No more than a
mile further along the track lies Nawakkulama, which was founded by
emigrants from Maha Ehetuwewa about 1950. A few miles further is
Tambiyawewa, which is claimed as an ancient Vedda site but which was
uninhabited for many years before emigrants from Kuda Ehetuwewa
settled it about twenty-five years ago. Tambiyawewa in turn has recently spawned two small settlements nearby, at Gonewewa and
Pathiyapothana, each the pioneering endeavor of a single family.

Finally, ten miles from Nikawewa junction, the jungle track ends
near Tantrimalai, the most remote of all the Vedda settlements and
quite inaccessible by vehicle during the rainy season. Tantrimalai is
famous as an ancient religious shrine, being reputedly the spot where
the bearers of the sacred Bo tree rested before proceeding to Anuradhapura. In recent years devout Buddhists from outside the area have
sponsored the restoration of the temple complex and have installed a
resident priest, who in turn has persuaded four Vedda families to settle
near him. These settlers came from further north, from the now abandoned village of Kongarayankulam on the other side of the Malwatu
River, which is here the border between the Northern and North Central provinces. The provincial border also roughly marks the boundary
between Tamil and Sinhalese communities, and the influence of the
former is strong among the Veddas of Tantrimalai, some of whom are
more fluent in the Tamil than in the Sinhalese language. But the Tamil
impact in language, custom, and even kinship has not been matched by
any significant penetration into economic life.

The reverse is the case in the area between the Malwatu and Kana-
dara rivers, where the Vedda villages are scattered among those of
other communities, among whom the Moslems predomonate. There
have been no marriages between Veddas and Moslems, but the Veddas
commonly work in Moslem fields while Moslems often control the
Veddas' own fields. Indeed the village of Hunupoloaygama has passed
entirely into Moslem hands, and its former inhabitants have dispersed to
found new settlements at Siyambalagaswewa (B),[3] Irigehewa, and
Peenigale. The other Vedda villages nearby, Wanniya Palugollewa,

3. As there is another Vedda village in Anuradhapura District that is also called
Siyambalagaswewa, these two villages are distinguished by the parenthetical letters
A and B, unless the context makes such indication unnecessary. The same applies
to the two villages called Nochchikulama. See map 2.1.

Kokkatiyawa, and Magurahitiyawa,[4] preserve a measure of independence, but here too the economic dominance of the Moslems is widely felt and resented.

Another cluster of Vedda village settlements lies between the Malwatu River and the track leading to Tantrimalai, of which Maha Ehetuwewa is the largest and longest established. Two of the others, Ihala Oyamaduwa and Andarawewa, have been settled in the last ten years by emigrants from Maha Ehetuwewa, while the third, Ihalawewa, has been pioneered by a family from Tambiyawewa whose older residents, it will be recalled, themselves migrated from Kuda Ehetuwewa. The latter village has been abandoned by the Veddas since control of its fields passed to outsiders.

Although Willachchiya is one of the most isolated parts of Anuradhapura District it has, during the last twenty years, increasingly felt the impact of the government's development projects. The establishment of the colonization scheme at Maha Willachchiya has had a widespread effect on the Vedda community. Improved communications have brought the Veddas into more intimate contact with the wider world. Only two Vedda men have actually been granted land in the colony, but the project provides an important source of income to others from wage labor. Moreover, although the Veddas still do not marry with their traditional neighbors who are not themselves Veddas, they have made a number of marriages with immigrants from more distant parts of Sri Lanka, many of whom are Sinhalese who came to the area in connection with the Willachchiya project. Other and more recent schemes, such as the development of Maha Nikawewa tank, the youth colonization project at Ethpethiyawa, and the new tile factory near Elayapattuwa, promise to extend these effects.

Such changes have not, however, been evenly felt in the Vedda community. Wanniya Helambewa, Maha Ehetuwewa, and Tambiyawewa now enjoy government schools, but few children attend from the smaller villages that are more than a mile or two from a school. Buses to Anuradhapura pass within a few hundred yards of Wanniya Helambewa, but a man from Tantrimalai must still walk nine miles to the nearest shop.

Some generalizations may yet be made. The Vedda villages in Willachchiya are smaller than those elsewhere, and the over-all density of population is lower. The greater distance between villages implies that jungle land is relatively plentiful, and this has two important

---

4. Magurahitiyawa is actually half a mile over the border in Pahala Wew *tulana*, but because of its proximity, intimate connections, and similar character, it is here grouped with the other Vedda villages of Willachchiya.

consequences. First, although the village tanks are small and unreliable, there is yet ample opportunity for working chenas, and it appears that chena cultivation is even more important in the economy of the Willachchiya villages than it is in the other Vedda villages such as Kukulewa. Second, it is still possible in Willachchiya, as it has almost ceased to be elsewhere, for an enterprising man to pioneer a new village in the jungle. Those who have done so have in most cases settled at the site of ancient tanks that have long been abandoned. But while the existence of these ancient works has facilitated the founding of new settlements and has directed their location, the Survey Department's finely detailed one-inch topographic maps suggest that very few of the more substantial sites still remain unexploited. There is also some suggestion that the superior jungle resources of Willachchiya make hunting a more rewarding activity than it has become in other areas.

THE GENERAL PATTERN OF MARRIAGE AND MIGRATION

It is already clear that the dominant theme in the recent demographic history of the Willachchiya Veddas has been one of growth. But several villages, notably Kuda Ehetuwewa, Suriyadamana, and Hunupolayagama, have also been abandoned by the Veddas during the last thirty years. In at least two of these cases, and possibly also in the third, abandonment followed the loss of control of the village lands to outsiders. Vedda expansion, then, has been taking place concurrently with a more gradual process of Vedda displacement. As a further qualification it should be emphasized that a number of the new settlements are as yet quite tentatively established. They have been founded by single families, and it is possible that several of them will prove abortive.

Nevertheless the expansion is genuine. The increase of the Willachchiya Vedda population from 94 to 813 between 1891 and 1970 represents a faster rate of growth than that of Sri Lanka as a whole, whose total population was enumerated at slightly over 3 million in 1891, rose to 8 million by the time of the 1953 census, and was projected to reach 13 or 14 million by 1970 (Abhayaratne and Jayewardene 1967, pp. 16-28; Selvaratnam 1961, pp. 33-49). Sri Lanka's population growth has been attributed largely to natural increase rather than migration differences, and since 1945 authorities have pointed to a dramatic reduction in the death rate that "has been occasioned mainly by the eradication of malaria (a major cause of morbidity and mortality in bygone years), the use of anti-biotics, better health facilities, improved sanitation and other public health measures" (Abhayaratne and Jayewardene 1967, p. 22).

The relatively isolated Veddas have not received the full benefit of all these innovations, yet their population has grown even faster than the national average. This apparent anomaly can be explained by migration differences, which have not been a decisive factor at the national level, but have had a significant effect on the Vedda subpopulation. Of the 178 marriages contracted between 1931 and 1970 by men and women raised in the Vedda villages of Willachchiya, 101 (57 percent) have been with people from outside the villages, and 76 of the 101 have been followed by residence within the community. Thus for every man or woman who has left the villages at marriage, three others have come in.[5]

Although there is a greater over-all frequency of virilocal than uxorilocal residence (table 5.2), Willachchiya has been scarcely less attractive to immigrant husbands than to immigrant wives. Thirty-seven of the fifty-two natal women (71 percent) who have found their husbands outside the Willachchiya Vedda community since 1931 have remained in the community.[6] The corresponding figure for men is thirty-nine out of forty-nine (80 percent) (tables 5.3, 5.4, 5.5, 5.6). The reasons for Willachchiya's ability to attract immigrant spouses have already been suggested. In a period when other villages have increasingly felt the pressure of population growth on their limited resources, Willachchiya has offered both sufficient jungle for chena cultivation and the opportunity to open up new paddy fields. Two large Vedda villages immediately east of Willachchiya, Medagama (26) and Tulaveliya (27), have been particularly important sources of immigration. In the last forty years twelve men and twenty-two women from these two

5. Of course, the significance of this migration difference for population growth rests less on the simple numerical predominance of immigrant over emigrant spouses than on the inclusion of the children of immigrant spouses among the local population and the exclusion of those of emigrants. Incidentally, confirmed cases of migration unassociated with marriage are limited to three families of immigrants and two young male emigrants, in addition to the three families that have moved to Maha Willachchiya colony.

6. This suggests a greater precision in dating the beginning of a marriage than is in fact possible. Few Vedda marriages are officially registered and there is therefore no written record of their date. The figures I give are estimates derived from informants' statements on the matter, and their declared ages, qualified by my own observations and in some cases checked against official records (since almost without exception births are registered), the declared and apparent ages of their children, and so on. Doubtless my estimates contain a number of errors, which are probably more frequent the further back one goes in time, but I think they are adequate to contrast, however roughly, the period from 1931 to 1950 with the twenty years since. Genealogical amnesia makes a further contrast with the period prior to 1930 unfeasible.

TABLE 5.2

POSTMARITAL RESIDENCE OF MEN AND WOMEN RAISED IN
WILLACHCHIYA VEDDA VILLAGES, 1931-50 AND 1951-70

	1931-50		1951-70	
	Number	Percentage	Number	Percentage
Duolocal	8	15.4	18	14.3
Virilocal	24	46.2	59	46.8
Uxorilocal	18	34.6	47	37.3
Neolocal	2	3.8	2	1.6
Total	52	100.0	126	100.0

villages have married and settled in the Vedda villages of Willachchiya, while only two men and six women have been received in return. Particularly prior to 1950 the marriage and kinship relations of the Willachchiya Veddas with the other Vedda villages were almost exclusively mediated through Medagama and Tulaveliya, and they are accordingly treated separately in the tables.

In the last twenty years the Willachchiya Vedda villages appear to have lost some of their appeal for immigrant spouses. Compared with the previous twenty years, the percentage of men and women who have married outside the Willachchiya Vedda community has risen from thirty-seven to forty-one, but the percentage of these marriages that have been followed by residence in the Willachchiya Vedda villages has fallen from eighty-two to seventy-three. In part this may reflect a tendency for those in the more distant past who married out of Willachchiya, and especially those who married out of the Vedda *variga*, to be dropped from informants' genealogies. But it is also partly a function of a general preference for virilocal residence, because in the earlier period Willachchiya Vedda men married outside more frequently than women, whereas in the last twenty years the reverse has been the case. Nineteen out of the forty-three men (44 percent), and nine out of the thirty-three women (27 percent), who were raised in the Willachchiya Vedda villages and who married between 1931 and 1950, found their spouses outside the villages. For the period from 1951 to 1970 the corresponding figures are thirty out of eighty-three men (36 percent) and forty-three out of ninety-six women (45 percent).

This shift in the balance of migration is also associated with a change in the character of marriages outside the Willachchiya Vedda communities. Twenty-two of the twenty-eight outside marriages made between 1931 and 1950 connected the Willachchiya Veddas with other Vedda villages. A further thirty-seven such marriages have taken place

TABLE 5.3

ORIGIN OF WIFE AND POSTMARITAL RESIDENCE IN MARRIAGES MADE
IN 1931-50 BY MEN RAISED IN WILLACHCHIYA VEDDA VILLAGES

Origin of Wife \ Postmarital Residence	Own Village	Uxorilocal	Neolocal	Total	Percentage
Own Village	8	0	0	8	18.6
Other Willachchiya Vedda Villages	7	9	0	16	37.2
Medagama or Tulaveliya	11	2	1	14	32.6
Other Vedda Villages	2	1	0	3	7.0
Non-Vedda	1	0	0	1	2.3
Unknown	1	0	0	1	2.3
Total	30	12	1	43	
Percentage	69.8	27.9	2.3		

TABLE 5.4

ORIGIN OF HUSBAND AND POSTMARITAL RESIDENCE IN MARRIAGES MADE
IN 1931-50 BY WOMEN RAISED IN WILLACHCHIYA VEDDA VILLAGES

Origin of Husband \ Postmarital Residence	Own Village	Virilocal	Neolocal	Total	Percentage
Own Village	8	0	0	8	24.2
Other Willachchiya Vedda Villages	9	7	0	16	48.5
Medagama or Tulaveliya	2	1	1	4	12.1
Other Vedda Villages	0	1	0	1	3.0
Non-Vedda	3	0	0	3	9.1
Unknown	1	0	0	1	3.0
Total	23	9	1	33	
Percentage	69.7	27.3	3.0		

TABLE 5.5

ORIGIN OF WIFE AND POSTMARITAL RESIDENCE IN MARRIAGES MADE IN 1951-70 BY MEN RAISED IN WILLACHCHIYA VEDDA VILLAGES

Origin of Wife \ Postmarital Residence	Own Village	Uxorilocal	Neolocal	Total	Percentage
Own Village	18	0	0	18	21.7
Other Willachchiya Vedda Villages	24	11	0	35	42.2
Medagama or Tulaveliya	9	0	1	10	12.0
Other Vedda Villages	7	2	0	9	10.8
Non-Vedda	5	5	0	10	12.0
Unknown	1	0	0	1	1.2
Total	64	18	1	83	
Percentage	77.1	21.7	1.2		

TABLE 5.6

ORIGIN OF HUSBAND AND POSTMARITAL RESIDENCE IN MARRIAGES MADE IN 1951-70 BY WOMEN RAISED IN WILLACHCHIYA VEDDA VILLAGES

Origin of Husband \ Postmarital Residence	Own Village	Virilocal	Neolocal	Total	Percentage
Own Village	18	0	0	18	18.7
Other Willachchiya Vedda Villages	11	24	0	35	36.5
Medagama or Tulaveliya	9	5	0	14	14.6
Other Vedda Villages	3	1	0	4	4.2
Non-Vedda	17	7	1	25	26.0
Unknown	0	0	0	0	0
Total	58	37	1	96	
Percentage	60.4	38.5	1.0		

since 1951, but this figure, while adequate to ensure continued inclusion in the larger network of Vedda kinship, represents a decline from
42 percent to 29 percent of all marriages. In contrast the number of
marriages outside the *variga* has risen from four (8 percent) to thirty-
five (28 percent).

That almost a third of recent marriages have crossed caste lines
indicates a serious, but not yet fatal, challenge to the rule of *variga*
endogamy. Almost every village has been affected and, indeed, very
few families can claim to be uncontaminated. There is, then, very little
tendency to seek alliance with a particular village on the grounds of its
superior purity. Some diehard traditionalists deplore and resist the
current state of affairs, but the individual application of private sanctions can do little to stem a tide of change that derives much of its
strength from political and economic developments outside the local
community.

I argued earlier, following Leach (1961a), that the demise of the
variga court, whose function was to prohibit and punish offenses
against the caste order, such as sexual liaisons across caste lines, was
linked to the abolition of the hereditary feudal office of Ratemahate-
maya in 1938 (see pp. 46-53). The Vedda *variga* court continued to
operate for some time after that, but I have no record of it having been
convened since the case in 1954 that Leach describes (1961a: 307-9). It
is precisely during the past fifteen years that cross-caste marriages have
become so frequent.

No less important in permitting this increase have been the new
opportunities and contacts afforded by economic developments in the
Willachchiya area, and particularly the wave of immigration that has
followed the establishment of projects such as the Willachchiya colonization scheme. Despite the removal of legal or quasi-legal sanctions
supporting the system of *variga* endogamy, neighboring villages of
different *variga* have preserved their traditional separation in matters of
sex and marriage. The outsiders who have married into the Vedda
community have not been natives of Willachchiya but have come from
more distant parts of the island, many of them in connection with one
or other of the government's development projects. Some have been
colonists, others laborers, most have been poor and landless men intent
on making a new life for themselves in Willachchiya. Already uprooted
from their native villages, more than two thirds of such men who have
married into the Vedda community have chosen to reside uxorilocally.

Improved communications and the prospect of making a living
outside their native villages have also encouraged, on a smaller scale, the
emigration of Vedda men. Five of the eleven men who have married

women of foreign or doubtful caste since 1951 live outside the community. These men, who even before marriage had left their villages to seek employment or advancement elsewhere, remain a small minority but represent a growing trend. There has not yet been any significant migration to Anuradhapura or other urban centers, but it is now recognized that a man's opportunities are not restricted to cultivation in his own or his wife's village. The Veddas have long labored in the fields of neighboring villages, and these traditional relationships, which were formerly recompensed by payment in kind, are now transacted on a cash basis. The conviction that wage labor is degrading has yielded to necessity, and it has become for many men the main means of making a living. Some have anticipated greater opportunities by moving from their villages. Regular employment remains a distant dream for the great majority, but the growing demand for casual labor, supplemented perhaps by a little petty trading, can provide for those in the right place and with the right contacts a better subsistence than does a fraction of an acre of paddy land in the home village.

In analyzing the structure of relations among the Willachchiya Vedda villages themselves, as distinct from their relations with outsiders, I shall not at first distinguish those settlements founded since 1950 from their parent communities. This reduces the complexity of the data but does not distort them because all the villages founded since 1950, with the single exception of Ihalawewa, have been within two or three miles of their parent communities, and the pioneer settlers have been able to continue to cultivate paddy fields in their former villages. Thus an argument relating choice of residence to cultivation prospects will not be affected by treating the new settlements, in the present context, as instances of village expansion rather than of fission and migration. For example, the man from Nochchikulama, who married uxorilocally a woman of Wanniya Helambewa, and who subsequently moved with his wife and her parents to the new village of Maha Helambewa, which his father-in-law pioneered a mile away, may be considered still to reside uxorilocally. Later, in order to assess the full extent and significance of residential mobility, it will be necessary to make finer distinctions.

As regards the villages founded between 1931 and 1950, the abandonment of Kuda Ehetuwewa (c. 1945) and Suriyadamana (c. 1950), and the establishment of new settlements at Tambiyawewa and Kuda Tammanawa, involved in each case the migration of a whole community. To this extent social continuity was not disturbed by physical removal and the new communities may be treated simply as extensions of the old, although under a new name. Nawakkulama, which was founded about 1950 by only a segment of the community at Maha Ehetuwewa, presents a special case. It is not distinguished from Maha Ehetuwewa in the discussion and tables dealing with the period from 1931 to 1950 (tables 5.7, 5.8), but is treated as a wholly independent settlement thereafter (tables 5.9, 5.10) so that, for example, its residents who have married since 1951 are considered to have married from Nawakkulama even though some of them may have spent most of their premarital lives in Maha Ehetuwewa.

Although in the abstract any one village is considered as suitable for marriage as any other, the distribution of marriages among the villages is not random (figure 5.1). In the first place marriages tend to take place between villages that are close together (table 5.11). Twenty-seven of the forty-five pairs of Vedda villages in Willachchiya have not been connected by marriage since 1930. Yet if two villages have been connected it is more than twice as likely as not (thirteen cases to five) that more than one marriage has taken place between them. Because villages are small and already composed of closely related kinsmen, this indicates a propensity to arrange marriages that reinforce existing relationships. Some have been marriages between first cross-cousins, as when the child of a man married uxorilocally returns in marriage to his father's natal village. Others have involved a pair of siblings, full or classificatory, marrying a pair of siblings from another village. Others again are less readily classifiable.

Of the 135 married couples resident in the Willachchiya villages in 1970, 15 (11 percent) are first cross-cousins. Previous students of Sinhalese kinship have interpreted higher percentages than this (13 percent or 16 percent) as "statistically a low frequency" (Tambiah 1965, p. 149) or as indicating that first cross-cousin marriages are "not very frequent" (Yalman 1967, p. 213). But it must be recognized that first cross-cousin marriage, however desirable it may be, is simply not available to a high proportion of men and women. Many people do not have first cross-cousins of the opposite sex. Even if they do, the age difference between them may be inappropriate, it being the normal cultural practice for a woman to marry a man who is older than herself but not more than about ten years older. Again a young woman may find that her first cross-cousin is already married to her elder sister. In these circumstances it is doubtful that a figure of more than 10 percent is properly to be considered "low."

Similar considerations apply to the incidence of marriage within a single village. In most of these villages, with immigrant spouses being the only likely exceptions, everyone is descended from a common ancestor no more than two or three generations back. Here an internal

TABLE 5.7

RESIDENCE OF MEN RAISED OR RESIDENT IN WILLACHCHIYA AFTER MARRIAGES MADE IN 1931-50

Postmarital Residence ↓ \ Premarital Residence →	Wanniya Helambewa	Maha Ehetuwewa	Kuda Ehetuwewa	Nochchikulama	Kuda Nikawewa	Suriyadamana	Hunupolayagama	Wanniya Palugollewa	Magurahitiyawa	Tulaveliya	Medagama	Other Vedda Villages	Non-Vedda	Unknown	Total
Wanniya Helambewa	5	1		1							1		1		9
Maha Ehetuwewa		8				2				1					11
Kuda Ehetuwewa	1	3	1					1	1						7
Nochchikulama			1										1		2
Kuda Nikawewa			1											1	2
Suriyadamana			1		5										6
Hunupolayagama			1				2	1							4
Wanniya Palugollewa							4				1		1		6
Magurahitiyawa								1							1
Tulaveliya									1	← Villages Outside Willachchiya					1
Medagama										1	Villages Outside Willachchiya				1
Other Vedda Villages										1	Villages Outside Willachchiya				1
Non-Vedda											Villages Outside Willachchiya				0
Total	6	9	5	2	2	5	4	7	3	2	2	0	3	1	51

NOTE: Included are three cases of neolocal residence: (1) a man from Tulaveliya married to a woman from Hunupolayagama, resident in Kuda Ehetuwewa; (2) a man from Hunupolayagama married to a woman from Tulaveliya, resident in Maha Ehetuwewa; and (3) a man from Tulaveliya married to a woman from another Vedda village, resident in Maha Ehetuwewa.

TABLE 5.8

RESIDENCE OF WOMEN RAISED OR RESIDENT IN WILLACHCHIYA AFTER MARRIAGES MADE IN 1931-50

Postmarital Residence \\ Premarital Residence	Wanniya Helambewa	Maha Ehetuwewa	Kuda Ehetuwewa	Nochchikulama	Kuda Nikawewa	Suriyadamana	Hunupolayagama	Wanniya Palugollewa	Magurahitiyawa	Tulaveliya	Medagama	Other Vedda Villages	Non-Vedda	Unknown	Total
Wanniya Helambewa	5			1						1	2				9
Maha Ehetuwewa		3					1			1	4	2			11
Kuda Ehetuwewa			3		1	1		1	1						7
Nochchikulama				2											2
Kuda Nikawewa					1						1				2
Suriyadamana						4					1			1	6
Hunupolayagama							2				1		1		4
Wanniya Palugollewa								3	2	1					6
Magurahitiyawa									0			1			1
Tulaveliya										*Villages Outside Willachchiya*					0
Medagama								1		*Villages Outside Willachchiya*					1
Other Vedda Villages						1				*Villages Outside Willachchiya*					1
Non-Vedda										*Villages Outside Willachchiya*					0
Total	5	3	3	3	2	6	3	5	3	3	9	3	1	1	50

NOTE: The cases of neolocal residence are as in table 5.7.

TABLE 5.9

RESIDENCE OF MEN RAISED OR RESIDENT IN WILLACHCHIYA AFTER MARRIAGES MADE IN 1951-70

Postmarital Residence \ Premarital Residence	Wanniya Helambewa	Maha Ehetuwewa	Nawakkulama	Tambiyawewa	Tantrimalai	Kuda Nikawewa	Kuda Tammanawa	Hunupolayagama	Wanniya Palugollewa	Magurahitiyawa	Tulaveliya	Medagama	Other Vedda Villages	Non-Vedda	Unknown	Total
Wanniya Helambewa	7			1		1					2			7		18
Maha Ehetuwewa	3	9							1		1					14
Nawakkulama			11											5		16
Tambiyawewa				10			1						1	4		16
Tantrimalai				2												2
Kuda Nikawewa				1										1		2
Kuda Tammanawa							9				1		1	1		12
Hunupolayagama		1	1				3				1					6
Wanniya Palugollewa									10	3	2	2		1		18
Magurahitiyawa										2		1	1			4
Tulaveliya																0
Medagama											Villages Outside Willachchiya					0
Other Vedda Villages				1			1									2
Non-Vedda	1	2		2												5
Total	11	9	14	11	4	3	10	5	11	5	7	3	3	19	0	115

NOTE: Included are four cases of neolocal residence: (1) a man from Tulaveliya married to a woman from Medagama, resident in Wanniya Palugollewa; (2) a man from Wanniya Palugollewa married to a woman from Medagama, resident in Maha Ehetuwewa; (3) a non-Vedda man married to a woman from Wanniya Helambewa, resident in Nawakkulama; and (4) a non-Vedda man married to a non-Vedda woman, resident in Tambiyawewa.

TABLE 5.10

RESIDENCE OF WOMEN RAISED OR RESIDENT IN WILLACHCHIYA
AFTER MARRIAGES MADE IN 1951-70

Postmarital Residence \ Premarital Residence	Wanniya Helambewa	Maha Ehetuwewa	Nawakkulama	Tambiyawewa	Tantrimalai	Kuda Nikawewa	Kuda Tammanawa	Hunupolayagama	Wanniya Palugollewa	Magurahitiyawa	Tulaveliya	Medagama	Other Vedda Villages	Non-Vedda	Unknown	Total
Wanniya Helambewa	13	1				1					1	1	1			18
Maha Ehetuwewa	1	4		3				2			1	2		1		14
Nawakkulama	2		10					1			1	1			1	16
Tambiyawewa	1	1		6	1		1	2					1	3		16
Tantrimalai				1	0									1		2
Kuda Nikawewa			1			1										2
Kuda Tammanawa	2			2			8									12
Hunupolayagama								3			1	1	1			6
Wanniya Palugollewa				1					11	1		2	2	1		18
Magurahitiyawa										2			2			4
Tulaveliya			1					2								3
Medagama			1							1		Villages Outside Willachchiya				2
Other Vedda Villages	1															1
Non-Vedda	2	2		2			1									7
Total	22	8	13	15	1	2	10	10	11	4	4	7	7	6	1	121

NOTE: The cases of neolocal residence are as in table 5.9.

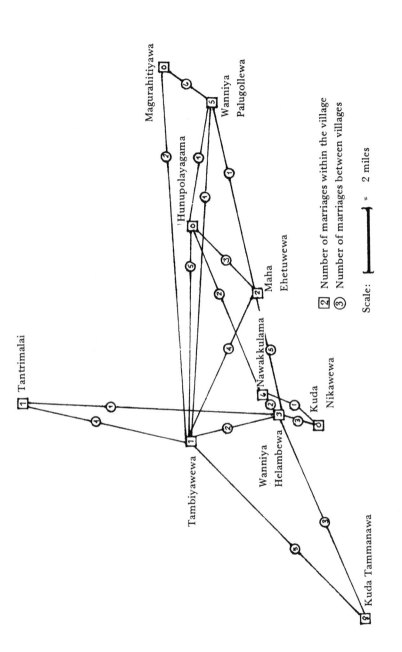

Fig. 5.1. Marriages within the Willachchiya Vedda Villages, 1931–70

Tantrimalai

Magurahitiyawa

Hunupolayagama

Wanniya
Palugollewa

Maha
Ehetuwewa

Nawakkulama

Kuda
Nikawewa

Tambiyawewa

Wanniya
Helambewa

Kuda Tammanawa

2 Number of marriages within the village
3 Number of marriages between villages

Scale: ⊢——⊣ = 2 miles

TABLE 5.11

THE RELATIONSHIP BETWEEN THE FREQUENCY OF MARRIAGE AND
THE PHYSICAL SEPARATION OF VEDDA VILLAGES IN WILLACHCHIYA

	Distance Apart in Miles					
	0-2	2-4	4-6	6-8	8-10	10+
Number of Pairs of Villages	3	8	6	9	6	13
Number of Marriages	11	12	11	6	8	3
Average Number of Marriages per Pair of Villages	3.7	1.5	1.8	0.7	1.3	0.2

union is also a marriage between first, or at most second, cross-cousins. There have been twenty-six marriages within a single village since 1931, representing 34 percent of the marriages within the Willachchiya Vedda community and 15 percent of all marriages made by Willachchiya Veddas. In view of the restricted possibility of its occurrence, it can be inferred from these figures that this type of marriage is welcomed.

Despite the tendency for marriages to reinforce existing relationships, a man can usually locate close kinsmen in most of the villages in the area. An example taken almost at random is that of M. Kandathe, the founder of Siyambalagaswewa (B). His direct descendants live in Tambiyawewa and Tulaveliya as well as in his own village. His siblings and their descendants live in Peenigale, Irigehewa, Maha Ehetuwewa, Ihala Oyamaduwa, Tambiyawewa, Diviyaubendewewa, and Gonewewa. His wife's siblings and their descendants live in several of the same villages, and also in Magurahitiyawa, Welewa, Wanniya Palugollewa, and Kokkatiyawa. A few short extensions of kinship would be sufficient to encompass the remaining Vedda villages in Willachchiya as well as a number of others elsewhere.

Thus the tendency to marry within villages with which one is already closely connected has not been so pronounced as to have divided the community into a number of exclusive and largely endogamous groups of kin. The pattern of relations is that of a single network. The bonds of kinship and marriage are drawn tighter in some parts of the network than in others, most notably within villages, but also between particular pairs of villages and between adjacent settlements. Yet although some villages are not directly connected with one another, their ties are nowhere remote. Despite the high frequency of marriages ouside the community the internal network remains unimpaired.

Because few men can marry within their own village, most face a choice of residence. Table 5.2 suggests that despite the changes of the last twenty years their choice has remained remarkably stable. This, however, is deceptive because between 1931 and 1950 more natal men married than did natal women, whereas since 1951 this pattern has been reversed. Table 5.2 in fact disguises an increasing tendency for both men and women who have been raised in the Willachchiya Vedda community to reside virilocally. This trend is clearly shown in tables 5.3, 5.4, 5.5, and 5.6, where it can be seen that the percentage of men remaining in their own villages after marriage has risen from seventy to seventy-seven, while that of women has declined from seventy to sixty.

The growing preference for virilocal over uxorilocal residence is statistical and economic rather than ideological or sentimental, and it reflects the sexual division of labor. A woman's occupations are mainly domestic and are little affected by whether she lives in her own or her husband's village. A man will probably find jungle suitable for chena cultivation in his wife's village as readily as his own, but he is unlikely to gain access to paddy fields there except as a dependent of his father-in-law, whereas in his own village he enjoys the prospect of direct inheritance.[7] The trend toward virilocal residence since 1951 is probably an expression of the increased importance of paddy cultivation in the village economy.

In support of this contention it will be recalled that the period since 1951 has indeed been one of expanded paddy cultivation, when many young men who would otherwise be landless, or who could expect no more than a fraction of the already small holdings of their parents, have received grants of paddy land on lease from the government (chapter 3). Leach (1961a, p. 84) has pointed out the correlation between these economic developments and the shift toward virilocality in Pul Eliya, where the process evidently began somewhat earlier. Most of the lease land obtained by the Willachchiya Veddas was not brought under cultivation until the late 1950s and 1960s.

If it has indeed been the recent acquisition of paddy land in their own villages that has persuaded an increasing proportion of men to reside virilocally, then it may also be true that this trend has now reached its peak. Despite the expansion of paddy cultivation since 1950 the ratio of land to people is hardly more favorable now than it was in 1930 (table 5.12). Because this expansion is now reaching the limits of what the available water supply can sustain, the successors of those who have made the recent acquisitions will find themselves in a similar position to those who married before 1950. Of course the situation

---

7. Note the special case of cross-cousin marriage between an immigrant man and his MBD in the village from which his mother emigrated at marriage. The mother may have exercised no rights in her natal village lands for a number of years, but her son may be able to assert a direct claim that is not mediated through his wife.

TABLE 5.12

THE EXPANSION OF POPULATION AND PADDY LAND IN
WILLACHCHIYA VEDDA VILLAGES, 1931-70

	1931			1970		
	Population	Acres of Paddy Land	Acres per Head	Population	Acres of Paddy Land	Acres Per Head
Wanniya Helambewa	17	7	0.4	136	17	0.1
Maha Helambewa	—	—	—	10	3	0.3
Maha Ehetuwewa	50	20	0.4	76	35	0.5
Nawakkulama	—	—	—	89	15	0.2
Ihala Oyamaduwa	—	—	—	25	8	0.3
Andarawewa	—	—	—	10	5	0.5
Kuda Ehetuwewa	38	8	0.2	—	—	—
Tambiyawewa	—	—	—	110	70	0.6
Ihalawewa	—	—	—	16	0	0.0
Pathiyapothana	—	—	—	8	3	0.4
Gonewewa	—	—	—	17	3	0.2
Nochchikulama	27	8	0.3	—	—	—
Tantrimalai	—	—	—	26	0	0.0
Kuda Nikawewa	10	1.5	0.1	13	9	0.7
Suriyadamana	29	30	1.0	—	—	—
Kuda Tammanawa	—	—	—	65	20	0.3
Heratgama	—	—	—	9	3	0.3
Katukeliyawa	—	—	—	10	5	0.5
Hunupolayagama	18	7	0.4	—	—	—
Siyambalagaswewa (B)	—	—	—	26	10	0.4
Irigehewa	—	—	—	12	2	0.2
Peenigale	—	—	—	12	2	0.2
Wanniya Palugollewa	22	9	0.4	68	34	0.5
Kokkatiyawa	—	—	—	46	15	0.3
Magurahitiyawa	13	4	0.3	29	19	0.7
Total	224	94.5	0.4	813	278	0.3

NOTE: To reiterate, my estimates of the extent of paddy land in these villages are not based on direct measurement and cannot be considered precise. They are derived from informants' statements of the extent of their individual holdings and of the total extent in their village, checked by brief inspection on the spot. Estimates of the acreages in 1931 were obtained by subtracting lease lands from the total, although it will be recalled that the Land Development Ordinance was not passed until 1935. Such errors as exist can be tolerated since it is not my purpose to rest the argument on the precise extent of expansion since 1931 or on the detailed differences that exist among the villages, but only to offer a gross indication of the expansion that has occurred.

may be affected by new employment opportunities, alternative methods of cultivation, or the intrusion of major irrigation projects, but in their absence the postmarital residential statistics of the period from 1951 to 1970 may appear as a temporary aberration from a more settled pattern and a balance between virilocal and uxorilocal residence may again be more nearly established.

SUMMARY

In summary, the most striking aspect of this one sector of the Vedda network of kinship and marriage is the accelerating rate of growth, both of the Vedda population and of the size and number of their villages. All other developments are related to these central facts. Population growth is attributable to both natural increase and migration differences, the Willachchiya Vedda community being one that has attracted immigrants. In recent years an increasing proportion of the immigrants have not themselves been Veddas. This change has been facilitated by general social and economic developments in the region and by the loosening of sanctions against cross-caste unions. On the other hand marriages that do take place among native community members do tend to reinforce existing ties and to link together villages that have been previously connected. Thus there are two opposed tendencies. One, which is increasing, is to extend the range of possible connections outside the Willachchiya Vedda community altogether. The other, which appears to have remained constant, is to concentrate alliances among those villages that are already close at hand, either in terms of geography or of kinship. Neither of these proclivities, however, nor their combination, has yet destroyed the integration of the Willachchiya Veddas within the wider network of the *variga* as a whole.

The possibility of marriage within one's own village is limited but, in combination with a balance of migration that has continued to favor the Vedda villages, it has been sufficient to enable a majority of both men and women raised in the community to remain after marriage either in their natal village or in a daughter settlement. In recent years virilocal residence has become increasingly popular, and this trend appears to be related to the improved prospects that young men enjoy of obtaining paddy land in their parents' villages. From a functionalist perspective one is inclined to emphasize the residential option and the practical modifications of strict and equal bilateral inheritance, whereby those children who remain in the village where parental property is located acquire a larger share of an inheritance than those who move away. These rules and practices provide an adaptive mechanism that can, to some extent, mitigate the concentration of property holding that would be otherwise entailed by a strict application of the rule of inheritance, together with the random demographic variations produced by differential fertility and mortality. In an imperfect way, and to the extent that in the aggregate married couples *do* tend to live where their prospects of inheritance are better, this mechanism provides a means of distributing paddy land more or less equably among the members of the community, or rather, of distributing personnel around the available land.

Doubtless this is so; at least my findings tend to support it (see e.g., table 5.12). But it is also only part of the story. For one thing, I have shown earlier that at least in Kukulewa, inheritance is not the dominant mode of transmitting possession of paddy land. Less detailed evidence from Willachchiya points in the same direction. Second, I have so far concentrated on the external relations of the Willachchiya villages, but have not yet described their internal structure. Third, I have related the pattern of marriage and migration to economic but not to political factors. To indicate the direction that further inquiry must now take, let us assume a hypothetical case where a man lives in village X, in which he holds one acre of paddy land. He has made some repairs to an abandoned tank Y, two miles away, and has there brought another acre under cultivation. He may now continue to live in X, or he may decide to leave it and establish a new settlement at Y. But he can as easily work both acres, whichever choice he makes. These, indeed, have been the grounds on which I have declined, up to this point, to treat separately the settlements established since 1951, for with one exception they all lie within two or three miles of their parent villages. But if our man does decide to move, if he leaves his former village and sets out consciously to create a new community at Y, this will be a political and symbolic act that separates him socially as well as physically from his kinsmen and erstwhile neighbors. It will be an act of secession that can express a political cleavage in the community, and it may mark a decisive stage in the process of village development. If this process is to be fully comprehended, such actions must be examined in their historical particularity.

6

Willachchiya: History and Process

WANNIYA HELAMBEWA AND MAHA HELAMBEWA

Wanniya Helambewa is one of the four Vedda villages in Willachchiya whose existence has been uninterrupted since 1891. During this period its population has grown from 8 to 136, although as recently as 1931 it had only 17 inhabitants. The rapid growth of the last forty years has been due to immigration as well as natural increase, but despite this the core of the village is still composed of a single group of siblings and their offspring.

In 1931 the village comprised the families of K. Banda and his sister K. Wallietana, who had both married immigrant spouses. The older children of these two couples were about to marry; one or two were perhaps already married (figure 6.1). By the early 1940s all twelve of these children were married. Wallietana's daughter and one of her sons married out of the village. Her other son married one of Banda's daughters, his MBD. All five of Banda's sons continued to reside in Wanniya Helambewa after marriage, as did two of his four daughters. In short, six of the seven men and two of the five women of this generation remained after marriage, giving a net gain to the village, after allowance is made for the internal union, of two women.

Approximately three-quarters of the next generation (twenty-five out of thirty-five) have also continued to live in Wanniya Helambewa after marriage (figure 6.2). Two marriages between first cross-cousins within the village have contributed to this relatively high figure, which is made all the more remarkable, in view of the general trend towards virilocal residence, by the preponderance of women

159

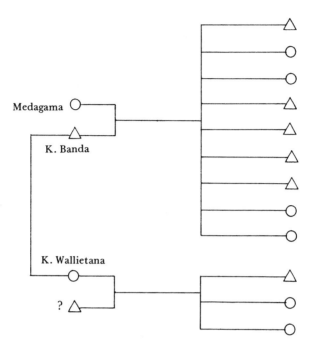

Fig. 6.1. Wanniya Helambewa in 1931

marrying here (twenty-two out of thirty-five). The key to this achievement has been the ability of the young women to attract non-Vedda husbands and to persuade them to settle in the village. No less than seven women of the younger generation have done this, as against only one who resides with her non-Vedda husband elsewhere.

The recent influx of outsiders can be largely attributed to the colony at Maha Willachchiya, four miles away. Four of the outsiders who married into Wanniya Helambewa were employed by one or other of the government departments involved in the Maha Willachchiya project. One now runs a small shop in Anuradhapura; the other three retain their government jobs. Another outsider who married into the village runs a shop at Nikawewa junction on the Anuradhapura road. Adding to these the two natal residents who are regularly employed, one by the survey department and the other at a cooperative store a few miles away, it appears that almost a third of the village's twenty-two householders derive their main income from sources other than cultivation.

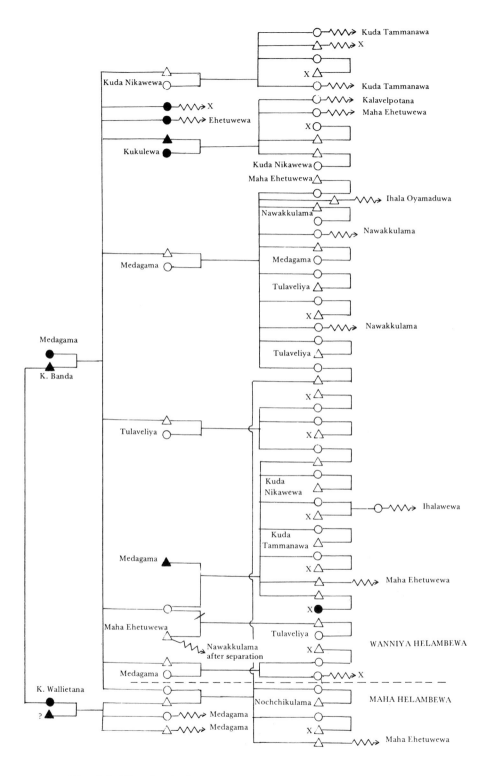

Fig. 6.2. Wanniya Helambewa and Maha Helambewa in 1970

In consequence, despite the rapid increase in population over the last forty years, there has been less pressure on the land than in other villages where few if any residents enjoy regular employment. There are only about seventeen acres of paddy land in Wanniya Helambewa, but only one family has emigrated.

This was the family of U. Punchirala, the one child of Wallietana's who had remained in the village after marriage. Punchirala moved in 1960 with his wife and children to Maha Helambewa, a long-abandoned tank about a mile from Wanniya Helambewa, where he had earlier worked a chena. There he has made some repairs to the bund and has attempted to restore to cultivation some of the land below the tank. Two of his children were married at the time Punchirala moved to Maha Helambewa. His eldest son had married a woman of Maha Ehetuwewa, where he now lives. His eldest daughter had brought her husband from Nochchikulama to live uxorilocally. Two more of his children have married in the last ten years. A daughter has married an outsider and moved away, while a second son has married his MBD and returned to Wanniya Helambewa. The latter is now the only descendant of Wallietana who still lives in Wanniya Helambewa. Thus although the population of Wanniya Helambewa is today precisely eight times as large as it was in 1931, the village is again entirely composed, as it was then, of a single group of siblings, their spouses, their descendants, and their descendants' spouses.

MAHA EHETUWEWA, NAWAKKULAMA, IHALA OYAMADUWA, AND ANDARAWEWA

Three and a half miles away through the jungle, Maha Ehetuwewa provides an interesting contrast. Like Wanniya Helambewa it is now inhabited by the descendants, and their spouses, of a single woman, who in this case is still living (figure 6.3; the one exception is discussed below). But unlike Wanniya Helambewa its population has grown by only 52 percent since 1931, from 50 to 76. However, during this period emigrants from Maha Ehetuwewa have founded three new villages whose combined populations reached 124 by 1970.

The first of these villages to be settled was Nawakkulama, an abandoned tank three miles from Maha Ehetuwewa and about a mile north of Wanniya Helambewa. The genealogical history of Nawakkulama has proved unusually difficult to reconstruct but it is evident that five married couples, with their children, moved to the village from Maha Ehetuwewa between 1945 and 1955 (figure 6.4). Two other couples came from elsewhere. Since that time the village has continuously expanded. Twenty-four children of the original settlers are now

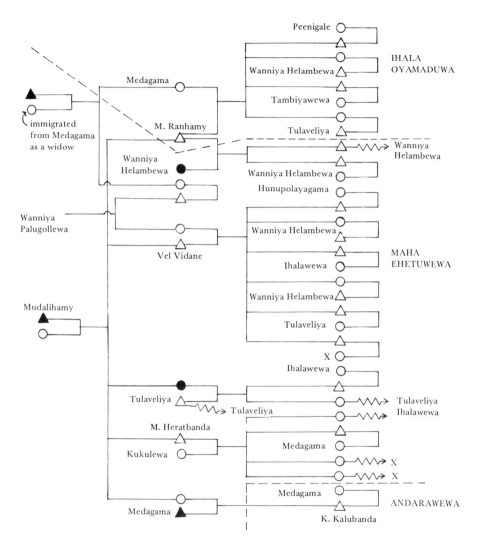

Fig. 6.3. Maha Ehetuwewa, Ihala Oyamaduwa,
and Andarawewa in 1970

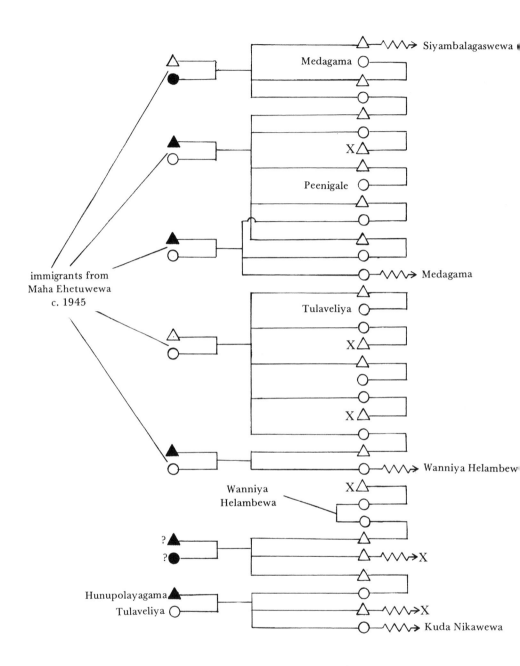

Fig. 6.4. Nawakkulama in 1970

married and eighteen of them are still resident. Five current marriages have been made within the village, serving to establish a closer network of kinship relations than appears to have obtained among the original settlers. Five men and three women have brought in spouses from outside, and three men and three women have left to take up postmarital residence elsewhere. With one of the original pioneering couples surviving and one young couple of recent immigrants, of which the wife's sister had already married into the village, there are now fifteen couples in Nawakkulama and a total population of eighty-nine.

The rapid growth of population has not been matched by rising economic prosperity. After the arrival of the original settlers the tank was restored and fifteen acres of paddy land under it were obtained on lease from the government. Almost all this land has since been privately, and illegally, mortgaged to the postmaster of a nearby village, as a result of which the villagers obtain for themselves no more than the equivalent of seven or eight acres' produce. Since this is far from adequate to support fifteen families, and no one is in regular employment, the villagers are mainly dependent on casual labor and their chena cultivation.

The departure of several families to Nawakkulama left Maha Ehetuwewa in the sole possession of a single group of siblings, the children of Mudalihamy, all of whom brought their spouses to live in the village. One of the siblings, who became the Vel Vidane (irrigation headman) is widely understood in other Vedda villages to have unduly exploited the powers and influence of his office to draw all the land in the village into the hands of his close kin. Whatever the means, the result is undoubted. No one in Nawakkulama now has any land in Maha Ehetuwewa.

In recent years the tendency has been to concentrate power and wealth even further into the hands of the Vel Vidane's family, but now increasingly to the benefit of himself and his children and to the exclusion of his siblings. He and his children now control approximately half the paddy land in the village. These economic and political developments are reflected in the recent marriage statistics of the village: although all six of the Vidane's married children live in Maha Ehetuwewa, only three of his siblings' thirteen married children do so.

There is one couple in Maha Ehetuwewa neither of whom is originally from the village. On the death of her husband in Medagama, M. Ranhamy's mother-in-law, accompanied by her younger and unmarried daughter, moved to Maha Ehetuwewa. A marriage was subsequently arranged between her youngest daughter and the Vidane's wife's brother from Wanniya Palugollewa. The couple were persuaded to settle in Maha

Ehetuwewa, where they remain, lacking any inherited claim, as clients of the Vidane.

Otherwise the trend is rather towards emigration. In 1962 M. Ranhamy, the Vidane's elder brother, with his second wife and their children founded a new village at Ihala Oyamaduwa, about two miles away. Once again the chosen site was that of an old abandoned tank. Ranhamy repaired the bund and has since brought about eight acres under cultivation. At the time of founding Ihala Oyamaduwa, Ranhamy's two children by his first wife were both already married to first cross-cousins from their mother's natal village of Wanniya Helambewa, where one now resides. The other has remained in Maha Ehetuwewa. Since the move four of the children of Ranhamy's second marriage have themselves married, and all have remained in the new village. Together with their parents they make up the five households of Ihala Oyamaduwa, whose population is now twenty-five.

In addition to what they have cleared in the new village Ranhamy and his family retain some land in Maha Ehetuwewa, and they live close enough to be able to continue to work this themselves. Informants in both villages, however, indicate that there is no cooperation and some hostility between the families of Ranhamy and the Vidane.

In the last two years K. Kalubanda, son and only child of the Vidane's widowed sister, has also moved with his family to found a new village. He has settled at Andarawewa, another abandoned tank within two miles of Maha Ehetuwewa where, with the help of his three oldest sons, he has cleared five acres. None of Kalubanda's children is yet married, but as with the founding of Maha Helambewa and Ihala Oyamaduwa, it is notable that the man has made the move at a time when at least some of his children are old enough to help him and are themselves at a marriageable age. One of Kalubanda's sons, who has recently obtained a job at the new tile factory on the road from Anuradhapura to Willachchiya, has remained in Maha Ehetuwewa where he lives with his grandmother. Kalubanda is confident that this old woman, his widowed mother, will shortly move to settle with him in his new village.

The Vidane's other sister is already dead. Only her son remains in Maha Ehetuwewa, her husband and daughter being both now married in the former's natal village of Tulaveliya.

Heratbanda, the Vidane's younger brother, still lives in the village but three of his four married children have left, and he is apprehensive of his brother's ambition, which he feels is now to acquire the whole village for himself and his children, Since the passage of the Paddy Lands Act of 1958, the Vidane holds no official authority, but his eldest son has become secretary of the local cultivation committee and now exercises most of the functions previously entrusted to the Vidane. During the 1960-70 cultivation season there were violent exchanges in the village following a dispute over the allocation of water for irrigation. Heratbanda and Kalubanda were both convinced that the irrigation policy implemented by the Vidane's family was intentionally being operated to their disadvantage.

Thus a pattern that could have been accidental in Wanniya Helambewa is seen to assert itself more dramatically in Maha Ehetuwewa. The core of each village is provided by a group of siblings. It does not seem likely, however, that this pattern will be maintained into the next generation at Wanniya Helambewa, where employment outside the community has mitigated the pressure on the village's own resources and has permitted a high proportion of native village members to remain in residence, But at Maha Ehetuwewa, where population growth has been kept in check by political processes within the village, the same pattern does promise to repeat itself in the future. Following the large-scale emigration to Nawakkulama, the village was in the sole possession of the Vidane's sibling group. Subsequently the Vidane, supported by his sons and sons-in-law, has come to dominate his siblings. These events have helped to provoke, on the part of the less successful siblings and their children, two recent attempts to found new settlements and a general tendency to move away from the village at marriage. The Vidane's children, all of whom have remained, will not have the village entirely to themselves, but they will surely dominate it. Is it too much to predict that, when their father's authority is withdrawn, they will engage in a new but not unprecedented struggle among themselves?

KUDA EHETUWEWA, TAMBIYAWEWA, IHALAWEWA, PATHIYAPOTHANA, AND GONEWEWA

Less than a mile from Maha Ehetuwewa is the former Vedda village of Kuda Ehetuwewa, whose inhabitants emigrated to Tambiyawewa about twenty-five years ago in circumstances that have left a persistent bitterness in their relations with the people of Maha Ehetuwewa. As at Nawakkulama today, their paddy fields had become heavily mortgaged to outsiders and they eventually lost possession. They accuse the Maha Ehetuwewa villagers of having actively connived in this process with the aim not of gaining outright control themselves but of enjoying the cultivation as tenants of the outsiders to whom the fields passed. In fact the fields are today neither owned nor cultivated by members of either village.

Tambiyawewa is situated about five miles away on the jungle road from Nikawewa to Tantrimalai. At the time the emigrants from Kuda Ehetuwewa settled there it was uninhabited, but it had earlier been the residence of the Vidane of Maha Ehetuwewa's grandfather, who was known as Tambarala. The Vidane of Tambiyawewa claims that the tank and its fields were obtained by the settlers from Tambarala's descendants at Maha Ehetuwewa in exchange for their remaining rights in Kuda Ehetuwewa. Tambarala himself is reputed to have come to Tambiyawewa from further north, that is to say, from the Tamil region, and the present Vidane of Tambiyawewa asserts that he was not merely a Tamil speaker but was actually of Tamil rather than Vedda extraction. Despite the tolerance of cross-caste marriages in the present, this charge expresses the hostility and social distance that exist between the people of Tambiyawewa and their former neighbors at Maha Ehetuwewa.

The settlement at Tambiyawewa was mainly the work of two brothers and their children who, with their spouses, provided seven of the nine couples that made the move. One of the others has since moved again to found a new village at Ihalawewa. The ninth couple came from other villages, the man being originally from Tulaveliya and the woman from Hunupolayagama (figure 6.5).

Only one of the two brothers' eleven children has married out of Tambiyawewa, and he has retained close connections with the village. Not only are three of his wife's first cross-cousins married into Tambiyawewa, but two of his own daughters have recently contracted marriages with their cross-cousins in the village. One daughter now lives at Tambiyawewa; the other has brought her husband to her mother's village (figure 6.6).

Other marriages reveal a similar tendency to consolidate existing relationships. Three men and two women who have married into Tambiyawewa already had siblings married into the village. One man has married within the village. Another has arranged an exchange marriage for his son and daughter, the daughter moving to her husband's village of Kuda Tammanawa while her brother brought her husband's sister as wife to Tambiyawewa.

Against this must be set a contrasting tendency toward marriage with complete outsiders, of which there have been six cases. As at Wanniya Helambewa the tendency has been for cross-caste couples to reside in the Vedda village. Five of the six couples do so at Tambiyawewa, and this has ensured that the balance of migration favors the village. The twenty-five marriages undertaken by people of Tambiyawewa and the villages founded from it since 1945 have brought in five men and nine women, while one man and nine women have left.

A further couple, both of whom were outsiders, settled in Tam-

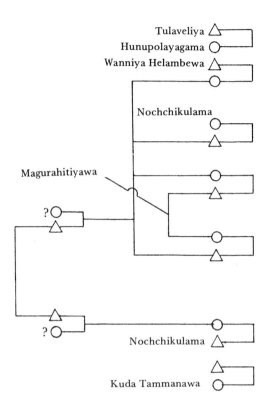

Fig. 6.5. Original Settlers in Tambiyawewa, 1945

biyawewa in 1967, following the wife's sister who was already married into the village. The husband died within a year, but his widow has remarried, and their eldest daughter has recently married a man of the village. On account of the family's recent immigration this marriage has here been considered as one between a man of the village and a woman from outside.

Turning to emigrants, Tambiyawewa lost two married couples when U. Appuhamy, one of the original settlers, left in 1967 to pioneer a new village at the abandoned tank of Ihalawewa. This tank is within a couple of miles of Maha Ehetuwewa and Appuhamy is alone among the settlers in having re-established good relations with the people of that village. Indeed his two daughters and one son, who were already married at the time he moved to Ihalawewa, had all married people from Ehetuwewa.

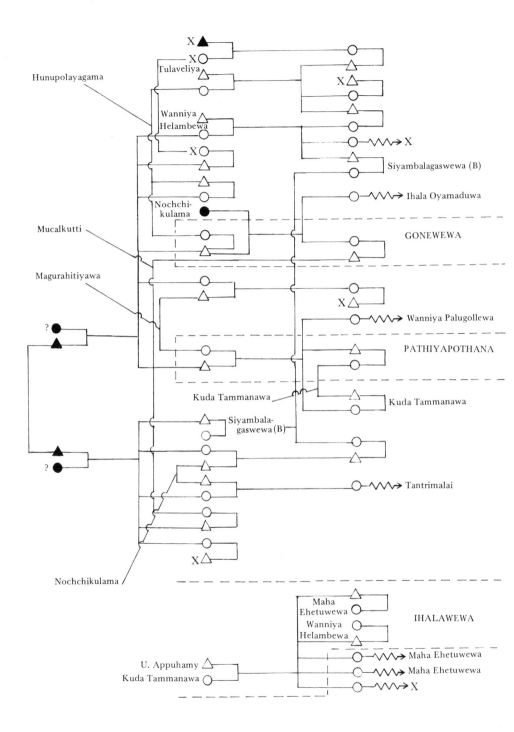

Fig. 6.6. Tambiyawewa, Ihalawewa, Gonewewa,
and Pathiyapothana in 1970

All three resided virilocally, and the married son moved with Appuhamy when he colonized Ihalawewa. Since then another son and another daughter have also married, again both virilocally, so that Ihalawewa now consists of three households and a population of sixteen (figure 6.6).

Tambiyawewa has spawned two other new villages in the last three years, but neither has involved such a decisive break as Appuhamy's move to Ihalawewa. Gonewewa and Pathiyapothana are both within a mile and a half of the parent village and their founders, who are brothers, continue to hold and work land in Tambiyawewa. As in the cases previously discussed (Maha Helambewa, Ihala Oyamaduwa, Andarawewa, and Ihalawewa), the pioneers are both middle-aged men whose older children are in their late teens and early twenties. Such marriages as their children have contracted are included in those discussed above. Pathiyapothana now has two households and a population of eight; Gonewewa has two households and a population of seventeen.

In contrast to the course of developments at Wanniya Helambewa, the influx of non-Vedda men into Tambiyawewa has done little to diversify the village economy. One immigrant derives part of his income from carpentry but no one in the village is regularly employed. More important is the colonization scheme at Maha Willachchiya, four miles away through the jungle, where many villagers go to find casual labor. Tambiyawewa's internal resources are also more adequate than those of many other Vedda villages in Willachchiya. There are about seventy acres of irrigated land, few of them apparently mortgaged, and the villagers are confident that this acreage can be increased. With eighteen households and a population of 135 in 1970 (including Gonewewa and Pathiyapothana) this represents a more favorable ratio of acres to people than is the case in the area as a whole.

These economic factors may help account for some of the peculiarities of Tambiyawewa's development that distinguish its history from that of Wanniya Helambewa or Maha Ehetuwewa. All but three of the eighteen married couples in Tambiyawewa (including Pathiyapothana and Gonewewa but excluding Ihalawewa, whose greater distance demands that it be treated separately) have at least one member who can claim to be directly descended from one of the two brothers whose children directed the founding of the village. Although this search for a common ancestor requires reference to a generation more remote than is necessary in either Wanniya Helambewa or Maha Ehetuwewa, a core of first parallel cousins is only one degree less intimate than the sibling core to be found at the other two villages. Like Maha Ehetuwewa, Tambiyawewa has spawned several daughter villages, but in the present case (with the possible exception of Ihalawewa) there are no signs that this process reflects the political and economic dominance of one sibling group over another, or of one man over his siblings. At Maha Ehetuwewa, cleavage in the sibling group and the emigration of the dominated were attributed to competition over scarce resources and the rivalry among siblings that in such circumstances follows the retirement of their father. In Tambiyawewa the prospect of further expansion within the village has alleviated this pressure, much as outside occupations have done at Wanniya Helambewa. But to a far greater extent than in the latter village, in Tambiyawewa the dilution of intimate kinship that is entailed by the passage of time and generations wherever relations are traced through common ancestry has been checked by the countervailing application of affinal ties.

TANTRIMALAI

Four families live at Tantrimalai, an ancient religious site deep in the jungle north of Tambiyawewa. They settled there in 1965 at the request of the priest who had himself been installed at Tantrimalai somewhat earlier and who is supported by the charity of Buddhists in other parts of the country. The four families came from Kongarayankulam, four miles further north on the other side of Malwatu Oya. Kongarayankulam had itself been a Vedda settlement for less than ten years, the inhabitants having moved there from Nochchikulama sometime in the late 1950s. Nochchikulama enjoyed a somewhat longer existence. It is first mentioned in the Census Report of 1921, where six inhabitants are recorded, but informants claim that it was originally settled from Ehetuwewa about twenty years before that.

The Veddas were encouraged in their migration by the loss of their lands, both at Nochchikulama and at Kongarayankulam. The former have passed to a Moslem, the latter to Tamils from Cheddikulam. Yet at Tantrimalai there are no paddy fields at all. However, the head of one of the four families, who is not himself of Vedda origin, is employed as the temple's caretaker. Otherwise the people live almost exclusively from their chenas, although occasionally a man of the village will go away for a spell of wage labor elsewhere.

The four families are those of a brother and sister, each of whom has a married son in the village. Figure 6.7 depicts these relationships as well as those with Tambiyawewa, with which the village is closely connected. But Tantrimalai also faces north, towards the Tamil villages across Malwatu Oya in the Northern Province.

Two such villages, Mucalkutti and Mayailmuttalyittakulam, are listed in the 1921 Census Report as containing a Vedda population, each of

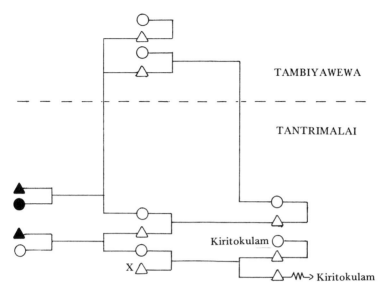

Fig. 6.7. Tantrimalai in 1970, showing Kinship and Marriage
Connections with Tambiyawewa

twenty-five persons. These populations have since become dispersed and
mainly absorbed into Tamil villages in the Northern Province such as
Cheddikulam, Puliyankulam, Mankandiya, and Kiritokulam. A brother
and sister from Mucalkutti have, however, married into Tambiyawewa
(see figure 6.6) and there have been two recent marriages between
Kiritokulam and Tantrimalai. The brother and sister in Tambiyawewa
use Sinhalese names, whereas their siblings in Kiritokulam and
Puliyankulam have Tamil names. But they themselves, like the young
woman from Kiritokulam who has married into Tantrimalai, remain
more fluent in the Tamil language.

The Veddas of Willachchiya consider these Tamil speakers to be of
their own caste or kind (*jati, variga*) but when asked to name the villages
occupied by members of the *variga*, they do not usually mention any
settlements north of Tantrimalai. But if the position of these Tamil-
speaking Veddas in the *variga* as a whole is distinctly marginal, when a
marriage is made with one of them, as in recent years has only been done
in Tambiyawewa and Tantrimalai, the propriety of their status is un-
questioned. Such marriages are thoroughly acceptable, much more so
than are unions with Sinhalese speakers who are not of Vedda origin,
although the latter are very much more numerous. In contrast to the
situation on the borders of the Eastern Province (see chapter 7), where

marriage alliance with Tamil speakers was formally ended a generation ago, language differences in northern Willachchiya have failed to develop into barriers to kinship and marriage comparable to those of caste. One is tempted to attribute this difference, at least partially, to the relative scarcity of population in Willachchiya and to the absence there of emulative models that neighboring Sinhalese communities might have provided. [1]

KUDA NIKAWEWA

Kuda Nikawewa is a small but long-established village located close to the junction of the Willachchiya and Tantrimalai roads. Its history reveals an uncharacteristic failure to expand. The present population is thirteen, which is precisely the figure given in the Census Report of 1901.

The tank is extremely small, and prior to 1950 only one and one-half acres were cultivated from it. In the last twenty years a further nine acres have been obtained on lease, but their irrigation remains unreliable. This has encouraged emigration, as has the proximity both of the road giving access to other villages and of the more prosperous Vedda settle-

1. This is intended as no more than a quick sketch of a problem of enormous interest and complexity that I hope to analyze more fully elsewhere. It is necessary, however, to justify my circumscription of the Anuradhapura Vedda *variga*, which may now appear to have been more arbitrarily defined than the facts would warrant. With respect to relations between the Willachchiya Veddas and the Tamil-speaking Veddas in the Northern Province, I have followed the practice of the Willachchiya Veddas of excluding Tamil-speaking communities from the list of Vedda villages while tolerating, and even approving, marriage with individual Tamil speakers whose Vedda ancestry can be asserted. In this, then, I have been as arbitrary as the Veddas themselves. I have also excluded the Tamil speakers in the Eastern Province, referred to in the text, since the Anuradhapura Veddas have not married with them in the last thirty years. There is also a third area, in the southeast of Anuradhapura District, where the boundary of the Vedda *variga* becomes somewhat indistinct. There have been several marriages between a group of Anuradhapura Vedda villages in this area and a number of settlements close to Dambulla, marriages that are declared to be proper on both sides. But whereas the Anuradhapura Veddas describe themselves unequivocally as Veddas, the Dambulla villagers describe themselves as Vedda by ancestry (*paramparawa*) but Goyigama by caste (*kula*), and justify this dual claim in terms of the occupational association of the caste names, Veddas being hunters and Goyigama people cultivators: "We are Veddas by ancestry but we long ago gave up hunting in the jungle to become paddy cultivators, so now we are Goyigama." The Anuradhapura Veddas are connected to these Dambulla villages by relatively few marriages (see chapter 7), and the latter are more closely related to other villages even further removed. In other words, the system is not fully closed here, but I treat it as such in order to keep my analysis within manageable dimensions.

ment at Wanniya Helambewa. Five of the eight living adults who were brought up in Kuda Nikawewa have moved away from the village, two of them completely out of the Vedda community and the other three into Wanniya Helambewa (figure 6.8). Two married couples and three households remain, those of a man, his sister, and son-in-law.

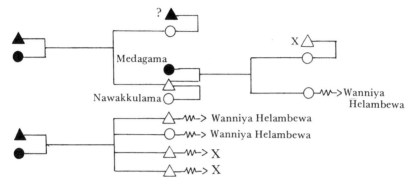

Fig. 6.8. Kuda Nikawewa in 1970

SURIYADAMANA, KUDA TAMMANAWA, HERATGAMA, AND KATUKELIYAWA

Kuda Tammanawa is located to the southwest of the Willachchiya road, in an area in which the Veddas form only a small proportion of the total population. The country west of the village is uninhabited, but Maha Willachchiya colony itself lies directly to the north, while to the south and east are a number of small traditional villages occupied by Sinhalese of various castes.

Kuda Tammanawa was founded about twenty years ago from Suriyadamana, which is claimed to be an ancestral Vedda village although it does not appear in census reports prior to 1911. Suriyadamana was supposedly abandoned following a prolonged outbreak of an infectious disease that took a heavy toll of life, but there is some suggestion, which I have been unable to verify, that this story masks a process that we have already encountered more than once, namely that mass emigration followed the loss of the village fields to outsiders. Certainly the present inhabitants of Kuda Tammanawa, which is only two miles away from Suriyadamana, do not now control any land in their former village. At the time of their arrival the tank at Kuda Tammanawa was in disrepair and was overgrown with jungle. The people repaired the tank and now cultivate about twenty acres that they have cleared below it. But this land is itself now mortgaged to inhabitants of the neighboring village of Kadurupitiya, who thus receive approximately half the produce. Under these conditions paddy cultivation is less important to the people of Kuda Tammanawa than are chena cultivation and, especially, wage labor, for which Maha Willachchiya colony and the more prosperous villages in the vicinity provide readier opportunities than are available, say, in Maha Ehetuwewa or Tantrimalai.

Since 1965 scarcity of land and a growing population have prompted the founding of two new villages from Kuda Tammanawa. Heratgama, a mile away, contains a single couple with adolescent children. Katukeliyawa, three miles away, contains the families of the founder and his two recently married sons. A daughter has also settled in Pathiyapothana in a sister exchange marriage with her brother's wife's brother. Further emigration has followed the grants of land in Maha Willachchiya colony to two men from Kuda Tammanawa. Three couples formerly resident in the village now live in the colony (figure 6.9).

In the twenty years since the village was founded, most marriages made outside Kuda Tammanawa (here taken to include Heratgama and Katukeliyawa) have been followed by residence inside the community. In this way three men and four women have been brought in, as against only one man and two women who have left. But this favorable balance of migration has been offset by the grants of land in Maha Willachchiya, for two couples who married inside the village since the move from Suriyadamana now live in the colony.

The most striking feature of the marital history of Kuda Tammanawa has been the high frequency of marriages within the village. Seven of the seventeen marriages made since 1950 have been of this type, and they have included four marriages between first cross-cousins. As a result, although the original settlers appear not to have been intimately related, the old man W. Sellathe now has descendants among all but one of the fifteen married couples of Kuda Tammanawa, Heratgama, and Katukeliyawa. Thus it can be seen, here as at Tambiyawewa, that affinal conections can concentrate relationships that would otherwise tend to diverge. The tendency for a village to be composed of the descendants of a single ancestor no more than a generation in the past can be the product not only of excision and emigration, as at Maha Ehetuwewa, but also of a pattern of marriages that might be called centripetal.

HUNUPOLAYAGAMA, SIYAMBALAGASWEWA (B),
PEENIGALE, AND IRIGEHEWA

Hunupolayagama lies about three miles northeast of Maha Ehetu-wewa on the other side of the Malwatu Oya. Claims that it was a Vedda village of long standing are supported by official records. The census

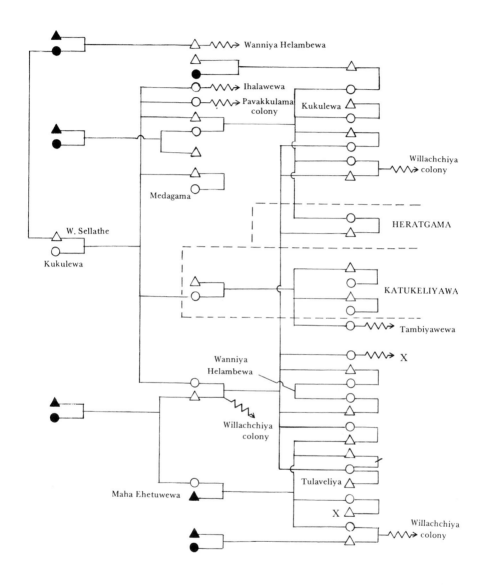

Fig. 6.9. Kuda Tammanawa, Heratgama, and
Katukeliyawa in 1970

Report of 1891, the earliest that provides figures for individual settlements, indicates that its population then was nineteen, and it was continuously inhabited thereafter until 1960. But by then the village lands had passed into the hands of neighboring Moslems and the Veddas abandoned them to found new villages at Siyambalagaswewa, Peenigale, and Irigehewa.

The Veddas claim that two other tanks a mile or two to the south, Pahiwalayagama and Relapanewa, had at one time also been Vedda settlements, but that control of them had passed to the Moslems at an earlier date. This claim is harder to substantiate. Relapanewa only appears in the census reports as an abandoned or uninhabited village. A population is consistently reported for Pahiwalayagama, but the Census Report of 1921, which is useful for its indication of the ethnic affiliation of the inhabitants of each village, describes it as a Moslem village. Whether or not the two villages were Vedda settlements at some time much earlier, the claim to their former possession expresses the feeling among the Veddas that they are being slowly but inexorably driven from their ancestral villages by a Moslem expansion. It is undoubtedly true that the Moslems, whose villages are larger and tanks more reliable, and who operate an extensive network of trading relations, dominate the economy of the local area.

The paddy fields at Hunupolayagama had been mortgaged for some years prior to 1960, but their Vedda owners had continued to cultivate them under the common arrangement whereby the produce is divided, after the deduction of expenses, almost equally between the mortgagee and the owner-cultivator. Later the Moslems decided to cultivate the fields themselves, as they were fully entitled to do under the normal mortgage agreement, which gives the mortgagee "right of possession in lieu of interest." The Veddas then sold out their remaining rights of ownership and abandoned the village.

Between 1891 and 1931 the population of Hunupolayagama remained more or less constant (table 5.l). In the last forty years, however, the population, now divided among the three daughter villages, has almost tripled. In this case the growth can be entirely attributed to natural increase since, as figure 6.10 shows, immigration has been balanced by emigration. There have been no marriages within the community.

The abandonment of Hunupolayagama repeated the course of events at Kuda Ehetuwewa and Suriyadamana in that the villagers all left at once. But the new pattern of settlements more closely resembles the establishment of small villages by individual families, such as has been described for Maha Helambewa, Ihala Oyamaduwa, Ihalawewa, and so forth.

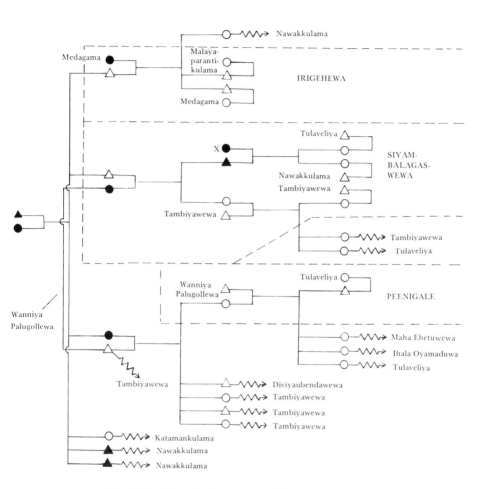

Fig. 6.10. Siyambalagaswewa (B), Irigehewa,
and Peenigale in 1970

The dispersal of the Hunupolayagama community was dictated by the limited economic potential of the new settlements. The largest of them, Siyambalagaswewa, has ten acres of paddy land, while at each of the other two, Peenigale and Irigehewa, only two acres have been brought under irrigation. Each of the three new communities is exclusively composed of the households of a living man and his descendants.

WANNIYA PALUGOLLEWA AND KOKKATIYAWA

Wanniya Palugollewa is another ancestral Vedda village. It lies four miles east of Hunupolayagama and is surrounded by Moslem communities. Kokkatiyawa is a formerly uninhabited site half a mile away into which a number of Wanniya Palugollewa families have moved in recent years. It contains its own restored tank and fields and may therefore be considered a distinct community, although ties with the parent village have not been broken.

The combined population of the two villages is now 114, an increase of more than 400 percent over that of 1931 when only 22 inhabitants were recorded. Migration differences have made a decisive contribution to this rate of growth, especially since 1951. Only 1 native has left the two villages at marriage in the last twenty years, while 13 immigrant spouses have been brought in. In addition, another couple, neither of whom was born in Wanniya Palugollewa although both are closely connected,[2] has also immigrated. In the earlier period the balance between immigration and emigration was very much more even (figure 6.11).

The ability of the two villages to attract immigrants is related to the expansion of paddy cultivation. Despite the rapid growth of population, the ratio of land to people is almost the same now as it was forty years ago (table 5.12). The government assisted in refurbishing the tank at Kokkatiyawa and in improving facilities at Wanniya Palugollewa, bringing under cultivation twenty-five new acres, held on lease, in the last fifteen years. Jungle land for chena cultivation is also still readily available.

Migration into Kokkatiyawa has left the families of B. Ukkubanda and his descendants as the sole inhabitants of Wanniya Palugollewa. In this case it does not seem that population movements are a direct expression of political cleavage. Three marriages in the last five years have connected Ukkubanda's children and grandchildren with the settlers in Kokkatiyawa. Most of the ancestral field at Wanniya Palugollewa is mortgaged to Moslems, while the government's recent distribution of

2. The husband is a native of Tulaveliya, but his stepfather is a native of Wanniya Palugollewa. The wife comes from Medagama where her mother, a native of Wanniya Palugollewa, settled virilocally.

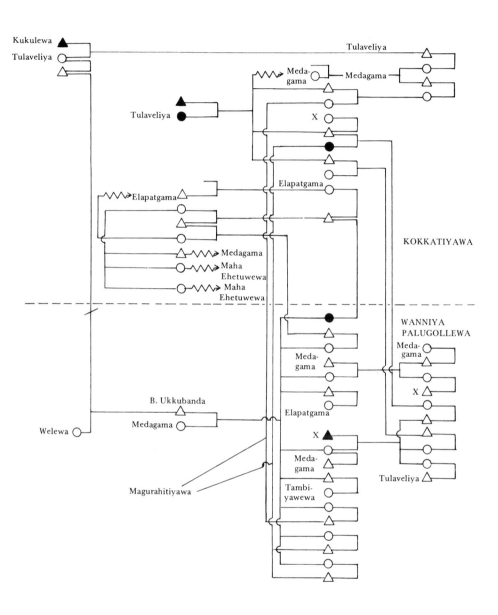

Fig. 6.11. Wanniya Palugollewa and Kokkatiyawa in 1970

lease land has not taken account of the residential separation of the two communities; that is, residents of Kokkatiyawa have obtained lease land under both Wanniya Palugollewa and their own tank, and Wanniya Palugollewa residents have likewise acquired land under both tanks. In short, if one emphasizes the physical separation expressed in migration and residence, one is inclined to speak here of two villages, but if one focuses on the social relations established through kinship, marriage, and land tenure, physical movement can perhaps better be described as part of a process of village expansion.

In any case, the achievement of B. Ukkubanda is remarkable. His nine married children (one of whom is now deceased) and his five married grandchildren have all remained with him. When writing earlier of cultivating units, I anticipated their dissolution soon after a group of siblings came to maturity and married. In the present instance, owing to Ukkubanda's continued vigor as well as to the acquisition of lease land, this process has been deferred; Ukkubanda is still in effective control although a number of his grandchildren are already adults. It is worth noting that Ukkubanda's four eldest children, including the two who themselves have married children, were women, and that women are commonly several years younger when they marry than are men. Thus the age difference between Ukkubanda and his oldest grandchildren is less than it would have been if his eldest children had been boys.

MAGURAHITIYAWA

Magurahitiyawa, a mile and one-half from Wanniya Palugollewa, is another long-established Vedda village, but its rate of growth in the last forty years has been much less rapid. A population of thirteen in 1931 has grown only to twenty-nine in 1970. During the period of reliable genealogical data (including all but the ancestral couple in figure 6.12) emigration has exceeded immigration while uxorilocal residence has been slightly preferred over virilocal. Three men have brought their wives to live in the village, and five have married out. Four natal women have resided in the village after marriage; another four have moved to their husbands' villages.

With one exception, Magurahitiyawa is composed of the descendants, and their spouses, of the couple who were the parents of the present senior generation. This couple had two sons and two daughters, of whom one son married away from the village. The children of one of the daughters, who had herself died, have also departed, leaving the village to a brother and a sister. Four of the sister's five children have married away, whereas all three of the brother's children who are married have

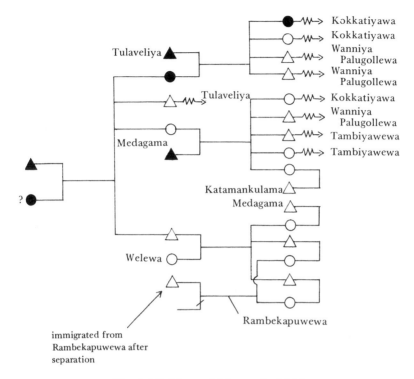

Fig. 6.12. Magurahitiyawa in 1970

remained. The brother, who was formerly the Vel Vidane and is now the local cultivation committee's agent for the Magurahitiyawa fields, is the acknowledged leader of the village and controls most of the ancestral fields. His sister's husband having died, the only other man of his generation is a landless divorcee from Rambekapuwewa settled near his two daughters who have married sons of the Vidane.

Thus the history of Magurahitiyawa displays its peculiar variation on a theme that has been encountered elsewhere. As a group of siblings comes to maturity, the formerly solidary interests of its members begin to diverge. Some of the siblings may leave the village at marriage, and of those that remain one comes to dominate the others. This man's children are likely to remain in the village after their marriages, while those of his less successful siblings are likely to leave. In the extreme case, which Magurahitiyawa approaches but does not quite achieve, the population of a village is composed, in each succeeding generation, of a single couple, their descendants and their descendants' spouses.

THE PROCESS OF VILLAGE DEVELOPMENT:
CONCENTRATION AND DISPERSION

Each village has its own unique history, but the particular form taken by any one of them is the product of factors that have also been operating in the others. One may therefore treat the structural history of each village as a particular variation on a common theme and assert that each village is "one of a kind." My concern here is with the more general features, the common theme of Willachchiya Vedda social history. I shall first present a brief statistical account of social and demographic developments over the last eighty years, and then compare two types of village structure, and examine the relationship between them in order to elucidate the structural history of the villages in "mechanical" terms that will complement the previous "statistical" account (cf. Lévi-Strauss 1953).

An examination of the partial social system constituted by the interrelated Vedda village communities of Willachchiya can emphasize one or more of three areas of analytical interest, none of which, however, can be wholly ignored. These are (1) the units, or elements, of the system, which in this case are the individual village communities; (2) the relations established among the elements; (3) the system as a whole, seen as the resultant of (1) and (2). Because relations among the Vedda villages (2) were discussed in the last chapter, the emphasis now will be on the village communities (1). Correspondingly, the Willachchiya Vedda community as a whole will be viewed more as the aggregate of such villages than as a system.

The general direction of development is already familiar and can be simply stated. Over the last eighty years there has been a significant increase both in the number of Vedda villages in Willachchiya and in their size.

Table 5.1 showed the increase of 138 percent that occurred in the total Vedda population in Willachchiya between 1891 and 1931. No villages were abandoned during this period, but four new ones were founded that by 1931 had a combined population of 144. Thus the new settlements absorbed more than the whole population increase, with the result that the average population of the villages fell from 18.0 to 16.0, a drop of 14.9 percent. On the other hand, the rapid growth of the new villages to an average size larger than that of the older communities meant that the over-all average population increased by 32.4 percent, from 18.8 to 24.9.

The rate of population growth since 1931 has been almost twice that of the previous forty years. The total population has grown from 224 to to 813, an increase of 589 (263 percent). Seventeen new villages have been founded, of which one (Kongarayankulam) has since been abandoned.[3] But four other villages that in 1931 had a combined population of 112 have also been abandoned, so that the average village population has risen from 24.9 to 38.7, an increase of 55.2 percent. Thus the growth of population has been so great that although there are now twenty-one Vedda villages in Willachchiya, as against the six that existed in 1891, the average village population is now more than twice what it was at the earlier date.

Nevertheless it is obvious that the possibility of founding new villages has done much to alleviate the pressure of population upon resources within the community at large. It is important to note, however, that new villages have been founded in two contrasting sets of circumstances. In one, that of displacement, the establishment of a new village has been part of a larger process that has also involved the abandonment of an old village. Vedda informants often associate this process of displacement with the persistence of infectious disease within the former community, but there are grounds for suspecting that often this explanation is a retrospective rationalization obscuring migration to a new location that has followed the loss of control over village lands to outsiders. Therefore displacement, as I have defined it, is not necessarily directly related to population growth within the Vedda community. On the other hand, those other caste or ethnic communities that have obtained possession of tanks and fields that were formerly in Vedda hands may well have been moved to do so by the pressure of their own increasing numbers on the resources available to them.

The second form that the establishment of new Vedda villages has taken is that of segmentation, which is more directly related to population growth within the Vedda community itself, although it may also be the result of political and economic processes within the village. In the case of segmentation, it has usually been one man, accompanied by his

3. In evaluating this comparison of the villages in 1931 and in 1970 it will be well to recall that my criteria (chapter 3) for defining a village are not precisely the same as those used by census officials. In particular it is possible that some of the pioneer settlements that I treat as independent villages in 1970 would not be considered separately from their parent communities in an official census. Similarly it is conceivable that the 1931 census figures conceal the existence of one or two pioneer settlements, which I would consider to be independent, by including them within their parent villages where the physical distance between them is not great, or where both lie within the same, administratively defined, *gama* (village). If this were so, the contrast between 1931 and 1970 would be that much reduced. But if any such pioneer settlements did exist in 1931, they have now disappeared both from the landscape and from the memories of present-day informants.

wife and children, one or more of whom may also be married, who has
split off from his former village to pioneer a new settlement. This contrasts with the characteristic pattern of displacement, in which a number
of independent families or households have moved together to found
the new village.

This correlation is too neat to be perfect, and the exceptions must
be noted. There have been ten instances of segmentation since 1931,
leading to the founding of the following settlements: Maha Helambewa,
Ihala Oyamaduwa, Andarawewa, Nawakkulama, Ihalawewa, Pathiyapothana, Gonewewa, Heratgama, Katukeliyawa, and Kokkatiyawa.
In all but two of these cases (Nawakkulama and Kokkatiyawa), the new
villages were indeed founded by one man, closely supported by his wife
and children, at least some of whom were mature enough to contribute
to the pioneering effort. Of the two exceptions, Kokkatiyawa is subject
to alternative interpretations, since the close ties, both social and physical, that it retains with its parent community, make it a case of village
expansion as much as of segmentation. In short, Nawakkulama, founded
by five married couples who moved together from Maha Ehetuwewa,
is the only clear-cut exception to the generalization that the founding of
a new village by segmentation has been the work of a single individual
assisted by his junior kinsmen.

Since 1931 there have also been five instances of displacement, in-
volving the abandonment by Veddas of the following villages: Kuda
Ehetuwewa, Nochchikulama, Kongarayankulam, Suriyadamana, and
Hunupolayagama. In four of these cases, the whole of the former community moved en masse to settle together in a new village—at Tambiyawewa (from Kuda Ehetuwewa), at Kongarayankulam (from
Nochchikulama), at Tantrimalai (from Kongarayankulam), and at
Kuda Tammanawa (from Suriyadamana). Hunupolayagama is therefore the exception here. Its abandonment, which followed the loss of
control over village lands, was clearly an instance of displacement, since
segmentation was immediately superimposed upon displacement, since
the former community split into three groups, each of which pioneered
a new settlement, and each of which was exclusively composed of the
households of a man and his descendants. This deserves to be treated as
an intermediate case, because the abandonment of Hunupolayagama
was an instance of displacement, while the subsequent founding of
Siyambalagaswewa (B), Irigehewa, and Peenigale displayed the characteristic aspects of segmentation.

The recent social and demographic history of the Willachchiya
Veddas is one of expansion, which has two aspects. There has been an
increase in the size of the individual villages, from a mean population of

18.8 inhabitants per village in 1891 to one of 38.7 in 1970. There has also been an increase in the number of villages, from a total of six in 1891 to a total of twenty-one in 1970. This implies an increase in the total Vedda population in Willachchiya from 94 in 1891 to 813 in 1970. There has also been a corresponding increase in the extent of irrigated land: accurate figures are not available for 1891 but since 1931 the total extent has been increased from approximately 94.5 acres to approximately 278 acres.

Because Vedda expansion has been taking place within a more gradual process of Vedda displacement, the Vedda villages, especially in Willachchiya but also elsewhere in Anuradhapura District, tend now to lie in or close to the arc of relatively sparsely populated territory that separates the Sinhalese villages of the district from the Tamil communities to the north and northeast (map 2.1). The historical evidence, however, is unfortunately insufficient to sustain the hypothesis that the direction of Vedda displacement has been consistently centrifugal, the result of pressures emanating from the more central and more densely populated areas of Sinhalese settlement.

These statistical trends have implications for the internal structure of the Willachchiya Vedda villages that can be assessed initially by isolating two mutually countervailing tendencies in village social organization, that toward concentration and that toward dispersion. In terms of kinship, a village may be said to be wholly concentrated when it contains someone who has at least one direct descendant in every other household in the village. It is wholly dispersed when none of the members of any one household shares a known ancestor in common with any of the members of any other household. In economic terms, a concentrated village is characterized by the monopolization of control of irrigated lands in the hands of one individual. In a dispersed village, every household controls an equal amount of irrigated land. In political terms, a concentrated village is characterized by autocracy, while in a dispersed village power is equally distributed among all the men, whose relations with one another produce a shifting pattern of factional alliance and competition.

Most of these extreme conditions are not encountered. But then the distinction between concentration and dispersion provides an ideal typical contrast that is not intended to be an accurate description of empirical reality. Nor is it, in itself, a theory that purports to explain historical events. Its purpose is heuristic. It is a means to the construction of appropriate concepts and hence of an analytical framework within which the complexities of history can be rendered intelligible. Thus, given the normative context of Vedda rules of inheritance, marriage, and residence, a village that is wholly dispersed in the aspect of kinship is hard even to envisage. But there *is* a discernible tendency towards dispersion that, if it were not met by a countervailing tendency towards concentration, might realize social forms that at least approximate a condition of complete dispersion. The objective is to examine these opposing tendencies, and to analyze them not only as the expression of external social, environmental, and demographic pressures (e.g., as the result of administrative decisions, population growth, and so on), nor simply as the automatic realization in social practice of traditional cultural norms, but also, and most decisively, as the outcome of strategic decisions made by groups and individuals within a definite natural and cultural environment.

In this perspective, it is not difficult to see that those Veddas who are most ambitious to monopolize the advantages of wealth and power that are potentially available to them seek to make themselves the central figures in concentrated villages. Those who are less ambitious, or who see no way to realize their greatest ambitions, strive to retain or ensure at least a tolerable measure of dispersion.

What is most remarkable about the Willachchiya Vedda villages is the degree to which, despite the boost that rapid population growth has given to the tendency towards dispersion, they remain highly concentrated. Of course, the possibility of founding new villages is also relevant since villages founded by segmentation are characteristically established in a highly concentrated state. Although the population of the average village has more than doubled since 1891, most Willachchiya Vedda villages are today dominated either by a single individual or by a group of siblings.

In order both to document this statement and to explain the facts it represents it is useful now to introduce some empirical types that realize in different combinations the contrary processes of concentration and dispersion. Maintaining the present emphasis on kinship structures, I shall distinguish two main types of village, the single-stem village and the multistem village. I do not here describe the members of a village as constituting a "kindred," but the overtonal reference to the concept of a "stem kindred" is intentional. A single-stem village is one in which a single known ancestor, living or dead, has at least one descendant in at least 90 percent of the households of the village. A multistem village is one in which this is not the case. The distinction is set at 90 percent in order to contain within the single-stem type those villages in which a neolocal couple has settled, usually in the status of client to the dominant man in the village, with whom there is often an affinal connection (e.g., Maha Ehetuwewa, figure 6.3). Within the general type of single-stem village it is also possible to distinguish subtypes according to the remoteness of the common ancestor. Thus a personal village is one in which the common ancestor is still living, a sibling village is one in which he is dead or departed but at least one of his children is resident, and a cousin village is one in which he and his children are dead or departed but at least one of his grandchildren is resident. Since Veddas normally have no knowledge of ancestors more remote than their grandparents there is no need to specify any further subtypes.[4]

It should be emphasized that the subtypes of single-stem villages are distinguished only by the range of kinship that connects their constituent households. In particular, it is not implied that power or wealth are more concentrated in personal villages than in sibling villages. Thus Kuda Tammanawa A (figure 6.9) is a personal village although wealth is quite widely distributed within it. Magurahitiyawa (figure 6.12) is a sibling village despite the concentration of power in the hands of the former Vel Vidane, and Maha Ehetuwewa (figure 6.3) is a personal village not because it is dominated by the former Vel Vidane but because his mother is still alive.

When the extant Vedda villages are classified according to this scheme it is seen that eighteen of them are single-stem villages, and only three (Nawakkulama, Tambiyawewa, and Kokkatiyawa) are multistem villages. And of the eighteen single-stem villages, fifteen are personal, three are sibling (Wanniya Helambewa, Kuda Nikawewa, and Magurahitiyawa), and none is a cousin village. Granted that eleven of the personal villages have been founded in the last twenty years by the process of segmentation, or, in the case of Siyambalagaswewa, Irigehewa, and Peenigale, by a combination of displacement and segmentation, it is nevertheless remarkable that, in an era of rapid population growth, the forces making for concentration should remain so powerful. To understand what lies behind these abstract social forces it is necessary to examine closely both demographic and more strictly sociological factors.

Demographically, the most pertinent consideration is that the more drastic effects of the rapid growth of population have yet to reveal themselves in my scheme of classification. The greatest increase in the rate of growth has occurred since 1931, among generations that are still living. While representatives of these generations remain alive, any tendency for personal villages to become sibling villages, or sibling

4. The reader may remember that the distinction between single-stem and multistem villages rests on *knowledge* or *ignorance* of a common ancestor, not on whether there was *in fact* a common ancestor.

villages to become cousin villages, or more generally, for single-stem villages to be transformed into multistem villages, will not express itself in my classification. Leaving aside the factor of immigration into the Willachchiya Vedda community at large, which is admittedly not negligible, population growth entails an increase in the size of sibling groups in successive generations. When the defining sibling group of a sibling village contains only two members, it requires only that the children of one sibling emigrate at marriage for the village again to take the form of a sibling village in the next generation. But the more members a sibling group contains, the higher the proportion of their children who must move out if the state of sibling village is to be retained. This is possible in a small number of cases but (still disregarding the possibility of marital migration across the boundaries of the Willachchiya Vedda community as a whole) these emigrant spouses must be immigrant spouses into other villages, in which therefore a corresponding high proportion of native members retain residence after marriage. Thus, for example, Wanniya Palugollewa (figure 6.11) is at present a personal village, but eight of B. Ukkubanda's children are married and still resident in the village, and some of them already have married children of their own. Everything indicates that Wanniya Palugollewa will become, first, a sibling village, and subsequently, a cousin village. Likewise Wanniya Helambewa is at present a sibling village, but the defining sibling group now has twenty married children resident in the village, and it is virtuallly certain that it will, in the not too distant future, become a cousin village.

There are, however, social strategies that can inhibit these demo-graphically induced tendencies. I have suggested that the passage of a village from one type or subtype to another, which, in systemic terms, would be described as its transformation from one state to another, is affected by marital choices and residential decisions, and I have shown earlier that these do not produce random patterns. It is useful now to recall my model of the developmental process of Vedda households and of basic cultivating groups. That model also describes at least a part, and sometimes the totality, of the developmental process of the village as a whole. In the more concentrated villages, that is, in personal and sibling villages, the structure of the basic cultivating group and that of the village as a whole may be identical. With respect to paddy cultivation, a personal or sibling village may be organized as a single basic cultivating group. This is most obviously the case in the villages recently established by segmentation, but although Wanniya Palugollewa is the only one of the older villages in which the identity of a single basic cultivating group

with the village as a whole is fully achieved today, it is closely approximated in several of the others, most notably in Maha Ehetuwewa and
Magurahitiyawa. And even in the more dispersed villages the developmental model of the cultivating group remains relevant since, in the absence of permanent corporate groups, the structure of the village as a
whole emerges from the articulation of its basic cultivating groups,
just as the structure of the latter is rooted in that of its constituent
households. Thus the strategic considerations that characterize the
development of the household and the cultivating group are no less
crucial to the development of the village.

I have shown that the successful Vedda man is one who retains the
allegiance and support of his sons and sons-in-law. Two measures of
success are residential proximity and continued participation, in a subordinate capacity, in the father's (or father-in-law's) productive activities. The support and allegiance of young men are retained by the distribution of present benefits and the prospect of further advantages in
the future. The successful Vedda is therefore a man of some substance
and, more especially, he is one who promises to become even wealthier.

Substantial wealth derives from access to the means of production
and, most decisively, from control over irrigated rice fields. At any given
time the amount of irrigated land in a village is more or less fixed, and an
ambitious man can only come to obtain more land by acquiring it from
his fellow villagers. In the smaller villages, most of his fellow villagers will
be either his siblings or his cousins. The image of the successful man
whose enterprise is expanding and whose sons and sons-in-law reside
close to him therefore requires as its complement that of his unsuccessful
kinsman whose wealth and prospects are declining. The latter's children
either strive to accelerate the intergenerational transmission of whatever
property they stand to inherit, or they are tempted to pursue their fortunes in the villages of their spouses. In combination, these characteristic
processes of domestic group and cultivating group formation and fission
produce, at the level of the village, a cyclical pattern in which a personal
village or a sibling village can reconstitute itself as such in successive
generations.

This possibility is encouraged in areas where there is also the prospect of founding new villages. Those who pioneer new settlements by
segmentation are usually enterprising and energetic men who have been
unable to realize their ambitions in their native villages. They either have
already experienced, or have grounds to fear in the future, the encroachment of more powerful neighbors and kinsmen. They cut their losses, as
the entrepreneurial metaphor has it, in order to make a new start else-

where. And they take their descendants with them, thereby further promoting social concentration within the community from which they detach themselves.

Concentration is further promoted, and hence the prospect of a personal or sibling village maintaining itself as such in successive generations is also further enhanced, by the opportunities that exist for village endogamy. In the smaller villages, most endogamous marriages are between first cross-cousins. In its political aspects, such a marriage may represent a decision by the parents to forego the chance of an undisputed dominance for the sake of a shared alliance. But although as brothers-in-law (*massinā / massinā*) the fathers of cross-cousins are status equals in the kinship hierarchy, there may also be real differences of power and wealth between them and apparent equality of status may mask a relationship of relative dominance and subordination.

It should also be emphasized that the concentration of kinship relations that results from village endogamy and cross-cousin marriage can be relatively independent of any concentration of power and wealth. This can be illustrated by reference to Kuda Tammanawa (figure 6.9), which was formerly a multistem village but which, on account of recent marriages within the village, has become a personal village. The old man W. Sellathe, although not himself wealthy, now has descendants among all but one of the fifteen married couples of Kuda Tammanawa and its daughter villages, Heratgama and Katukeliyawa.

In most cases, however, there is a more positive association between kinship and political and economic concentration. This derives from factors inherent in the developmental process of the village, which in turn is based on the developmental processes of the household and the cultivating group, whose dynamic aspect is determined by the strategic decisions made by social actors who are endeavoring to realize distinct, and often conflicting, interests. To the extent that strategies aimed at the monopolization of wealth and power are successfully implemented, a village also becomes more concentrated in the dimension of kinship. But the environmental and demographic factors remain critical. The ability to create differences of wealth and power within a village results in more concentrated social forms, but the massive growth of populations has been a powerful force promoting dispersion. If the Vedda villages of Willachchiya remain distinctly concentrated, this is largely due to the possibility of founding new villages by segmentation, a process that characteristically establishes the pioneer settlements in a highly concentrated state while also promoting concentration in the village of origin.

I have implied a conviction that the Vedda villages of Willachchiya were no less concentrated in the past than they are today. This is difficult to document conclusively, but it is the most plausible interpretation of the available evidence. Genealogical data can give the main outlines of the kinship composition of the villages over the past forty years, but their deficiencies become rapidly more glaring as one moves back in time. One is therefore forced to rely increasingly upon the demographic data from the censuses.

In 1891, as I have noted, the average population of the villages was 18.8. More than half the total population was at that time contained in Wanniya Palugollewa, and all the other four Vedda villages had populations of less than twenty. Even allowing for the smaller sibling groups of a period before the rapid growth of population, it seems reasonable to infer that these four villages, at least, were probably personal or sibling villages. Similarly in 1931, when the average village population had risen only to 24.9, it seems likely that a majority of villages fitted into either the personal or the sibling type. The demographic data are somewhat less compelling here, but the genealogical data are at least consistent with this interpretation (see, for example, figure 6.1).

It becomes possible, then, to outline a historical model of cyclical village development that cannot be advanced with conviction of absolute certitude, but is plausible in the light of the available evidence. The small villages of the past were mostly personal and sibling villages that, through the developmental process I have analyzed, were able to reconstitute themselves as such in successive generations. There would, of course, have been numerous movements back and forth, as personal villages became sibling villages and vice versa. Indeed, in ideal terms, these two types can be seen as mutually successive stages in the cycle, the personal village corresponding to the concentrated stage in the development of the household when a middle-aged man in his prime is closely attended by his sons and sons-in-law, and the sibling village corresponding to the stage of dispersion when he has died or retired and his sons and sons-in-law are moving apart.

Caution in interpreting a largely inaccessible past should be matched by a circumspect attitude toward an unknown future, especially because it is no necessary part of the social anthropologist's enterprise to predict or explain events that have not yet occurred. Nevertheless, provided always that there are no radical changes in the external social environment, it seems inevitable that the growing trend toward dispersion will be accentuated in the future. As the new generations, with their larger sibling groups, replace the old, personal villages will turn into sibling villages, sibling villages will become cousin villages, and so on. There is no evidence that the rate of population growth has begun to slacken, although governmental action may eventually achieve this. Moreover, as suitable locations for founding new villages have become scarce, the prospect of maintaining intravillage concentration by means of segmentation is slight.

I have attempted here to analyze the countervailing tendencies toward concentration and dispersion, the environmental and cultural factors that condition the ability to realize them and the social strategies that promote them. The different aspects of concentration and dispersion are partly independent of one another, but the extremes of concentration may be said to be expressed in a single-stem village, especially a personal village, which contains only one basic cultivating group, and whose political structure is given by a pattern of cyclical autocracy. Dispersion, by contrast, is represented by a multistem village in which there are many distinct basic cultivating groups, and in which the political structure is one of persistent multicentrism.

7

The Larger Villages: Autocracy
and Multicentrism

THE VILLAGES

Medagama (26)[1] and *Tulaveliya* (27) have already been encountered as the two villages through which the marital relations connecting the Willachchiya Vedda villages with the rest of the *variga* are largely mediated (chapter 5). It can be seen from tables 7.1 and 7.2 that seven of the eleven currently married men and women who were raised in Willachchiya and who have moved at marriage to Vedda villages elsewhere are living either in Medagama or Tulaveliya. Correspondingly thirty-one of the forty-one immigrants currently married into Willachchiya from Vedda villages elsewhere have come either from Medagama or Tulaveliya. The two villages are alike in being much larger than any village in Willachchiya (table 7.3; cf. table 5.1), but they differ in one significant respect. Medagama lies alongside the Colombo-Jaffna railway (map 2.1), and a number of railway workers' living quarters have been built within the village. Marriages between the railway workers and the villagers, eight of whom are themselves employed on the railway, make up the majority of the relatively large number of unions in Medagama that cross *variga* lines. Tulaveliya, which is more remote from the industrial world, will be of interest to anthropologists because of its close proximity to Pul Eliya (Leach 1961a). More than fifty years ago a couple from Tulaveliya founded a new settlement nearby at *Kalavelpotana* (28), which is now

---

1. Numerals and letters in parentheses refer to map 2.1.

TABLE 7.1

PREMARITAL AND POSTMARITAL RESIDENCE OF CURRENTLY (1970) MARRIED ANURADHAPURA VEDDA MALES AND POSTMARITAL RESIDENCE OF OTHER MALES CURRENTLY MARRIED TO VEDDA FEMALES AND RESIDENT IN VEDDA VILLAGES

Postmarital Residence \ Premarital Residence	Wanniya Helambewa	Maha Ehetuwewa	Nawakkulama	Tambiyawewa	Tantrimalai	Kuda Nikawewa	Kuda Tammanawa	Hunupolayagama	Wanniya Palugollewa	Magurahitiyawa	Pandiggama	Welewa	Diviyaubendewewa	Medagama	Tulaveliya	Kalavelpotana	Kukulewa	Elapatagama	Siyambalagaswewa (A)	Kirimetiyawa	Elapatwewa	Kanugahewa	Rambekapuwewa	Bogahawewa	Dambagahabpota	Migahapattiya	Maha Migaswewa	Halmillewa	Pusdiwulwewa	Moragoda	Rotawewa	Malayaparanikkulama	Kalamankulama	Adampane	Bakmikada	Dambulla Vedda villages	Colony; Vedda by birth	Non-Vedda village; Vedda by birth	Non-Vedda by birth
Wanniya Helambewa	12	1	–	1	1	1	–	–	–	–	–	–	–	–	2	–	–	–	–	–	–	–	–	–	–	–	–	–	–	–	–	–	–	–	–	–	–	–	7
Maha Ehetuwewa	3	13	–	–	–	–	–	–	–	–	–	–	–	–	1	–	–	–	–	–	–	–	–	–	–	–	–	–	–	–	–	–	–	–	–	–	–	–	4
Nawakkulama	1	11	11	–	–	–	–	–	–	–	–	–	–	–	–	–	–	–	–	–	–	–	–	–	–	–	–	–	–	–	–	–	–	–	–	–	–	1	3
Tambiyawewa	1	–	–	11	2	–	–	–	–	–	–	–	–	–	1	–	–	–	–	–	–	–	–	–	–	–	–	–	–	–	–	–	–	–	–	–	–	1	4
Tantrimalai	–	–	–	3	3	1	–	–	–	–	–	–	–	–	–	–	–	–	–	–	–	–	–	–	–	–	–	–	–	–	–	–	–	–	–	–	–	–	1
Kuda Nikawewa	–	–	–	–	1	1	–	–	–	–	–	–	–	–	1	–	–	–	–	–	–	–	–	–	–	–	–	–	–	–	–	–	–	–	–	–	–	–	–
Kuda Tammanawa	–	–	–	–	–	–	12	–	–	–	–	–	–	–	–	–	–	–	–	–	–	–	–	–	–	–	–	–	–	–	–	–	–	–	–	–	–	–	1
Hunupolayagama	–	1	–	–	–	–	–	3	1	–	–	–	–	–	2	–	–	–	–	–	–	–	–	–	–	–	–	–	–	–	–	–	–	–	–	–	–	–	1
Wanniya Palugollewa	–	2	–	2	–	–	–	–	13	3	–	–	–	–	–	–	–	–	–	–	–	–	–	–	–	–	–	–	–	–	–	–	–	–	–	–	–	–	–
Magurahitiyawa	–	–	–	3	–	–	–	–	3	3	–	–	–	–	1	–	–	–	–	–	–	–	–	–	–	–	–	–	–	–	–	–	1	–	–	–	–	–	1
Pandiggama	–	–	–	–	–	–	–	–	–	–	35	5	–	–	1	–	5	–	–	–	–	2	–	–	–	–	–	–	–	–	–	–	3	1	–	–	–	–	1
Welewa	–	–	–	–	–	–	–	–	–	–	5	46	2	3	2	1	2	–	–	–	1	1	–	–	–	–	–	–	–	–	–	–	–	–	–	–	–	1	2
Diviyaubendewewa	–	–	–	–	–	–	–	–	–	–	–	2	17	–	1	–	–	–	–	–	–	–	–	–	1	–	·	–	–	–	–	–	1	–	–	–	–	–	2
Medagama	1	–	–	–	–	–	–	–	–	–	–	3	–	36	1	–	–	–	–	–	2	–	–	–	–	–	–	–	–	–	–	–	1	1	–	–	–	–	8
Tulaveliya	–	–	–	–	–	–	–	–	–	–	–	2	–	–	40	2	–	–	–	–	1	–	–	–	–	1	–	–	–	–	–	–	1	–	–	–	–	–	2
Kalavelpotana	–	–	–	–	–	–	–	–	–	–	–	–	–	–	2	4	1	–	–	–	–	–	–	–	–	–	–	–	–	–	–	–	–	–	–	–	–	–	2
Kukulewa	–	–	–	–	–	–	–	–	–	–	–	5	–	–	1	–	66	5	–	–	1	1	2	–	2	2	–	1	–	–	–	–	1	–	2	–	–	–	3
Elapatagama	–	–	–	–	–	–	–	–	–	–	–	–	–	–	–	–	5	10	–	3	1	–	1	–	–	–	–	–	–	–	–	–	–	–	–	–	–	–	1
Siyambalagaswewa (A)	–	–	–	–	–	–	–	–	–	–	–	–	–	–	–	–	–	7	7	10	–	1	1	–	–	–	–	–	–	–	–	–	–	–	–	–	–	–	1
Kirimetiyawa	–	–	–	–	–	–	–	–	–	–	–	–	–	–	–	–	4	–	–	4	3	–	–	–	–	–	–	–	–	–	–	–	1	–	–	–	–	–	–

TABLE 7.1—Continued

Postmarital Residence \ Premarital Residence	Wanniya Helambewa	Maha Ehetuwewa	Nawakkulama	Tambiyawewa	Tantrimalai	Kuda Nikawewa	Kuda Tammawa	Hunupolayagama	Wanniya Palugollewa	Magurahitiyawa	Pandiggama	Welewa	Diviyaubendewewa	Medagama	Tulaveliya	Kalavelpotana	Kukulewa	Elapatgama	Siyambalagaswewa (A)	Kirimetiyawa	Elapatwewa	Kanugahewa	Rambekapuwewa	Bogahawewa	Dambagahaulpota	Migahapattiya	Maha Migaswewa	Halmillewa	Pusdiwulwewa	Moragoda	Rotawewa	Malayaparantikulama	Katamankulama	Adampane	Bakmikada	Dambulla Vedda villages	Colony; Vedda by birth	Non-Vedda village; Vedda by birth	Non-Vedda by birth
Elapatwewa	—	—	—	—	—	—	—	—	—	—	—	1	1	—	—	—	5	—	1	—	23	1	1	1	—	—	—	—	—	—	—	—	—	—	—	—	—	—	—
Kanugahewa	—	—	—	—	—	—	—	—	—	—	1	2	2	—	1	—	—	—	—	—	—	25	7	—	—	—	—	—	—	—	—	—	1	—	—	—	—	—	—
Rambekapuwewa	—	—	—	—	—	—	—	—	—	—	2	2	1	2	1	—	2	—	—	—	—	—	23	—	—	—	—	—	—	—	—	—	4	—	—	—	—	—	1
Bogahawewa	—	—	—	—	—	—	—	—	—	—	—	2	1	—	—	—	—	—	—	—	—	1	2	30	—	—	—	—	—	—	—	—	4	1	1	—	—	—	2
Dambagahaulpota	—	—	—	—	—	—	—	—	—	—	1	2	—	—	—	—	2	—	—	—	—	—	1	—	11	1	—	—	—	—	—	—	—	—	—	—	—	—	4
Migahapattiya	—	—	—	—	—	—	—	—	—	—	—	1	—	—	—	—	—	—	—	—	—	—	—	—	1	26	—	—	—	1	1	—	—	—	—	2	1	—	5
Maha Migaswewa	—	—	—	—	—	—	—	—	—	—	—	—	—	—	—	—	—	—	—	—	—	—	—	—	—	—	18	—	—	3	1	—	—	—	—	1	—	—	—
Halmillewa	—	—	—	—	—	—	—	—	—	—	—	1	—	—	—	—	1	—	—	—	—	—	—	—	—	2	—	15	26	3	4	—	—	—	—	1	1	—	2
Pusdiwulwewa	—	—	—	—	—	—	—	—	—	—	—	—	—	—	—	—	1	—	—	—	—	—	—	—	—	1	3	1	26	1	2	—	1	—	—	—	1	1	4
Moragoda	—	—	—	—	—	—	—	—	—	—	—	—	—	—	—	—	—	—	—	—	—	—	—	—	—	—	—	2	5	5	2	—	1	—	—	1	—	1	2
Rotawewa	—	—	—	—	—	—	—	—	—	—	—	1	—	—	—	—	1	—	—	—	—	—	—	—	—	1	1	4	2	—	53	—	—	—	—	1	—	—	6
Malayaparantikulama	—	—	—	—	—	—	—	—	—	—	2	—	—	—	—	—	—	—	—	—	—	—	—	—	—	—	—	—	—	—	—	16	1	—	—	—	—	—	2
Katamankulama	—	—	—	—	—	—	—	—	—	—	2	1	—	7	2	—	3	—	—	—	—	2	3	2	1	—	—	—	1	—	2	1	39	17	3	—	1	—	—
Adampane	—	—	—	—	—	—	—	—	—	—	1	—	—	1	—	—	3	—	—	—	—	3	2	2	3	—	—	—	—	—	2	—	—	—	2	—	—	1	—
Bakmikada	—	—	—	—	—	—	—	—	—	—	1	—	—	—	—	—	3	—	—	—	—	2	2	2	3	—	—	—	—	—	—	—	—	2	29	—	—	—	—
Dambulla Vedda villages	—	—	—	—	—	—	3	—	—	—	—	4	—	—	—	—	—	1	—	—	1	2	1	—	—	2	—	—	—	—	—	—	—	—	—	—	1	1	2
Colony; Vedda spouse	—	—	—	—	—	—	—	—	—	—	—	2	—	—	—	—	—	—	—	—	—	—	—	—	—	—	—	—	1	—	—	3	8	—	—	—	—	1	—
Non-Vedda village; Vedda spouse	—	—	—	—	—	1	—	—	—	—	—	1	—	—	—	—	—	—	—	—	—	—	—	—	—	1	—	2	2	3	3	—	1	—	—	—	—	1	—
Colony or non-Vedda village; non-Vedda spouse	1	—	2	—	—	2	—	—	—	—	—	—	—	—	—	—	—	—	—	—	—	—	1	—	1	1	—	—	—	—	—	—	—	—	2	—	—	—	—

NOTE: Villages founded since 1950 are not treated independently from their parent communities.

TABLE 7.2

PREMARITAL AND POSTMARITAL RESIDENCE OF CURRENTLY (1970) MARRIED ANURADHAPURA VEDDA FEMALES AND POSTMARITAL RESIDENCE OF OTHER FEMALES CURRENTLY MARRIED TO VEDDA MALES AND RESIDENT IN VEDDA VILLAGES

Postmarital Residence \ Premarital Residence	Wanniya Helambewa	Maha Ehetuwewa	Nawakkulama	Tambiyawewa	Tantrimalai	Kuda Nikawewa	Kuda Tammanawa	Hunupolayagama	Wanniya Palugollewa	Magurahitiyawa	Pandiggama	Welewa	Diviyaubendewewa	Medagama	Tulaveliya	Kalavelpotana	Kukulewa	Elapatgama	Siyambalagaswewa (A)	Kirimetiyawa	Elapatwewa	Kanugahewa	Rambekapuwewa	Bogahawewa	Dambagahalpota	Migahapattiya	Maha Migaswewa	Halmillewa	Pusdiwulewewa	Moragoda	Rotawewa	Malaiyaparanikkulama	Katamankulama	Adampane	Bakmikada	Dambulla Vedda villages	Colony; Vedda by birth	Non-Vedda village; Vedda by birth	Non-Vedda by birth
Wanniya Helambewa	16	—	—	1	—	2	—	—	—	—	—	—	—	3	3	—	—	—	—	—	—	—	—	—	—	—	—	—	—	—	—	—	—	—	—	—	—	—	1
Maha Ehetuwewa	1	4	—	3	—	—	—	2	1	—	—	—	—	4	1	—	1	—	—	—	—	—	—	—	—	—	—	—	—	—	—	—	—	—	—	—	—	—	1
Nawakkulama	2	9	—	—	—	—	—	—	—	—	—	—	—	1	1	—	—	—	—	—	—	—	—	—	—	—	—	—	—	—	—	—	—	—	—	—	—	—	1
Tambiyawewa	1	10	—	—	1	—	—	1	—	1	—	—	—	—	—	—	—	—	—	—	—	—	—	—	—	—	—	—	—	—	—	—	—	—	—	—	—	1	2
Tantrimalai	1	—	—	2	—	1	—	3	—	—	—	—	—	—	—	—	—	—	—	—	—	—	—	—	—	—	—	—	—	—	—	—	—	—	—	—	—	1	—
Kuda Nikawewa	—	—	1	2	1	—	—	—	—	—	—	—	—	—	—	—	—	—	—	—	—	—	—	—	—	—	—	—	—	—	—	—	—	—	—	—	—	—	—
Kuda Tammanawa	2	2	—	—	—	—	9	—	—	—	—	—	—	1	1	—	1	—	—	—	—	—	—	—	—	—	—	—	—	—	—	—	—	—	—	—	—	—	—
Hunupolayagama	—	—	—	—	—	—	—	5	—	—	—	—	—	1	1	—	—	—	—	—	—	—	—	—	—	—	—	—	—	—	—	—	—	—	—	—	—	—	—
Wanniya Palugollewa	—	1	—	—	—	—	—	—	12	2	—	1	—	3	1	—	—	—	2	—	—	—	2	—	—	—	—	—	—	—	—	2	4	—	—	—	—	—	1
Magurahitiyawa	—	—	—	2	—	—	—	—	2	—	—	—	—	—	1	—	—	—	—	—	—	—	—	—	—	—	—	—	—	—	—	—	—	—	—	—	—	—	—
Pandiggama	—	—	—	—	—	—	—	—	—	—	34	2	—	—	2	—	—	—	1	—	1	3	—	—	—	—	—	—	—	—	—	—	—	—	—	—	—	—	—
Welewa	—	—	—	—	—	—	—	—	—	1	7	44	13	—	—	—	—	—	1	—	—	1	—	—	—	—	—	—	—	—	—	—	1	—	—	—	—	—	1
Diviyaubendewewa	—	—	—	—	—	—	—	—	—	—	—	4	—	—	—	—	—	—	—	—	—	—	—	—	—	—	—	1	—	—	—	—	—	—	—	—	—	—	—
Medagama	1	1	—	—	—	—	—	—	—	—	—	1	—	36	4	—	1	—	1	1	1	—	—	—	—	—	—	—	—	—	—	1	1	—	—	1	—	—	6
Tulaveliya	—	—	—	2	—	—	—	—	—	—	6	1	—	3	27	—	—	—	1	—	1	—	1	—	—	—	—	—	—	—	—	4	3	—	—	—	—	2	2
Kalavelpotana	1	—	—	—	—	—	—	—	—	—	—	—	—	—	5	—	—	—	—	—	—	—	—	—	—	—	—	—	—	—	—	—	—	—	—	—	—	—	—
Kukulewa	—	—	—	—	—	—	—	—	—	—	1	8	—	1	1	5	57	1	5	3	3	—	3	—	3	—	—	—	—	—	—	1	1	—	—	—	2	—	1
Elapatgama	—	—	—	—	—	—	—	—	—	—	—	2	—	2	1	—	2	11	1	1	1	—	1	—	1	—	—	—	—	—	—	—	—	—	—	—	—	—	—
Siyambalagaswewa (A)	—	—	—	—	—	—	—	—	—	—	—	—	—	—	1	—	3	1	2	—	1	—	1	—	—	—	—	—	—	—	—	—	—	—	—	—	—	—	—
Kirimetiyawa	—	—	—	—	—	—	—	—	—	—	—	3	—	—	—	—	13	3	—	13	1	—	—	—	1	—	—	1	—	—	—	—	—	—	—	—	—	—	—

TABLE 7.2—Continued

Postmarital Residence \ Premarital Residence	Wanniya Helambewa	Maha Ebetuwewa	Nawakkulama	Tambiyawewa	Tantrimalai	Kuda Nikawewa	Kuda Tammanawa	Hunupolayagama	Wanniya Palugollewa	Magurahitiyawa	Pandiggama	Welewa	Diviyabendewewa	Medagama	Tulaveliya	Kalavelpotana	Kukulewa	Elapatgama	Siyambalagaswewa (A)	Kirimetiyawa	Elapatwewa	Kanugahewa	Rambekapuwewa	Bogahawewa	Dambagahaulpota	Migahapattiya	Maha Migaswewa	Halmillewa	Pusdiwulwewa	Moragoda	Rotawewa	Malayaparantikulama	Katamankulama	Adampane	Bakmikada	Dambulla Vedda villages	Colony; Vedda by birth	Non-Vedda village; Vedda by birth	Non-Vedda by birth
Elapatwewa	—	—	—	—	—	—	—	—	—	—	3	2	2	—	—	—	5	—	—	4	17	1	—	—	—	—	—	—	—	—	—	—	—	—	3	—	—	—	—
Kanugahewa	—	—	—	—	—	—	—	—	—	—	—	—	—	—	1	—	—	—	—	—	—	20	5	2	—	—	—	—	—	—	—	—	—	—	—	—	—	—	—
Rambekapuwewa	—	—	—	—	—	—	—	—	—	—	5	2	—	—	—	—	—	—	—	1	1	—	23	4	1	—	—	—	—	—	—	—	—	—	—	—	—	—	—
Bogahawewa	—	—	—	—	—	—	—	—	—	—	2	3	—	—	—	—	2	—	—	—	1	—	6	25	—	—	—	—	—	—	—	—	—	—	—	3	—	—	3
Dambagahaulpota	—	—	—	—	—	—	—	—	—	—	1	—	—	1	—	—	2	—	—	1	—	—	—	—	13	3	2	2	3	—	—	—	—	—	—	—	—	—	7
Migahapattiya	—	—	—	—	—	—	—	—	—	—	—	—	—	—	—	—	—	—	—	—	—	—	—	—	4	13	2	4	2	—	—	—	—	—	3	3	—	—	—
Maha Migaswewa	—	—	—	—	—	—	—	—	—	—	—	—	—	—	—	—	—	—	—	—	—	—	—	—	1	2	7	4	—	—	—	—	—	—	—	2	—	—	—
Halmillewa	—	—	—	—	—	—	3	—	—	—	—	—	—	—	—	—	—	—	—	—	—	—	—	—	1	—	5	16	5	—	—	—	—	—	—	3	—	2	2
Pusdiwulwewa	—	—	—	—	—	—	—	—	—	—	—	—	—	—	—	—	—	—	—	—	—	—	—	—	—	—	1	4	21	1	—	—	—	—	—	2	—	2	2
Moragoda	—	—	—	—	—	—	—	—	—	—	—	—	—	—	—	—	—	—	—	1	—	—	—	—	1	1	—	—	6	6	6	—	—	—	—	—	—	1	1
Rotawewa	—	—	—	—	—	—	—	—	—	—	—	—	—	—	—	—	—	—	—	—	—	—	—	—	—	—	—	7	4	—	48	—	—	—	—	—	—	—	2
Malayaparantikulama	—	—	—	—	—	—	—	—	—	—	1	—	—	1	1	—	—	1	—	—	—	—	—	—	1	—	—	—	—	—	—	7	3	—	—	—	1	—	—
Katamankulama	—	—	—	—	—	—	—	—	—	—	4	—	—	1	2	—	—	—	—	—	—	—	—	—	1	—	—	—	—	—	—	—	46	1	—	—	—	—	—
Adampane	—	—	—	—	—	—	—	—	—	—	1	—	—	—	—	—	3	—	—	2	3	1	1	2	1	5	2	—	—	—	—	—	—	20	7	—	1	—	—
Bakmikada	—	—	—	—	—	—	—	—	—	—	1	—	—	—	—	—	—	—	—	—	—	—	—	—	—	—	—	1	—	—	—	—	—	—	33	6	—	—	—
Dambulla Vedda villages	—	—	—	—	—	—	—	—	—	—	—	1	—	—	—	—	—	—	—	—	—	—	—	—	—	—	—	—	—	—	—	—	1	—	6	—	—	—	—
Colony; Vedda spouse	2	—	—	—	—	—	3	—	—	—	3	3	—	1	2	—	2	—	—	2	1	1	1	2	1	1	2	—	—	—	—	—	9	—	—	1	—	—	—
Non-Vedda village; Vedda spouse	2	—	—	—	—	—	2	—	—	—	2	2	—	1	—	—	1	—	—	1	—	—	—	—	1	1	—	—	—	—	—	—	—	—	—	9	—	—	—
Colony or non-Vedda village; non-Vedda spouse	2	2	—	—	—	—	—	—	—	—	—	2	—	2	2	—	1	1	—	1	—	—	—	2	2	4	—	—	—	—	—	—	—	1	1	—	—	—	—

NOTE: Villages founded since 1950 are not treated independently from their parent communities.

TABLE 7.3

POPULATION OF ANURADHAPURA VEDDA VILLAGES OUTSIDE
WILLACHCHIYA, 1891, 1931, AND 1970

	1891	1931	1970
Pandiggama	36	132	256
Gallewa	0	0	0
Welewa	135	148	384
Diviyaubendewewa	0	0	152
Medagama	44	99	331
Tulaveliya	73	94	345
Kalavelpotana	0	7	60
Kukulewa	108	207	552
Elapatgama	0	21	145
Siyambalagaswewa (A)	0	21	58
Kirimetiyawa	0	25	129
Elapatwewa	37	56	192
Kanugahewa	28	62	213
Ihala Tammenawa	20	14	0
Rambekapuwewa	53	77	223
Manakande	18	13	0
Kohombagaswewa	32	0	0
Nochchikulama (B)	9	0	0
Bogahawewa	30	49	240
Dambagahaulpota	40	59	194
Migahapattiya	60	76	263
Maha Migaswewa	74	63	147
Halmillewa	38	98	161
Pusdiwulwewa	17	52	242
Moragoda	0	34	69
Rotawewa	55	105	434
Gallinda	60	0	0
Kurundankulama	56	0	0
Malayaparantikulama	0	31	119
Katamankulama	0	171	375
Adampane	31	39	217
Bakmikada	0	68	299
Total	1076	1821	5800
Number of villages	22	26	25
Average population	48.9	70.0	232.0

SOURCES: 1891-1931, official censuses; 1970, author's census.
NOTE: Gallewa was founded after 1891 and was already abandoned by 1931.

inhabited by their children and grandchildren. Several outsiders have married into this village, including the man whose *variga* court case is described by Leach (ibid., pp. 307-9; see also p. 38 for the Kalavelpotana villagers' tenancy of their fields).

Katamankulama (44) and *Malayaparantikulama* (43) are two Vedda villages that lie just over the border in the Northern Province, a few miles from Vavuniya town. Katamankulama, which is also known as Etambagaskada, was founded at the end of the nineteenth century from the former Vedda village of *Kurundankulama* (R). A few years later, between 1901 and 1911, the remaining inhabitants of Kurundankulama moved to a new settlement at Malayaparantikulama that, however, has remained a smaller and less prosperous village than Katamankulama. The inhabitants of these two villages are Sinhalese speakers, but many of the neighboring villages are Tamil, and the Veddas are said by their fellows elsewhere to show some Tamil influence, especially in their industrious devotion to paddy cultivation. On the other hand, Katamankulama is the only Vedda village that contains both a Buddhist temple and a resident priest.

To the southwest of Katamankulama, on the border of the North Central and the Northern provinces, are the sites of two villages that are said to have once been Vedda settlements. According to the census records *Nochchikulama* (B) (N) was abandoned between 1911 and 1921 and *Kohombagaswewa* (F) between 1901 and 1911. Most of the survivors moved either to Katamankulama or to Pandiggama.

To the southeast of Katamankulama, *Pandiggama* (21), *Rambekapuwewa* (34) and *Kanugahewa* (33) reveal less distinctive features. All have been continuously inhabited by Veddas since before 1900, and all have received a modest influx of immigrants from three other Vedda villages that have been abandoned during the present century. *Gallewa* (H) appears to have been founded in the last decade of the nineteenth century, but it flourished for less than thirty years before its inhabitants moved, or returned, to Pandiggama. *Ihala Tammenawa* (G) and *Manakande* (J) were in existence earlier and survived longer, but both were abandoned during the 1930s. The surviving inhabitants of Manakande moved to Rambekapuwewa, which is only a couple of miles away, while those of Ihala Tammenawa dispersed to Pandiggama and Kanugahewa as well. As in Willachchiya, the abandonment of these villages is said to have followed severe and prolonged outbreaks of sickness, but there is also some suggestion that the loss of control over village lands to outsiders was a decisive factor.

Bogahawewa (35), another traditional Vedda settlement, lies to the northeast of Rambekapuwewa on the new road that leads to Padaviya colony. This is one of the largest of the government's colonization projects, and the Bogahawewa villagers have been much affected by it. Some have gone into trade by the roadside, others have found wage labor in the colony, and most complain that their ancestral fields are now flooded by the restored tank at Padaviya. A number of villagers were offered land in the colony, but most of them have not taken up or asweddumized their allotments. The village has also received attention from a Buddhist charity organization, which has put up about twenty small concrete houses for the villagers.

Since his reference is to Padaviya, it seems likely that it was at Bogahawewa that Parker encountered the "Wanniyas" he described in *The Taprobanian* in 1887. There can be little doubt that this "race of hunters," whose territory extended "from Padaviya tank to Tantrimalai," and who claimed to occupy seventeen villages in the North Central Province and another in the southern part of the Northern Province (Kurundankulama?), were the ancestors of the people I am describing as the Anuradhapura Veddas, for it will be recalled that the latter also refer to themselves as *"Wanni minissu."*

Welewa (22), with a population of 135, was the largest Vedda village at the time of the 1891 census, but this figure remained more or less stable until 1931, since when the village has grown rapidly. Around 1950 two families from Welewa established a new village a few miles away at *Diviyaubendewewa* (23), and the daughter village now also has a population of more than 150. Several other families from Welewa have settled at Kadahate, where they form a small minority in a Goyigama village.[2]

Kukulewa (30) has been discussed previously (chapters 2, 3, and 4). It has been the largest Vedda village throughout the present century, and its central position in the territorial distribution of the Vedda villages gives it a strategic location in the *variga* network as a whole. Kukulewa has also spawned three new villages in the last seventy years. *Elapatgama* (24), founded between 1901 and 1911, and *Siyambala-gaswewa* (A) (29), founded between 1921 and 1931, were both established in the manner widely documented in Willachchiya, that is, by a middle-aged man accompanied by his young adult sons and some-

2. This development contravenes the normal practice, described earlier, whereby a village is inhabited by members of only one *variga*. There are a few other instances of one or two Vedda families settling in villages of other *variga*, where they usually work as tenant cultivators. Such villages are not considered here as Vedda villages. The marital connections linking them with the Vedda villages are subsumed in the rows marked "Non-Vedda village; Vedda spouse" and the columns marked "Non-Vedda village; Vedda by birth" in tables 7.1 and 7.2. On the other side, a number of Vedda villages contain one or two families of non-Vedda *variga*. In these cases the immigrants have usually been shopkeepers. They have not been included in the tables unless a marriage has been established between them and the Veddas.

times also by his sons-in-law. Elapatgama is now largely in the hands of the founder's grandchildren and great-grandchildren, while Siyam-balagaswewa remains in the hands of the children and grandchildren. *Kirimetiyawa* (31) was apparently also founded in the 1920s, but does not appear as an independent village in the census of 1931. The Veddas say they obtained the site, which as elsewhere was that of an abandoned tank, from the members of the Goyigama village within whose boundaries it lay. The Vedda population in 1931 was probably reported as a part of that of the administrative village within which Kirimeti-yawa lies, and the figure given in table 7.3 is my own estimate based on genealogical data. In this case the village was either founded by two families that were not closely related, or the single founding family was shortly joined by a second. There is some disagreement on the matter.

Elapatwewa (32) is a long-established Vedda village near Horuwopo-tana, and lies a mile off the Anuradhapura-Trincomalee road. It is also within a mile of the Vanniyar aristocrat's *valavva* ("manor-house, or dwelling of a chief," Pieris 1956, p. 309) at Morakewa, and the Veddas work in the Vanniyar's extensive fields. The village is at present inter-nally dominated by a *kapurala-anumetirala* (priest-spirit medium), whose reputation extends over a wide area and well beyond the bounds of the Vedda community.

Adampane (45) and *Bakmikada* (46) are further to the northeast, over the border in Trincomalee District. Bakmikada was founded from Adampane at about the turn of the century, but has since become larger than its parent village. These are the two villages that up until a generation ago maintained kinship and marriage relations with Tamil-speaking Veddas at Kuchchaveli on the east coast. This memory may have provided the basis for the assertion of Wickremasinghe et al., made in their analysis of Vedda blood groups and hemoglobins (1963, p. 118), that the people of Adampane and Bakmikada enjoy "free intermarriage with Tamils." In fact they are as clearly integrated into the Vedda *variga* as are the people of any other village. Likewise the statement that the people of Adampane and Bakmikada "speak only Tamil" is not correct today. There are certainly a number of people in the two villages who *can* speak Tamil, but the first language in both is Sinhalese.

There are six Vedda communities in the neighborhood of Hurulu-wewa, the site of another major governmental attempt to refurbish and colonize an ancient tank. One of them, *Moragoda* (38), was founded by an immigrant family from Elapatwewa between 1911 and 1921, and remains in the hands of the children, grandchildren, and great-grand-children of the founders. The other five are all longer established; that is, they were already inhabited by Veddas at the time of our earliest records from the nineteenth century, and are claimed to be ancestral villages by their present residents. Two of them, *Dambagahaulpota* (L, 37) and *Migahapattiya* (K, 36), have recently been displaced, as the traditional villages lay in the former tank-bed of Huruluwewa and have been submerged by the restoration scheme. The villagers were offered land in the colony and were given house sites and houses in two adjacent and self-contained sections of it, which now bear the names of the former communities. Many villagers are doubtful that they have bene-fited from their upheaval. Each family has been given paddy land on lease, but irrigation at Huruluwewa has not always been reliable, and cultivation has not always been possible, or, if it has been attempted, not always successful. Furthermore, the Veddas feel uncertain of the permanence of their tenure, and they resent those restrictions on the disposition of their fields that directly contradict their traditional rules of inheritance. Finally, the scale of the colonization scheme requires that the Veddas go several miles to find jungle for chena cultivation and even for firewood.

The three other Vedda villages in the area, *Maha Migaswewa* (40), *Halmillewa* (39) and *Pusdiwulwewa* (41), have not been so directly affected by the Huruluwewa project, and they preserve a more tradi-tional way of life.

The last community in the Anuradhapura Vedda *variga* is *Rotawewa* (42), which lies to the southeast of Huruluwewa in Polonnaruwa District. This is the only community in the Anuradhapura *variga* that is men-tioned in the Seligmanns' account of the Veddas (1911, pp. 56, 74, 177-78). The village is also briefly mentioned in a report on an exploration of ancient irrigation works written by Bailey and others in 1855, which is worth quoting in full:

> At the Weddah village of Rotawewa we found the people most primitive. They had been settled here from a long period, and said that they once owned all the adjoin-ing lands. This village and that of Potane they told us are presided over by a Weddah chief, who bears the title of the Rangdoon, or the 'Golden Bow.' Unfortunately for us, this chief was from home on a shooting expedition, and we had not an oppor-tunity of making his acquaintance, but we saw his quiver, full of arrows, which he had left behind. [Adams, Churchill, and Bailey, quoted in Brohier 1934, p. 46]

The restoration of irrigation works in the area finds Rotawewa now compressed between the major tanks of Kaudulla and Minneriya. The villagers have derived some advantages from these developments, notably improved communications and access to casual employment, and they have lost few of their traditional paddy fields, but as at Huruluwewa they particularly resent the new difficulties that restrict chena cultiva-tion. Indeed they must now go so far for chena cultivation that many families move their whole households into the jungle, and during the chena season the permanent village is largely deserted.

Another Vedda village near Minneriya, called *Gallinda* (M), was as large as Rotawewa at the time of the 1891 census, but was abandoned for unknown reasons between 1901 and 1911.

THE GENERAL PATTERN OF MARRIAGE AND MIGRATION

The most striking factor in the demographic history of these villages, as in Willachchiya, has been the rate of population growth (table 7.3). In 1891 the Vedda population of 1076 was distributed among twenty-two villages. By 1931 the population had risen by 69.2 percent to 1821, nine new villages had been founded and five abandoned.[3] The average village population had thus risen from 48.9 to 70.0. Since 1931 the population has increased by 218 percent to 5800, two villages have been abandoned and one new one founded. The average village population is now 232.0.

The rate of population growth, both between 1891 and 1931, and between 1931 and 1970, has been less rapid than that of the Willachchiya Vedda community, which is partly attributable to the balance of migration between the two areas. I have already noted that more people, both men and women, have migrated into the Willachchiya community than have moved out of it into Vedda villages elsewhere, owing in part to the greater availability of new lands to cultivate in Willachchiya and particularly to the possibility of founding new villages at uninhabited and abandoned tanks. Outside Willachchiya, where the general population is much denser, this possibility is now virtually nonexistent. Only one new Vedda village has been founded since 1931. Consequently almost all the swollen population has had to be contained in the existing villages, the average population of which is now more than three times what it was forty years ago, and nearly five times what it was eighty years ago.

The general pattern of marriage and residence resembles that of Willachchiya, but with some differences (tables 7.1, 7.2, 7.3). As in Willachchiya a number of marriages are tolerated that cross *variga* lines, and these are most frequent where traditional life has been most directly affected by external developments, such as a colonization project (Migahapattiya, Dambagahaulpota, and Rotawewa) or, as in Medagama, by the railway. Veddas do not marry with neighboring and traditional communities of different *variga*.

Among current marriages, virilocal residence is preferred over uxorilocal (table 7.4), as in Willachchiya, and neolocal residence is uncommon, being less than 4 percent in both areas. Duolocal residence is significantly more frequent outside Willachchiya than within it. This is

3. These figures include Gallewa, which was both founded and abandoned during this period.

TABLE 7.4

POSTMARITAL RESIDENCE OF COUPLES IN THE ANURADHAPURA VEDDA VILLAGES, 1970

	Duolocal	Virilocal	Uxorilocal	Neolocal
Pandiggama	20	15	14	0
Welewa	32	14	12	1
Diviyaubendewewa	6	11	7	2
Medagama	19	17	17	0
Tulaveliya	17	23	10	1
Kalavelpotana	0	4	5	0
Kukulewa	37	29	20	1
Elapatgama	3	7	8	2
Siyambalagaswewa (A)	0	7	2	1
Kirimetiyawa	4	6	9	1
Elapatwewa	10	13	7	2
Kanugahewa	12	13	8	2
Rambekapuwewa	12	12	11	2
Bogahawewa	12	18	13	1
Dambagahaulpota	2	9	11	6
Migahapattiya	2	24	11	3
Maha Migaswewa	6	12	1	0
Halmillewa	6	9	10	1
Pusdiwulwewa	10	16	11	1
Moragoda	0	5	6	0
Rotawewa	31	22	17	0
Malayaparantikulama	4	12	3	0
Katamankulama	22	17	24	1
Adampane	3	14	17	2
Bakmikada	15	14	18	1
Wanniya Helambewa	3	9	13	0
Maha Ehetuwewa	0	13	4	1
Nawakkulama	6	5	3	1
Tambiyawewa	1	10	9	1
Tantrimalai	1	2	1	0
Kuda Nikawewa	0	1	1	0
Kuda Tammanawa	6	6	3	0
Hunupolayagama	0	3	5	0
Wanniya Palugollewa	4	9	8	1
Magurahitiyawa	0	3	2	0
Total	306	403	321	35
Percentage	28.7	37.8	30.1	3.3

NOTES: (1) N = 1065; (2) Residential reference is to village, not household; (3) Figures for villages founded since 1950 which, with one exception are all within three miles of the village from which they were settled, are included with those of the parent community.

largely a matter of opportunity. Those villages in which duolocality is the most common form of residence (Pandiggama, Welewa, Medagama, Kukulewa, Rambekapuwewa, and Rotawewa) are among the most populous and, from the point of view of an aspiring spouse, may therefore be expected to contain a greater number of persons of appropriate sex and age who are not excluded as permissible partners by the cross-cousin marriage rule. These figures tend therefore to support my contention that "close" marriage, where "closeness" is defined either locally (marriage within the village) or in terms of kinship (first or second cross-cousin marriage), is not avoided by the Veddas but is often welcomed where it is available.

It must be emphasized, however, that this remains a matter of preference and inclination. It is not so pronounced that it threatens to create "microcastes" by fission within the *variga* as a whole. The latter remains a single network of kinship and marriage. As in Willachchiya there are certainly areas of concentration or intensity within the network, places where the net of kinship and marriage is drawn tighter, so to speak, and these can be described in terms either of kinship (marriage with a "close" cross-cousin, brother-sister exchange, etc.) or of locality. In the latter case one points first to the frequency of marriage within a single village, expressed in duolocal residence, and secondly to the frequency of marriage within a cluster of adjacent villages as, for example, among the villages close to Huruluwewa (Dambagahaulpota, Migahapattiya, Maha Migaswewa, Pusdiwulwewa, Halmillewa, and Moragoda; tables 7.1, 7.2, 7.4). On the other side, there are a number of villages, particularly the large and more centrally located ones, that maintain marital relations over an extensive area. Natives of Kukulewa, for instance, are married and living in twenty other Vedda villages, and there are seven other communities (Pandiggama, Welewa, Medagama, Tulaveliya, Rambekapuwewa, Dambagahaulpota, Katamankulama), whose native sons and daughters are resident in ten or more villages within the *variga*. Correspondingly there are six villages (Tulaveliya, Kukulewa, Bogahawewa, Dambagahaulpota, Katamankulama, and Adampane) that have attracted immigrant spouses from ten or more communities. Thus while there is no record of a marriage directly connecting Rotawewa with Katamankulama, which is more than fifty miles distant, each of these villages is currently connected to Kukulewa, Welewa, and Bogahawewa, and the integrity of the *variga* network is thus maintained.

The residential choice that is available when a marriage takes place between natives of different villages can compensate for demographic fluctuations and permit a more or less equable ratio of population to cultivable land among the various villages. An estimate of this ratio in 1931 and 1970 is offered in table 7.5, but I must again warn the reader

TABLE 7.5

Paddy Land Holdings Per Capita in the Vedda Villages Outside Willachchiya, 1931 and 1970

	1931			1970		
	Popu-lation	Paddy land acres	Land per capita	Popu-lation	Paddy land acres	Land per capita
Pandiggama	132	44	0.3	256	96	0.4
Welewa	148	88	0.6	384	124	0.3
Diviyaubendewewa	—	—	—	152	36	0.2
Medagama	99	10	0.1	331	85	0.3
Tulaveliya	94	30	0.3	345	170	0.5
Kalavelpotana	7	3½	0.5	60	18	0.3
Kukulewa	207	66	0.3	552	130	0.3
Elapatgama	21	7	0.3	145	35	0.2
Siyambalagaswewa (A)	21	1½	0.1	58	3	0.1
Kirimetiyawa	25	12	0.5	129	46	0.4
Elapatwewa	56	16	0.3	192	126	0.7
Kanugahewa	62	12	0.2	213	67	0.4
Ihala Tammenawa	14	?	3	—	—	—
Rambekapuwewa	77	10	0.1	223	60	0.3
Manakande	18	?	?	—	—	—
Bogahawewa	49	6	0.1	240	16	0.1
Dambagahaulpota	59	35?	0.6	194	95	0.5
Migahapattiya	76	90?	1.2	263	135	0.5
Maha Migaswewa	63	15	0.2	147	25	0.2
Halmillewa	98	42	0.4	161	52	0.3
Pusdiwulwewa	52	13	0.3	242	26	0.1
Moragoda	34	8	0.2	69	21	0.3
Rotawewa	105	7	0.1	434	72	0.2
Malayaparantikulama	31	8	0.3	119	56	0.5
Katamankulama	171	58	0.3	375	138	0.4
Adampane	39	18	0.5	217	98	0.4
Bakmikada	68	18	0.3	299	138	0.4
Total	1821	618+?	0.3?	5800	1868	0.3

that my estimate of land extents in all villages other than Kukulewa is crudely derived and in one or two cases may be seriously in error (see chapter 5, footnote 8). As in Willachchiya the extension of paddy land has roughly kept pace with the expansion of population over the last forty years. Clearly the ratio of people to land shows significant differences between certain villages, but it may be admitted that the residential option provides a mechanism whereby the differences that do emerge can be mitigated.[4] Other things being equal, Vedda couples tend to reside in the village of the partner who stands to gain access to the greater amount of paddy land. The aggregate effect of many such decisions is to approach a ratio of population to land that is the same for all villages.

This result may be described as a function of residential norms and practice. But to do so does not adequately explain the particular residential decisions that Veddas make, for these decisions are made by individual couples in each case, and there is no evidence that individual Veddas are oriented toward their collective effect. On the contrary, Veddas decide where to live in terms of their own private interests and satisfactions. Accordingly, throughout this study I have played down the "functionalist" perspective that would emphasize the socially adaptive effects of residential decisions, and have chosen to examine these decisions as being themselves the result of other social factors, particularly of political and economic processes within the different villages.

In earlier chapters I have demonstrated that the developmental processes both of the Willachchiya villages (chapters 5 and 6) and of the basic cultivating groups in Kukulewa (chapter 4) are rooted in that of the household. If the focus had been on political rather than economic matters, I would have emphasized that the basic cultivating groups in Kukulewa could equally have been described as factions, or as the cores of factions. Members of the same basic cultivating group act together in political affairs, and the play of village politics ranges loosely allied clusters of basic cultivating groups in competition with one another, with the wealthier proprietors usually providing whatever leadership the factional alliances display. These alliances can be no more permanent than the basic cultivating groups that are their constituent units. Indeed they are often a good deal less so, as groups that are allied on one issue may be opposed on another, although it is also true that some groups seem almost always to ally with one another. What *is* more or less permanent is the pattern, or form, of factional alliances, the structure of the basic cultivating groups that compose them and the developmental process through which the basic cultivating groups pass. Particular groups

---

4. Fox (1967, pp. 152-53) has emphasized this point in a general context.

come and go, and alliances are made and broken, but at any one time the structure of Kukulewa politics is largely given by the alliances and conflicts that currently obtain between a number of basic cultivating groups.

Much of this also applies to the Willachchiya villages, with the important difference that there the number of basic cultivating groups is not infrequently reduced to one. This removes the necessity—or, rather, the possibility—of making political alliances within the village, and it indicates the more or less complete concentration of productive property in the hands of one man. This extreme state can be reproduced in successive generations, as has been shown, giving a temporal pattern that can be described, in political terms, as one of *cyclical autocracy*. This pattern is also characteristic of Kukulewa, but not at the level of the village as a whole. Each basic cultivating group possesses the same internal structure and dynamics as the autocratic village, but because Kukulewa contains a number of such groups, the structure of the village itself has a strikingly different character. This pattern, where in each generation power and property are dispersed among a number of competing groups, and where no one man is able to impose an autocratic dominion, may be described as one of *persistent multicentrism*.

These labels are intended to designate the extreme types, and it is not to be expected that all the villages can be adequately described exclusively in terms of one or the other. Villages move from one extreme to the other, and at any given time may lie somewhere between the two poles, so that they are best described in terms of both types and the opposition between them. Thus it is possible, for example, for a dominant pattern of cyclical autocracy to accommodate a multicentric period of intense factionalism between the removal of one autocrat and his succession by another. Several general tendencies may nevertheless be noted. The over-all trend of the Vedda villages, largely but not wholly on account of the population factor, has been one of movement from the autocratic extreme towards persistent multicentrism. Many of the Willachchiya villages, however, and especially those that are single-stem villages, remain closer to the pole of cyclical autocracy, while most of the villages considered in the present chapter, like Kukulewa, approach the opposite pole of persistent multicentrism. I shall not attempt to support this last assertion by detailed examination of the history of all the Vedda villages outside Willachchiya, but I shall use both new and familiar data from Kukulewa to emphasize the necessary contrast with the pattern of cyclical autocracy and to assess the various factors that have tended to move the villages toward one or other of the extreme types.

FACTORS PROMOTING CYCLICAL AUTOCRACY AND PERSISTENT MULTICENTRISM

One of the dynamic forces underlying Vedda social processes is the conflict between the desire of parents to retain the support of their adult children and the children's preference for autonomy. The former is realized by the continued ability to direct the children's labor and is expressed by their continued residence close to the parents. The latter is realized by independence in productive activities and is expressed by residential separation. Because the support of adult children is more easily retained by those parents whose economic operations are still expanding, children are persuaded to continue investing their labor and allegiance in their parents' enterprises in expectation of the enhanced rewards, including a greater inheritance, that will thereby accrue to them. Thus a young couple's choice between virilocal and uxorilocal residence is affected not simply by the relative prosperity of the two sets of parents at the time the residential decision is made, but by a further assessment of the parents' prospects of expansion in the future.

These considerations apply to all the Vedda villages, in some of which, however, control of paddy land is autocratically concentrated while in others it remains dispersed among the heads of a number of kin-based factions. Obviously the simple extent of a village's paddy lands and the size of its population are major determinants of the degree to which wealth and power become concentrated. Other things being equal, the greater the extent of paddy land and the larger the population, the more difficult it is for a single individual to acquire autocratic dominion. Thus the rapid growth of population in the villages and the expansion of the acreage under permanent cultivation during the period covered by this study have, in themselves, made village autocracy harder to establish and have ensured a statistical trend towards the predominance of the multicentric type. This trend has been most pronounced where there have been few opportunities to found new villages that could draw off a segment of the increased population. But there have also been other historical factors that have qualified and affected this tendency in various ways.

First, one must note the changes in the terms under which newly irrigated land is held. Almost all the land brought under cultivation since the implementation of the Land Development Ordinance of 1935 is held on crown lease under conditions that prevent the cultivator from selling his holding and that severely curtail his right to mortgage it. Illegal mortgages are admittedly already common but nevertheless, to the extent that current land policy *is* effectively implemented, the concentration of property holding is restricted.

Other economic changes, and particularly the increasing penetration of the monetary economy, act in the opposite direction. A number of economic possibilities that were formerly forbidden or inhibited by the ethics of kinship can now be realized on a cash basis. It has become tolerable, for instance, for one villager to hire another's labor for a daily wage.

It is difficult, however, to specify precisely what effect increasing liquidity has had on the market for land. The significant extent to which paddy land has changed hands *inter vivos* in recent years tempts one to infer that in earlier times a lesser volume of money, combined with cultural constraints on its use, would have inhibited the concentration of property in land. On the other hand, the historical evidence I have cited for Willachchiya shows that, notwithstanding the norm of bilateral inheritance, enterprising men *were* able to place themselves in exclusive possession of at least the smaller villages, and this suggests that the transmission of landed property *inter vivos,* and even among members of the same *variga*, has not been wholly dependent on the increased liquidity of recent years.

Perhaps the most decisive economic change has been in the organization of trading and shopkeeping. Until about fifteen years ago the only successful traders in the Vedda villages that were large enough to support a shop were outsiders from some other *variga* (cf. Leach 1961a, p. 131; see also chapter 4). Native shopkeepers were evidently unable to resist their kinsmen's demands for excessively favorable credit terms, and sooner rather than later they went bankrupt. Since that time conditions have changed sufficiently for at least the shrewder Vedda entrepreneurs to sustain quite flourishing businesses. K. Wannihamy, the man who now controls the most land in Kukulewa, also runs a successful shop, and at least half the householders in the village are at one time or another in his debt, many of them chronically so. As trader and moneylender, the successful shopkeeper is well placed to take advantage of the villagers' increasing demand for consumer goods, and he is the man most likely to acquire paddy land on mortgage.

A third source of change affecting the degree to which control of paddy land becomes concentrated has been administrative. Prior to the Paddy Lands Act of 1958 the only representative of official authority normally resident in any of the Vedda villages was the Vel Vidane, or irrigation headman. It is plain enough, from the accounts I gave of the Willachchiya villages, that those men who were able to dominate their villages very frequently also occupied the office of Vel Vidane, and the evidence from the other Vedda villages equally supports a modified extension of Leach's finding that, in Pul Eliya, "throughout the period under review the village was dominated by the holder, for the time being, of the office of Vel Vidane" (1961a, p. 193). In the larger villages outside Willachchiya, however, this domination was not absolute. Power and wealth were shared among a number of prominent householders, among whom the Vel Vidane enjoyed peculiar advantages since, as in Pul Eliya, his authority and privileged relationship with external officials often "gave him the power to manipulate the processes of property succession in his own favour" (Leach 1961a, p. 193). But since the early 1960s the Vel Vidane's rights and duties have been transferred to cultivation committees, whose members are elected by secret ballot for a term of three years. Committee members are largely drawn from among the wealthier proprietors, but because their continued tenure of office depends upon the electoral support of their constituents they are to that extent discouraged from exploiting their official position to acquire property at the expense of their fellow villagers.

These last two factors can be illustrated by comparing the careers and styles of leadership of two men in Kukulewa, H. V. Bandathe, the former Vel Vidane, and K. Wannihamy, the presently successful shopkeeper, a discussion that will pull together some earlier strands of the argument by using the drama of individual ambition to summarize the changing terms and context of Vedda social life.

Bandathe's father was a man from Pandiggama who settled uxorilocally in Kukulewa. He brought no wealth with him to add to the little that his wife inherited. Nevertheless in the 1920s Bandathe's mother, along with her brother and sister, were able to begin to buy small pieces of paddy land in the village. During the same period Bandathe's elder sister, Kaluhamy, left the village and was married across caste lines to a man who employed by the local Ratemahatmaya. Detractors of Bandathe insinuate that this marriage was merely a formal convenience that masked a more intimate relationship between Kaluhamy and the Ratemahatmaya, a relationship they allege was the basis of Bandathe's appointment to the office of Vel Vidane when he was still less than thirty. By this time Bandathe had himself married across caste lines (see figure 3.2). His affines were the Fernando family of Low Country Sinhalese Catholics who had established themselves as small traders in the village.

As Vel Vidane during the period before 1938, when the Ratemahatmaya's authority was finally translated into the bureaucratic routine of the Divisional Revenue Office, Bandathe learned to operate within a predominantly traditional political order. He cultivated his patrimonial relationships with members of the old Vanniyar aristocracy, who were still prominently represented at the local levels of the colonial administration. In the Ratemahatmaya's *valavva* (manor house) and in the offices and courtrooms of the government he came to represent Kukulewa, and later the Vedda *variga* as a whole. Indeed, even in 1970, years after his office was abolished, he was still the only Kukulewa villager that many officials in Anuradhapura knew by name. His unique standing made him the man upon whom officials came to rely in their dealings with the Veddas, and this in turn enabled him to sway administrative decisions in the direction of his private interest. To his fellow villagers he became a powerful and apparently sophisticated neighbor who enjoyed access to official authorities and whose assistance could smooth the way towards obtaining, say, a gun license or a title deed, but whose enmity could herald unfavorable administrative decisions and unwelcome official harassment.

Bandathe's first wife died in the early 1940s, and he subsequently married a young girl from Dambagahaulpota who has since borne him a dozen children. The earlier marriage produced only one child, a son who has married a woman from Katamankulama and who continues to live in Kukulewa. This son inherited all the land that Bandathe acquired during the course of his first marriage, and he maintains an independent household, although he combines with his half-brothers to cultivate both the fields that have passed to him and those that are still in his father's hands. Bandathe himself takes little interest in paddy cultivation, and seems to have retained only the formal respect of his children. The eldest son and daughter of his second marriage are both now married, the latter living with her husband in Migahapattiya, the former living independently in Kukulewa. Bandathe's failure to hold his married children in continued close dependency is at least partly attributable to his inattention to paddy farming. Cultivation of his lands is now largely supervised and financed by his eldest son, who has himself acquired control of all that he can expect to inherit, while the children of the second marriage are so numerous that despite the volume of Bandathe's holdings, their individual inheritance prospects are very modest.

After the Paddy Lands Act abolished the office of Vel Vidane, Bandathe was able to get himself elected to the first cultivation committee, but he was subsequently removed by his fellow members (see pp. 54-56). He had identified himself too strongly with the external hierarchy of the traditional order, and as that order changed and the secret ballot was introduced he found himself almost without support in his own village. In part this was a reaction to his overbearing manner and the personal ends to which he had bent the privileges of office, but these traits were shared by some former Vel Vidanes whose authority and wealth have not been significantly diminished by the abolition of their office. A more basic cause of failure was Bandathe's lack of interest in paddy cultivation. He did acquire land while he was Vel Vidane, but much of it was new or marginal land that he never seriously attempted to bring under permanent cultivation. Nor, despite his affinal ties to the Fernando traders, did he take on a significant number of mortgages. He did not therefore build up any extensive following of clients, dependents, and employees whom he could bind to himself by virtue of his direct control of the means of production. His power had a political, not an economic, base and when the political order was altered, it crumbled.

Bandathe has subsequently again sought political support at the polls, but without success. He has become a somewhat embittered old man who no longer cultivates his own fields and who appears to be losing his ability to control his appetite for alcohol. Nevertheless he still retains the respect of some who remember his fluency in the older political idiom and who yet seek to take advantage of the contacts he has maintained outside the village. Likewise administrators in Anuradhapura still suppose him to be a man of considerable unofficial authority—a supposition of which he does nothing to disabuse them—and he was, for example, the first Vedda to whom we were introduced. And on occasion he can still put on an effective performance. Barefoot, dressed in the traditional white shirt and white sarong, with his long hair tied up on top of his head and a hand towel draped over his shoulder, his confident and commanding voice and deep, quick eyes can still lend him an impressive appearance. It is part of a style and manner that express the values of the traditional order, and it is only, I suppose, where such a traditional order has been long and deeply entrenched that its exponents can at once appear both so dignified and so obsequious.

K. Wannihamy's career has been quite different. Born in Kukulewa of virilocal parents who held little property, his youth was, by his own admission, wild and violent. As a young man he lived and worked outside the village for some time, during which he acquired a rudimentary commercial skill and made the acquaintance of local traders (*mudalalis*). In the mid-1950s he opened a shop in Kukulewa, the continuing success of which has been the basis of his subsequent prosperity. He now controls almost thirteen and one-half acres of paddy land in the village, all but three of which is land that he holds on mortgage, and his other credit relations are even more extensive. My estimate is that at one time or another during the year at least half his fellow villagers are in his debt.

Wannihamy's wife is a native of Kukulewa whose mother spent a few months in jail following a fight over an inheritance in which she found herself on the opposite side to H.V. Bandathe Vel Vidane. Wannihamy and Bandathe are dedicated enemies who will now have nothing to do with one another, as I discovered early in my field work when, having been introduced into the village by Bandathe, my attempt to take an initial census was thwarted by the shopkeeper's refusal to speak to me. With reference to national political alignments, Wannihamy is an enthusiastic supporter of Mrs. Bandaranaike's Sri Lanka Freedom Party (SLFP), while Bandathe is loyal to the United National Party (UNP), which in Anuradhapura District is still dominated by the old aristocracy. And in the cultivation committee elections that took place in 1968, Bandathe was the chief organizer of the slate of candidates that attempted to dislodge the incumbent members, whose Kukulewa representatives included Wannihamy (the treasurer) and his son-in-law.

Wannihamy's prosperity reflects his skill both in commerce and in the still powerful idiom of kinship, which he has successfully contained within limits that do not threaten his entrepreneurial activities. He supports his elderly parents-in-law, but although he offers employment to his wife's sisters' husbands (his "brothers"), the terms of these relations are strictly contractual; that is, although the kinship connection may enhance the possibility of securing employment or patronage from Wannihamy, it confers no privileges in the terms of the relationship itself. Wannihamy has also been comparably successful both in constraining the alliances formed by the marriages of his children within narrow limits, and in holding those children within the confines of his economic activities. Two of his children are married to children of his widowed sister and two others to children of A. Dingiribanda. These sons and sons-in-law, who remain in Kukulewa, live close to him and work, for the most part, under his direction, preferring to defer the pleasure of independence for the sake of continued participation in a successful and expanding enterprise.

In contrast, then, to the political basis of Bandathe's former influence, which rested predominantly on traditional status relationships, Wannihamy's power is more strictly economic and is exercised through contractual relationships. This is reflected in his physical appearance. His hair is cut short in the modern style, he favors the colored sarongs and the *mudalali's* prominent money belt, and he has deposited part of his savings in the gold teeth that distinguish the adult members of his family. Again Wannihamy is largely unknown among the old aristocracy and the officials in Anuradhapura with whom Bandathe has long been familiar. Wannihamy's associations outside the village connect him instead with the *mudalalis* who control a large but undetermined share of the regional economy and who operate away from the English-speaking centers of officialdom (chapter 4, note 15).

Wannihamy's replacement of Bandathe as the most powerful man in Kukulewa indicates quite starkly some of the changes that have been occurring in recent years. And although the particular personalities and events have, of course, been different in other villages, my sketch of their careers illuminates some general themes. Vedda relations with the outside world have been gradually, but with increasing rapidity in recent years, transformed from a traditional and more or less feudal basis to one that is increasingly commercial and democratically representative. In former times the influence of prominent Veddas rested in considerable measure on their position within the traditional status system, whether as Gamarala, officer of the *variga* court, or as occupant of the mixed feudal and bureaucratic office of Vel Vidane. They were often thereby enabled, at least in the smaller villages, to exercise a virtually autocratic authority over their neighbors and kinsmen. The rapid growth of population and the difficulty, outside Willachchiya, of founding new villages, have dramatically increased the average size of Vedda communities, and have made exclusive domination more difficult to establish. The effect of government policy, especially the Land Development Ordinance and the Paddy Lands Act, has been in the same direction. On the other hand the concurrent monetization of the village economy has brought new opportunities of advancement to the native entrepreneur who may yet, even in the expanded villages, establish a dominion that is no less extensive than that of his less commercially inclined predecessors.

It remains to be seen whether these changes will foster the emergence of a more rigid class structure among the Veddas. Within the hierarchical structure of the traditional order, status differences among the Veddas were minimal, and although the Gamarala and the Vel Vidane were often able to take economic advantage of their offices, they were nevertheless still kinsmen of their fellow villagers and thus, in a fundamental sense, their status equals. Relationships within the kinship system were, and are, typically inegalitarian, but all Veddas have equally enjoyed the prospect, for some part of their lives, of occupying all the positions available to members of their sex. At the same time the private possession of paddy land has always permitted differential access to the means of production. But the operation of the kinship system, as I have described it, as well as the continuing importance of chena cultivation and the opening up of new lands to paddy cultivation, have served to prevent wealth differences from crystallizing into a structure of opposition between more or less permanently established classes of landowners and landless laborers.

At present kinship remains the dominant idiom in which Veddas express their social relations, and the most successful men continue to find their most reliable supporters among their close kin. The groups that dominate village life still rise and fall with the individuals who lead them. And just as in the past there were no corporate kin groups that endured through the generations, so in the present there are, as yet, no business firms or corporations that survive the entrepreneur's retirement from active management. Thus the developmental cycle of the household is still the fundamental structural process in Vedda village society.

But the recent reduction of the area in which the claims of kinship privilege override those of "rational" economic calculation represents a replacement of status principles by those of class, and the new entrepreneur enjoys an advantage over traditional leaders that may yet permit him to acquire a more extensive dominion, an advantage that lies in his command of economic resources that can bind clients, supporters, and employees beyond the range wherein the reciprocal prospects and obligations of kinship are compelling. Were corporate forms of organization to be adopted whereby an entrepreneur's assets were not inevitably dispersed among his heirs at his retirement or death, a division of the Veddas into two clearly defined and opposed classes might well develop. Given the present scarcity of new lands to bring under cultivation and the increasing acceptance of contractual market relations even among close kinsmen, not only the temporary concentration of productive paddy land, but also its permanent possession, in the hands of a few enduring corporate groups, become a real possibility. In such hypothetical but not implausible circumstances, one might then anticipate the subsequent withering of kinship and marriage relations across the class division between the landed and the landless and the elaboration of status differentials that emphasize that division.

Whether the increasing prominence of class principles will eventually lead to such a starkly defined structure of classes will probably depend on national developments.[5] Up to now the prevailing ideology within the national elite has continued, on the whole, to favor individual property rights in a competitive market economy. This liberal ideology, however, has had to contend both with attempts to implement socialist principles, as expressed for example in the Paddy Lands Act of 1958, and with nationalistic longings for the restoration of an idealized past in which the local peasant community was free from antagonisms, as well as with the increasingly urgent pragmatic concern to raise agricultural productivity. As a result, the sanctity of individual property rights has already been seriously qualified. And while legislative enactments and political decisions in Colombo have not often been immediately translated into

5. For analyses of national politics since independence, see Wriggins 1960, Singer 1964, Kearney 1973. Herring (1972) gives an interpretation of ideological differences within the elite in relation to land policy. For accounts of the insurrection of 1971, see Arasaratnam 1972, Warnapala 1972, Halliday 1972, Obeyesekera 1973, and Obeyesekere 1974.

Anuradhapura District was one of the centers of insurrection, but on the evidence available to me the Veddas seem not to have been deeply involved in it. This is probably because the insurrectionists were predominantly educated rural youth (Obeyesekere 1974, p. 374), and the educational level of the Veddas is well below the average. The only two young men from Kukulewa to be detained after the insurrection were also the only two who were attending high school at the time of my field work.

social and economic change in the remote Vedda villages, the national government continues to be increasingly disposed to effect change at the village level and increasingly able to do so. It would thus be imprudent to predict that class relations will inevitably develop in the manner suggested. Only if agriculture continues to be increasingly commercialized, and if the ideal of the individual peasant proprietor continues to dominate policy making, is the development of clearly defined classes of landlords and landless laborers among the Veddas at all probable. But surely one lesson of the insurrection in 1971 is that there are also other, and more radical, possibilities.

8

Theoretical Implications

My analysis of the operation of Anuradhapura Vedda social institutions has implications for the general understanding of the kinship systems of South India and Sri Lanka. This is a topic that has long attracted the attention of anthropologists and one that in recent years has inspired both lively debate and sophisticated analysis.

Much of the analysis has focused on the interpretation of the so-called Dravidian terminology, the common use of which is the most evident expression of unity within an area that is characterized by an apparent diversity of forms of kin group.[1] This is already to pose, in one of its aspects, the Dravidian "problem": how is a single terminological system accommodated to such a variety of group structures?

It was Lewis Henry Morgan (1871, 1963) who both brought the Dravidian terminology to the attention of anthropologists and raised the general question of the relationship between systems of terminology and forms of social organization. Morgan noted that the same terminological system was shared by the main Dravidian languages, which

1. To avoid any confusion it should be made clear that in the context of kinship studies the term *Dravidian* refers in the first instance to a type of terminological system rather than to a language family. The terminological system is common to the Dravidian languages of South India and Sri Lanka but is not restricted to them. For example, the structure of the Sinhalese terminology is of the Dravidian type, although Sinhalese is an Indo-European language. The particular form that the terminology takes among the Sinhalese-speaking Veddas of Anuradhapura District has been described in chapter 3. The present discussion focuses on the kinship systems of South India and Sri Lanka and will make only occasional reference to Dravidian systems that have been studied in other parts of the world.

he assigned to the Dravidic class of the Turanian family (1871, pp. 385 ff., 521 ff.). He also pointed out the similarities between this system and that which he called the Ganowanian, which is now most commonly known as the Iroquois system (Murdock 1949, Lounsbury 1964), and he used these similarities to support the theory of the Asian origins of the American Indian (1871, pp. 498-508).[2] In *Ancient Society* the Turanian or Ganowanian system of "consanguinity," that is, terminology, was given its determinate place in Morgan's scheme of general social evolution according to the theory that the development of systems of consanguinity follows changes in the forms of marriage and family structure, which they record. The development of the Turanian terminology was there ascribed to "the organization into gentes [i. e., clans] and the punaluan family" (1963, pp. 396-98).

But Morgan's theoretical attempt to show the determining effect of social organizational forms on systems of kinship terminology won little acceptance among his contemporaries. In Britain McLennan's famous retort was that kinship terms formed merely a code of "mutual salutations" (1876, p. 331), while in the United States there was a reaction against Morgan that culminated in Kroeber's assertion that "terms of relationship are determined primarily by linguistic factors, and are only occasionally, and then indirectly, affected by social circumstances. [They] reflect psychology, not sociology" (1909, pp. 83-84). More than anyone it was Rivers who restored the problems broached by Morgan to the forefront of anthropological interest, and, most relevantly, in doing so he depended heavily on arguments derived from his study of Dravidian kinship. While the substance of Rivers's hypotheses has in most cases been found wanting, it has rarely since his time been doubted that there is some relationship between systems of terminology and forms of social organization. The problem has been to discover the precise character of this relationship, and in the continuing process of this discovery, Dravidian kinship systems have presented an outstanding challenge.

For the Dravidian terminology is not only found over a wide geographical area but is employed by peoples with seemingly very different forms of social and kinship organization. Within the area of South India and Sri Lanka alone it is found, for example, among the patrilineal Coorgs (Srinivas 1952), the matrilineal Nayars (Gough 1952, 1955, 1959) and the bilateral Kandyan Sinhalese (Leach 1960, 1961a; Tambiah 1958, 1965; Yalman 1960, 1962, 1967). In the face of this

2. As noted in chapter 3, it has only recently been recognized that the similarities between Dravidian and Iroquois terminology serve to obscure some fundamental differences. See Lounsbury (1964), Keesing (1975, pp. 105-12), Goodenough (1968), Scheffler (1971).

ethnographic diversity is it necessary to revert to McLennan and Kroeber and to assert that there need be no relationship between a terminological system and the form of social organization with which it is
found, or at least that the relationship is devious and indirect? Or, alternatively is it possible that a matrilineal, a patrilineal, and bilateral
kinship system have more in common than the anthropological development of kinship theory would have us believe? Or again, may it be
that the Dravidian terminology is unusually flexible and can be adapted
to an extraordinary variety of social systems?

In approaching these problems in a South Asian context, Rivers
abandoned Morgan's evolutionism but retained a historical orientation
that looked for the determinants of kinship terminology in antecedent
social conditions. He did not challenge the conventional wisdom of the
time that matrilineal descent preceded patrilineal descent, in South
India if not universally, but in seeking to interpret the important relationship between a mother's brother and a sister's son among the
Todas, his familiarity with the kinship terminology suggested to him
that the relationship was to be explained, not simply as a vestige of
"Mother Right," but also by the practice of cross-cousin marriage
(1907, 1914; pp. 47-49). He discovered that the same term was applied
in the languages of South India both to the mother's brother and to the
father-in-law, and often also to the father's sister's husband. The simplest way to explain this was to posit an identity; and if the mother's
brother *is* the father-in-law, then the system is one of cross-cousin
marriage. But it should be noted that Rivers thought that cross-cousin
marriage was not widely practiced in the present; the terminology reflected an archaic pattern rather than contemporary practice.

A few problems remained. Rivers was firmly convinced of the fundamental structural importance of exogamous unilineal descent groups,
but this obliged him also to explain why *both* kinds of parallel cousins
were prohibited marriage partners. This explanation he also found in
history. Most South Indian societies were patrilineal, and this accounted for the prohibition against FBD marriage. But they had been
matrilineally organized at some earlier time, or so at least Rivers argued,
and the prohibition against MZD marriage, like the terminological
identification of mother's brother and father-in-law, could thus be interpreted as a vestige of an earlier form of organization.

The argument was taken a stage further. He had accounted for the
prohibition against parallel cousin marriage, but why was cross-cousin
marriage *prescribed*? Why marry a cousin at all? Why not marry someone previously quite unrelated? Rivers here turned to one of his fa-
vorite hypotheses and postulated the earlier existence of dual organiza-

tion. With a rule of moiety exogamy cross-cousins would be permissible spouses while parallel cousins would be prohibited.

It is interesting that in advancing this argument, which he based on the association of cross-cousin marriage with dual organization in Australia, Rivers seems to have appreciated that what was at issue was categorical and not necessarily first cross-cousin marriage (unless he envisaged only one family in each moiety!). But his explanation of the terminological identification of mother's brother and father-in-law appears to be based on the idea that the same *individual* was both mother's brother and father-in-law. Had he recognized that the term for mother's brother/father-in-law (like that for cross-cousin) denoted a category rather than an individual, he might also have recognized that while, as he asserted, first cross-cousin marriage was relatively rare in South India, nevertheless categorical cross-cousin marriage was yet widely practiced.

The major deficiency of Rivers's interpretations, however, lies elsewhere. While his recognition of the association between Dravidian terminology and cross-cousin marriage and his emphasis on descent and exogamy indicated the direction that subsequent analysis would take, his explanations in terms of hypothetical historical antecedents place him as firmly at the end as at the beginning of a tradition. Within a few years the social anthropological investigation of kinship and social organization was dominated by "structural" and "functional" approaches that, at least in principle, abjured historical and quasi-historical explanations of the kind that Rivers offered.

Nevertheless Rivers had shown the association, in South India, of the Dravidian terminology and (categorical) cross-cousin marriage, which at least made sense of the lumping within the same kin category of certain affinal types and certain kin types (e.g., mother's brother and father-in-law). Given the marriage rule, and given the continued emphasis on unilineal descent, the focal problem remained to explain why both kinds of parallel cousins were placed together in the same category of ineligible marriage partners. With patrilineal descent a man's FBD would be a lineage mate and hence prohibited by the rule of exogamy, but why was MZD also prohibited? Likewise, with matrilineal descent, why was FBD prohibited? Rivers's answer, as we have seen, was to claim that these prohibitions were vestiges of a former matrilineality. Later analysts came up with different answers. Thus the Toda kinship system, which Rivers had described as patrilineal (1906), was reinterpreted by Emeneau as one of double descent (1937, 1941), although this revision has subsequently been challenged by Yalman (1962, p. 560, 1967, pp. 336-43). Others fell back into Rivers's own position and looked to the survivial of ancient forms. Thus Gough describes the southern Tiyyar as basically patrilineal, but she also identifies residual matrilineages in order to explain the prohibition of MZD marriage, even though the prohibition itself constitutes almost the whole evidence for the existence of the matrilineages: "My informants knew nothing about these clans except that they were once exogamous. . . . Though the clans have died out, marriage is prohibited between known matrilineal kin" (1955, p. 60). Others again seem scarcely aware of the structural problem. Thus Srinivas, describing the Coorgs, is content to assert that the prohibition against MZD marriage is simply "an attempt to balance the enormous importance accorded to paternal relatives in a kinship system the foundation of which is the patrilineal, patrilocal *okka* (descent group)" (1952, p. 145).

These and other particular interpretations share certain features in common. As Yalman demonstrates (1967, 1969), they all rely on dubious assertions about descent, lineages, and exogamy to explain the marriage rule, and they all look to features peculiar to the particular society under investigation to explain a marriage practice that is, nevertheless, general in South India and Sri Lanka. They therefore have little to offer in the explanation of the marriage rule in societies that share the Dravidian terminology but that lack, for example, a system of double descent. The apparently universal association of the terminology with cross-cousin marriage in South India and Sri Lanka invites a general interpretation, but such does not seem able to emerge from a one-sided emphasis on unilineal descent.

Progress out of this impasse has come in recent years from the application of a theoretical orientation owing much to Lévi-Strauss (1949) that has been dubbed "Alliance Theory" in contrast to the "Descent Theory" developed, after Rivers, principally by Radcliffe-Brown and his followers. A comprehensive discussion of Descent and Alliance Theory would be out of place here (see Dumont 1961, Schneider 1965, Buchler and Selby 1968, Fox 1967, Keesing 1975, etc.). It will be sufficient to indicate in broad terms that whereas descent theorists have commonly emphasized the internal organization of descent groups and have looked to marriage as a means of ensuring the continuity of such groups through succeeding generations, alliance theorists have focused on the structure of relations established among groups that are more or less permanently linked to one another by recurrent marital exchanges. Alliance theory has been most effective in the understanding of so-called prescriptive systems, which systems are characterized by one of the several possible forms (bilateral, matrilateral, etc.) of cross-cousin marriage. In the analysis of the Dravidian kinship systems of South India and Sri Lanka the most comprehensive and ambitious studies that have been at least partly inspired by Alliance

Theory have been those of Dumont (1950, 1953a, 1953b, 1957a, 1957b, 1961, 1964, 1966) and Yalman (1962, 1967, 1969).

Dumont maintains the traditional distinction in his formula: "Kinship = kin (or consanguinity) + affinity" (1957b, p. 26, 1961, p. 81), but affinity is here raised to a power equal to that of consanguinity. Whether kinship is organized matrilineally or patrilineally, the crucial point is that the relationship between a man's father and his mother's brother is one of affinity and that, in Dravidian systems, just as descent group membership is inherited, so the affinal relationship between brothers-in-law is inherited by their children, that is, by cross-cousins. Affinity is thus placed on a par with descent as an equally enduring institution that is transmitted from generation to generation:

To say that an alliance relationship is inherited is the same as to say that a certain marriage regulation is observed. . . . [W]hat we are accustomed to call cross-cousin marriage is nothing but the perfect formula for perpetuating the alliance relationship from one generation to the next and so making the alliance an enduring institution. . . . [1953a, p. 38]

Yalman, on the other hand, rejects Dumont's distinction between kin and affines, and prefers to describe what Dumont calls affinity as "rights and obligations between brother and sisters" (1967, p. 357). This, he is persuaded, enables him to go beyond Dumont, who "is still operating with the concept of 'exogamous' lineages, which are primary units in the system" (ibid.). Yalman argues that it is the "claims of the brothers and sisters upon each other which are the fundamental principle . . . in South Indian kinship" (ibid., p. 359). The claims of cross-cousins upon one another are not, as Dumont suggests, to be seen as a matter of inherited affinity, the transmission to the next generation of the alliance between brothers-in-law, but are the expression of the mutual claims of the two parents who are siblings. Whereas Dumont interprets the claims that a man has upon his mother's brother's daughter as a generational transmission of the marriage alliance between his father and his mother's brother, Yalman sees them as the claims that a woman has upon her brother being expressed by her son (1967, pp. 358-59). Thus, for Yalman, the inheritance of such claims is always bilateral in Dravidian systems. In this situation it is inappropriate to emphasize a distinction between "kin" and "affines" because the latter are already kinsmen. The more basic distinction is between "siblings" (including parallel cousins) and "cross-cousins," and this serves simply to segregate those kin with whom sexual relations would be incestuous from those other kin with whom sexual relations are permitted and marriage is prescribed. Cross-cousins are in fact "in a permanent relationship of 'marriage' by virtue of their positions in the kinship framework" (1962, p. 565).

In general Yalman rejects as inadequate the traditional explanations of Dravidian terminology by recourse to exogamous unilineal descent groups, and argues instead "that the terminology is directly related to small, largely endogamous social units" (ibid., p. 567). At the same time he recognizes that shallow unilineal descent groups may coexist with these bilateral and largely endogamous kindreds, although "there is clearly a separation of the spheres of activity in such cases" (ibid., p. 568). In other words societies employing Dravidian terminology may contain both endogamous kindreds, which include cross-cousins, and exogamous unilineal descent groups, which exclude them. The relative importance of these groups may vary from one social context to another, and from one society to another.

Criticism of Yalman's thesis (Dumont 1964; Tambiah 1965; Obeyesekere 1967, 1968) has mainly focused on the question of the relationship between the terminological system, the forms of social group, and actual behavior. Tambiah argues that although Yalman "specifically states that he is analyzing the properties of Dravidian kinship categories as a terminological system, he frequently shifts his frame of reference so that the logical implications of the terminological system are also treated as rules of actual behaviour" (1965, p. 134). Similarly Obeyesekere argues that "Yalman's 'hypothesis' commits the fallacy of deducing behavioural regularities from a terminological system," and that "it is not possible *a priori* to predict behaviour or the type of social system from the set of terms alone" (Obeyesekere 1967, pp. 248, 251). Likewise Dumont, although his reference is to group structure rather than to behavior, is making a similar point when he asserts that terminology and "corporations" are two different aspects that

tell us quite different stories which have first of all to be told as they are, and analyzed. Any attempt to reduce one to the other is vain, as should be explicit in the fact that kinship terminologies have not as their function to register groups.

Dumont goes on to state that

it is clear from the material available that a terminology of the Dravidian type accompanies different sorts of group organizations. . . . The only correlation that the analysis of the terminology points out [that with 'cross-cousin' marriage] holds good everywhere. The variability of other features simply shows that the type of terminology, although part and parcel of the social order, is not necessarily linked with one particular kind of group organization. [Ibid., p. 78]

Thus Dravidian terminology may be employed in societies possessing either unilineal descent groups (and, on a larger scale, clans), or endogamous kindreds (and on a larger scale, castes and subcastes) or both. Now the formation of either such group isolates a particular "kind" of person. They differ in that the endogamous kindred includes "affines" (in this case "cross cousins") as the same kind of persons as "kinsmen" (i. e., consanguines), while the unilineal descent group excludes them. Dravidian terminology distinguishes between "cross" and "parallel" cousins anyway, but recognition of unilineal descent reinforces this distinction. Thus, from the point of view of marriage relations, those groups that have adopted unilineal descent are simply emphasizing, to a greater extent than do those that are organized into endogamous kindreds, that one marries a different "kind" of person. In Dravidian systems, the actual kinship category of persons from whom a man selects his spouse remains the same (his female "cross-cousins"), but the distance and difference between a man and his in-laws may be either emphasized or muted.

Yalman's argument, however, is that despite the evident variations in group structure among societies that employ the Dravidian terminology there are, nevertheless, also commonalities at this level. He claims that while an ideology of unilineal descent is often found in the societies of South India and Sri Lanka, the unilineal groups thus identified are often not effective corporate units but that everywhere, underlying the shifting patterns of descent and often unnamed, there are to be found bilateral and largely endogamous kindreds. He discerns what he calls the "general structure" of Dravidian systems, which he describes as

the most general theme of South Indian kinship systems stripped of all structural embellishments . . . . Descent concepts are not stressed; the choice of locality [i.e., post-marital residence] is theoretically open; inheritance is equally divided among sons and daughters; authority depends on the head of the household and can be exercised by the MB or even the F-in-L; dowry is not emphasized, but bridewealth is disapproved. What stands out is the insistence on cross-cousin marriage and on a small circle of endogamy—that is, microcastes in the form of *pavula* or *variga*. [1967, p. 279]

Yalman discovers this unembellished structure among the Kandyan Sinhalese. Of course he recognizes that not all Dravidian systems exhibit these features with equal intensity, but where, for example, a society chooses to elaborate an ideology of unilineal descent, this is to be treated as one of many possible variations on the general theme. The model of the general structure thus allows for considerable variation in particular features, which are seen to function as "structural indices to distinguish communities from one another" (1967, p. 360).

Elsewhere, however, Yalman employs his concept of the general structure rather differently. Discussing the possibility of comparing two systems, he claims that "we are justified in isolating the common structural elements in the two systems and speaking of the underlying pattern as the general structure" (ibid., p. 305). This is ambiguous. If the general structure describes what is held in common then the characterization given of it earlier must be abandoned, for there are a number of Dravidian systems in which descent *is* stressed, inheritance is *not* equally divided, dowry *is* emphasized, and so on. Perhaps the two usages can be integrated, but it remains somewhat unclear whether in Yalman's view the general structure is shared and manifested by all the systems, or whether it is to be located, in some sense, behind or underneath them all, but does not necessarily overtly express all its elements in any particular one of them. Yalman's Introduction (ibid., pp. 3-7) indicates that he takes the latter view, which derives from Lévi-Strauss (1953), but if this is so one would think that the general structure might be better composed out of more abstract elements.

Perhaps this ambiguity helps explain why Yalman presents his general structure in predominantly negative terms. But in any case it adequately represents the kinship system of the Anuradhapura Veddas, with the exception of the final and most forceful statement, which is problematic. In the first place, as I have emphasized previously, cross-cousin marriage among the Anuradhapura Veddas is categorical and often ex post facto; that is, when a marriage is made the Veddas place their newly acquired affines, if they are not already so placed, in kinship categories that are consistent with the presumption that the husband and wife are cross-cousins. Thus whatever kinship relation existed between them prior to the marriage, a man will place his WF in the same kinship category as his MB and his FZH. I would therefore rephrase Yalman's formulation to read: " . . . what stands out is the insistence that marriage be treated as if it takes place between cross-cousins. . . ."

More troublesome, perhaps, is the notion of "microcastes" and the bringing together of *pavula* and *variga*. Both these terms are used flexibly by the Anuradhapura Veddas, but they rarely overlap. *Pavula* may refer to a man's wife alone, or to his wife and children, or to all his close kin (a bilateral kindred), but it will rarely include more than a couple of dozen people. *Variga,* on the other hand, is most commonly used to describe the whole caste group within which marriage is permitted. This group today numbers more than six thousand individuals. Where then is the "microcaste," within which there is an "insistence on . . . a small circle of endogamy"? And how small is "a small circle"?

Not only do *pavula* and *variga* describe groups of different size; they also refer to groups with very different functions. If the Vedda *variga* is to be considered a group at all, it is as a corporation that maintains its intrinsic perpetuity by "exclusive recruitment to restricted membership . . " (Fortes 1969, p. 306; see chapter 3). The *variga* does not act as a single collectivity, nor does it now have representative leaders who can act on its behalf. On the other hand the Vedda *pavula* commonly does act as a group, for example as a unit of production and of consumption. But the usage is flexible and the range of reference is determined by the context. In paddy cultivation *pavula* may describe a group of cooperating kinsmen that is larger than a single household, while the *pavula* that gathers after a man's death to conduct his funeral may contain individuals, such as adult brothers, who have not cooperated economically for many years.

Moreover, neither the Vedda *variga* nor the *pavula* forms a closed "circle of endogamy." There is indeed a tendency towards endogamy among the Veddas, as there is in other societies in South India and Sri Lanka, but it can only be misleading to confuse this tendency with a structure of endogamous groups. Certainly the Vedda *variga* is ideally endogamous, but there are no Vedda groups that are in practice wholly endogamous. Yalman's emphasis on "the insistence . . . on a small circle of endogamy" conjures up an impression of closed networks of kinship and marriage, which in turn facilitates the presentation of Dravidian societies as being composed of discrete endogamous groups (kindreds, or microcastes), whereas, at least among the Anuradhapura Veddas, a more accurate representation is that of an observable preference of varying intensity for marriage among close kin that does not go so far as to divide the *variga* as a whole into more than one marriage isolate. In other words, as applied to the Anuradhapura Veddas, Yalman's formulation reifies into a structure of groups what is no more than a matter of preference and statistical pattern. The tendency toward forming endogamous circles within the *variga* can be described in terms either of kinship or locality, but it would be misleading to assert that endogamy is insisted upon, since in order to bring a higher proportion of marriages within the circle one must always expand its radius, and one must go even beyond the boundaries of the *variga* if one wants to include all the marriages. Thus, as I have shown, about 10 percent of Anuradhapura Vedda marriages are between first cross-cousins, and almost one in three are between native members of the same community. One could draw the circle a little wider and say that a higher proportion of men and women marry within a radius of five or ten miles of their native village, or one could take the whole *variga* as the "circle of endogamy" and say that in about 85 percent of the marriages in which Vedda men and women are currently engaged both parties are native members of the *variga*.

These concentric circles of relative endogamy are the statistical result of a great many individual marital decisions. They undoubtedly reflect group strategies, but they do not in themselves adequately define group boundaries. Moreover their lack of closure makes clear that if there is a centripetal tendency to form small circles of endogamy (microcastes) that are more narrowly circumscribed than that of the *variga* as a whole, this tendency is not fully realized, which is to say that Yalman's "insistence" meets some resistance. There is also a centrifugal tendency that prevents the *variga* from dividing into smaller circles and that ensures that even the *variga* itself is not a closed system. From another perspective, and to anticipate somewhat, this is to acknowledge that those who are involved in creating a marriage enjoy a measure of choice, and that analysis can focus on the goals they seek and the strategies they employ.

In general it appears that the results of the prolonged attempt to identify a single form of kin group structure in all the societies of South India and Sri Lanka that employ the Dravidian terminology have been disappointingly negative. Yalman has performed the invaluable critical service of sweeping away the lingering insistence on associating the terminology with some kind of unilineal descent, but his attempt to substitute endogamous kindreds or microcastes for the rejected descent groups is much less persuasive.[3] He has amply demonstrated the common importance of bilateral kin groups within the region, but his assertion that "the Dravidian kinship categories . . . exist in order to regulate sex, marriage, and other kinds of behavior *within* bilateral kin groups" (1967, p. 219; emphasis added) exaggerates the incidence of endogamy in such groups. It unwarrantably transforms marriage between close cross-cousins from an option that may, under certain circumstances, enjoy strategic advantage, into the central principle of

3. It must be admitted that Yalman's analysis leaves some scope for different interpretations. At the beginning of *Under the Bo Tree* he asserts that it is "not exogamous lineages or the organization of kin that determines the terminology of kinship" (1967, p. 9). This may seem like a retreat from his earlier position that "the terminology is directly related to small, largely endogamous social units" (1962, p. 567), made perhaps in response to Dumont's criticism that the terminology "is not necessarily linked with one particular kind of group organization" (1964, p. 78). But as Yalman's analysis develops, it becomes clear that group structure does retain its importance in accounting for the terminology in his theory. See quotations in the text and his statement that "the Dravidian kinship categories . . . are not related to exogamy but exist in order to regulate sex, marriage, and other kinds of behavior within bilateral kin groups. The bilaterality of the groups should be stressed. . . . [1967, p. 219]

group definition and group maintenance in Dravidian systems. The twin conclusions must rather be that, as Dumont has argued, "the type of terminology . . . is not necessarily linked with one particular kind of group organization" (1964, p. 78), and that, whatever anomalies remain to trouble those anthropologists who seek a perfect fit between the terminology and the group structure, the Dravidian terminology has proved itself, in practice, adaptable to a notable variety of group structures. This conforms to the findings of those who have studied Dravidian terminologies in other parts of the world where they are even to be found without any form of cross-cousin marriage rule (Scheffler 1971).[4]

This is in no way to impugn the many virtues of the kind of comparative study that Yalman has presented. His penetrating analysis of Dravidian kinship systems as logically intelligible transformations of one another retains its value quite independently of the importance that is sometimes forced upon endogamous kindreds or microcastes. To revert to an earlier point about the ontological status of the "general structure" that he discerns, I am arguing only that the structural analysis of transformations does not require, and is even impeded by, the simultaneous attempt to identify substantive commonalities, that is, at the empirical level, common group structures, among all the systems being considered.

An alternative approach to the comparative problem has been adopted by Tambiah (1973) in a study that gives much greater weight to economic factors. Yalman is doubtless correct in his argument that the "marriage rules as we find them in South India and Ceylon are not related to any particular economic or group features of special communities" (1967, p. 9), since, as he points out, "we find the same rules in communities that exhibit every conceivable variation in ecology,

---

4. But one problem in the general interpretation of Dravidian-type terminology is that of deciding whether a given terminology belongs to the type. In his review of the Melanesian data, Scheffler even treats as "Dravidian" certain terminologies that lack the equivalences between "consanguineal" and "affinal" relatives that almost invariably appear in South India and Sri Lanka. Not surprisingly, where these equivalences are absent, there is commonly also an absence of the classificatory cross-cousin marriage rule. An interesting exception to the usual pattern in South India and Sri Lanka. has recently been described by Stirrat (1975). The Karaava caste people of Wellagoda, a Christian fishing village on the west coast of Sri Lanka, use the Sinhalese kinship terms. but they have devised a strikingly variant system that distinguishes "consanguines" from "affines." For example, "cross-cousins" are here classed with "siblings" and "parallel cousins," while the terms that elsewhere are used to refer to both "cross-cousins" and "siblings-in-law" are reserved for the latter alone. Marriage here repeats no previous affinal tie and is "outside the range of second cousins." [1975, p. 605]

economy, caste structure, lineage, and so on" (ibid.). But this is not to claim that the economic and group features are not related *among themselves*. Tambiah's wide-ranging study leads out from a discussion of traditional Indian legal concepts relating to property and its transmission to encompass a number of cases from Burma as well as India and Sri Lanka that show that systematic relations among such institutions as bridewealth, dowry, inheritance, descent, and postmarital residence produce a series of structures that can profitably be treated as transformations of one another, or as "dominant and variant (s) within the same family" (1973, p. 137). Thus, for example, he argues that

the most general Indian pattern of dowry in movable wealth and of an intricate pattern of affinal prestations etc. is associated with and occurs in conjunction with the norm of patrilocality (or avunculocality). In contrast the definition that a woman's dowry rights includes [sic] inheritance of land (and other patrimonial immovable wealth) which she shares equally with her brother can only occur in conjunction with matrilocality or duolocality . . . or ambilocality . . . as the main form of residence. It can also plausibly be argued that shifts towards egalitarian property rights between male and female siblings and toward an open residence pattern of virilocality or uxorilocality or of living with the husband's or wife's parents can create (if pushed far enough) a shift from unilineal descent to bilateral kinship. [Ibid., p. 109]

It must be emphasized that these kinds of variation occur not only between different regions or communities but also within individual villages. The variations, and their association with differences in economic standing, have been particularly well documented in a number of Sinhalese case studies (e.g., Leach 1961a, Tambiah 1965, Yalman 1967, Obeyesekere 1967, Robinson 1968, 1975). Leach, for example, shows that *"(b)inna* (uxorilocal) marriages are, by and large, those of over-privileged females or of underprivileged males" (1961a, p. 85), while Yalman makes the point that "(t)he most important fact about inheritance . . . is that rich and poor families do not act in the same way" (1967, p. 131). Thus we are not dealing with a situation in which social practice can be adequately described simply by showing that it is in conformity with, or that it deviates from, some single, uniform set of norms. Social practice must be seen as the execution of strategies the availability and attractiveness of which vary with social, and particularly economic, position, and the goals of which include, most prominently, the acquistion of wealth, social status, and political power. In other words, while Yalman is correct in his assertion that "marriage rules . . . are not related to any particular economic or group features of special communities" (1967, p. 9) marriage *practices* undoubtedly are so related, as has nowhere been more clearly demonstrated than in Yalman's own ethnographic analyses.

If the forms of inheritance, affinal prestation, marriage, residence, and hence group formation, are related to wealth, then the case of the Anuradhapura Veddas may be of particular comparative interest, since they are clearly the poorest of all the Sinhalese communities that have yet been described in detail. They seem to be located somewhat beyond the Sinhalese extreme that Tambiah envisages when he argues that

[t]he Kandyan Sinhalese . . . show a wide latitude as regards marriage—ranging from the giving of substantial dowries among the aristocratic (*radala*) or wealthy categories to the complete ignorance of dowry among the poor and perhaps in the extreme event the dispossession of daughters who have gone away on marriage. [1973, p. 132]

Among the Veddas, as was most clearly shown in the analysis of the Willachchiya communities, there is scarcely a hint of the "patrilineal tendency" that would dispossess daughters who have married out in order that immovable property might be reserved for the sons. Rather the pattern is that those who stand to inherit least, whether males or females, are most likely to marry out and abandon their potential inheritance, while among the children of the more prosperous Veddas, sons tend to marry virilocally, daughters tend to settle uxorilocally, and both sons and daughters tend to claim an inheritance. Nevertheless, with the minor qualification that his hypothetical "extreme" should be stripped of its "patrilineal" bias in order to encompass the present case, the Anuradhapura Veddas may be seen to fit comfortably into Tambiah's general scheme as another "variant."

Besides being offered as a further case study that can be used to test the general structural models of Yalman and Tambiah, my account of the Anuradhapura Veddas attempts to deal with two problems, the methodological significance of which deserves some emphasis. First, there is a problem of sampling. Social anthropologists have been well aware that a single village, in Sri Lanka or South India, does not normally constitute a closed circle of kinship and marriage, yet when discussing patterns of marriage they have been content to generalize from the intensive study of a single village. The problem of the typicality of the particular village selected for study has been largely ignored. For example, Tambiah's analysis of "Kinship fact and fiction among the Kandyan Sinhalese" (1965) explores the sociological implications of the peasant's choice between an intravillage and an extravillage orientation, but the findings appear to be based on data collected within the one village of Rambukkolawa. However, these data seem to show that in Rambukkolawa, among members of the Goyigama caste, marriage brings a new resident into the village three times as frequently as it persuades a native villager to leave (ibid., p. 145, table 5a). In his sample of seventy-three Goyigama caste marriages of which at least one partner was born in Rambukkolawa, all the native males who married women from outside the village resided virilocally, while almost half the native women who married men from outside chose to reside uxorilocally. Rambukkolawa is evidently attractive to spouses from outside and one infers, therefore, that there must be other, contrasting, villages within the circle of endogamy that lose at marriage more residents than they gain. If this is so, then no one village can be considered typical of the network as a whole, and a satisfactory analysis must comprehend a number of villages, and preferably all of them. This is what I have attempted to do for the Anuradhapura Veddas.

Secondly, and less originally, in its application of developmental models of kinship systems, my account includes the time dimension as an integral part of the analysis. Such models have been widely used elsewhere (see, e.g., Goody 1958) and their value is in no sense restricted to Dravidian systems, but they are perhaps particularly appropriate, and even indispensable, in the analysis of societies that lack effective descent groups. In the absence of enduring corporate groups there may yet be a persistently observable structure that is the product, for example, of shifting relations among a number of impermanent factional groups, but a synchronic structural analysis is unable to comprehend the process of these groups' formation and dissolution and thereby fails to penetrate adequately their character and dynamics. Moreover, in societies in which there are no corporate kin groups that serve in some measure to bind the interests of their members throughout their careers, there may commonly be structurally significant shifts in the relationships among kinsmen that remain undiscovered by synchronic analysis but can be elucidated by a developmental approach. This point can be illustrated by addressing a crucial problem in Sinhalese kinship studies, that presented by comparing the relationship between brothers (*aiya/malli*) with the relationship between cross-cousins or brothers-in-law (*massinā/massinā*).[5]

Let us begin with Leach's formulation.

"Brothers" are always in elder-brother/younger-brother relationship. It is a relationship of inequality and polite respect. In contrast, "brothers-in-law" (*massinā*) are in a standing of equality and may joke together.

The reason for this difference in expected behaviours is plain. Brothers are expected to be co-resident; brothers-in-law are not. Co-residence implies joint-heirship to a common estate; joint-heirship is a relationship of restrained rivalry. Although brothers in this society are often seen to be rivals this does not derive from any intrinsic principle of kinship; the rivalry is manifest only in so far as they

5. Reference here is to "full" brothers, first cross-cousins, and actual brothers-in-law.

are competitors for managerial control of the same piece of parental property. It is only because brothers are expected to reside virilocally (*dīga*) that personal relations between them are expected to be difficult.

Brothers-in-law do not ordinarily have managerial interest in the same piece of land, and it is for this reason that they are able to cooperate on a basis of equality without strain. [1961a, p. 188]

Commenting upon this in the light of his own study of Rambukko-lawa, Tambiah agrees that "(t)he relationship between brothers-in-law (*massinā*), especially if they live in the same village, may be said to be the most solidary relationship connoting cooperation in diverse activities" (1965, p. 161). But he goes on to point out that

in Rambukkolawa and its related villages it would not be correct to say that brothers-in-law do not have interest in the same block of property. We have seen that a son-in-law is often endowed (on behalf of his wife) with some land by his father-in-law.

This calls into question the general applicability of Leach's hypothesis, and thereby complicates the issue as to how these *massinā* can cooperate despite competitive interest in land. [Ibid.]

Tambiah acknowledges that his criticisms "have only complicated the issue which hence requires a more complex answer" (ibid., p. 162). Perhaps a developmental perspective supplies the necessary complexity, but first, a comment on the kinship categories may be useful.

It has often been pointed out, as Leach does, that while brothers (*aiya/malli*) are always in elder-brother/younger-brother relationship, the terms used by brothers-in-law or cross-cousins of the same sex are reciprocal (*massinā/massinā; nāna/nāna*). This contrasts the "equality" of the latter relationship and the "inequality" of the former. But if we introduce a third party, the father or the father-in-law, the pattern changes. From the father's perspective all his sons, although they are *aiya* and *malli* to one another are placed in the same category, that of *puta*, which is distinguished from that of *bāna*, in which all his sons-in-law are included. Thus two men who enjoy the reciprocal *massinā* relationship are placed in separate categories by the man who is father to one and father-in-law to the other, while those whose relations among themselves are asymmetrical find themselves in the same category.

This additional complexity suggests the direction of a developmental analysis. While the father is still exercising authority, the relationship between him and his sons overshadows that between the sons themselves, whose mutual inequality and rivalry are veiled by their common subordination to their father. The category of sons is distinguished from that of sons-in-law, but members of these junior categories can stress the reciprocal and egalitarian *massinā* relationship between themselves. When the father's authority is removed, restraints on the underlying inequality between *aiya* and *malli* are withdrawn as brothers struggle over the disposition of their parental property. Their sisters' husbands (*massinā*), if settled with their affines, may also engage in this struggle but despite the disadvantages of uxorilocality they do so as status equals (*massinā/massinā*). And, of course, brothers-in-law enjoy the prospect, forbidden to brothers, of transforming their rivalry into the marriage alliance of their children.

This is not to be construed as an assertion that the kinship structure itself and, *a fortiori*, the kinship terminology, compel two kinsmen to cooperate at one stage of their careers and be rivals at another. I insist, and here I follow Leach and Tambiah rather than Yalman, that kinship is not a "a thing in itself" (Leach 1961a, pp. 304-5, Tambiah 1965, p. 133), but that it has to be understood in relation to practical concerns such as that of access to productive resources. Thus my analysis fits the Vedda case, but I would expect it to require modification where access to land is ordered differently. For example, the relationship between brothers-in-law may go through quite different phases in those Sinhalese communities in which daughters receive their inheritance in the form of dowry.

More generally, the developmental models employed in this thesis, those of the household, the basic cultivating group, and the village society, are the central features of an attempt to articulate the analysis of nonrepetitive historical change with that of persistent structural processes that have continued to repeat themselves, within certain limits of variation, throughout the time period under consideration. This endeavor has involved a synthesis of both "historical" and "systemic" approaches to the understanding of Vedda society, using these terms to describe two ideal types constructed from elements that distinguish the terms of other comparable oppositions, such as those between the cultural sciences and the natural sciences, ethnography and ethnology, the idiographic and nomothetic approaches, historicism and positivism, and so forth. In broad terms the historical approach attempts to comprehend discontinuous historical events in all the richness of their local, cultural particularity, while the systemic, or naturalistic, approach aims to identify continuous social trends and cross-cultural regularities, producing empirical generalizations that have sometimes misleadingly been described as sociological laws. The systemic approach is analytical and atomistic, attempting to break some phenomenon down into its component elements that can then be shown to be systematically related to one another. The historical approach is synthetic and holistic, and attempts to understand some phenomenon by accurately locating it within its context. In studies of social structure, the systemic approach treats men and women as objects whose behavior is shaped by the cultures and social structures that constrain them, whereas the historical approach treats men and women as subjects whose actions produce whatever culture or social structure the observer is able to discern. Any particular scholar usually combines aspects of both approaches, but a brief historical sketch may serve to clarify the necessary distinctions.

The self-confident optimism of nineteeth-century anthropologists derived in large measure from their naïve appreciation of the problems confronting the systemic, or naturalistic, approach, to which most of them were committed. Tylor's epigrammatic statement that "if law is anywhere, it is everywhere" (1920, p. 24) is less useful as a conclusion, which is how he presents it, than as a rallying cry that signals the point of departure for systemic analysis. But while Tylor, Morgan, Spencer, McLennan, and their contemporaries undoubtedly produced order out of chaos, a hundred years later sociological laws still elude the grasp or crumble at the touch, and Morgan's "stages" are of little use after the first week of an introductory course. Boas, as is well known, was tireless in exposing the limitations of "the comparative method," but his was a rearguard action, and anthropologists have since plunged happily into the pitfalls against which he warned. Radcliffe-Brown also attacked the evolutionists and diffusionists but, as Evans-Pritchard tartly remarks, "the functionalist critics should have challenged them, not for writing history, but for writing bad history. As it was, they dropped the history and kept the pursuit of [sociological] laws, which was often precisely what had made the history bad" (1964, p. 173). In fact, for all their differences, Boas and Radcliffe-Brown shared important assumptions and goals with their predecessors. They both agreed that a science of society or culture, in what Kroeber calls "the strict sense," was in principle possible. The more radical historian's critique was left to Kroeber in the United States and Evans-Pritchard in Britain. Kroeber asserts that "the total work of science must be done on a series of levels" (1952, p. 121), of which the highest is that of culture, and he goes on to argue that

the more basic a level is in the hierarchy, the more successfully do its phenomena lend themselves to manipulation by the methods of science in the strict sense— methods resulting in uniformities, repetitive regularities, and therefore predicta- bility. But on the contrary, the higher the level, the more recalcitrant are its phenomena to treatment by methods homologous or perhaps even analogous to those of physics and chemistry; whereas they yield readily . . . to intellectual treatment similar in principle to that which historians follow . . . . Instead of dis- solving them away into laws or generalizations, the historical approach preserves its phenomena . . . and finds its intellectual satisfaction in putting each preserved phenomenon into a relation of ever widening context with the phenomenal cosmos. [Ibid., pp. 122-23]

Evans-Pritchard's similar thesis is that

> social anthropology is a kind of historiography, and therefore ultimately of philosophy or art . . . it studies societies as moral systems and not as natural systems . . . it is interested in design rather than process and . . . it therefore seeks patterns and not scientific laws, and interprets rather than explains. [1964, p. 152]

A fundamental dilemma stems from the anthropologist's ambitious determination to talk both about man in general and about particular men. Individual men are like ourselves, and we cannot fail to observe them acting purposefully, which is to say freely, but man in general is a remote and ethereal abstraction that we are less reluctant to see as the passive plaything of natural (which here include social) forces. And while abstract man, or man in general, can only be the *object* of our studies, even the grossest sympathy compels us to recognize that the men and women whom we meet and about whom we write are *subjects* like ourselves; that is, they are actors, or agents.

It may be true, as Tylor suggests, that "law is everywhere," but we are a very long way from specifying the laws that make us act the way we do, and in the meanwhile we want to understand what various people have been doing. When we isolate and examine a number of social facts such as norms of kinship behavior or child-rearing practices, and then present them in a systematic way as "social structure," a "culture" or whatever, we appreciate the condition of the people whose behavior is said to be molded by these forces, but we do not recognize them as ourselves. They have become puppets.

The systemic, positivistic approach has always led in this direction. Of course every kind of study abstracts from what actually takes place and is therefore partial, and it would be ridiculous to deny the immense rewards that have accrued from dealing with roles rather than with people, but this approach does run into problems. One of the most intractable has been that of social change, to account for which positivistic anthropologists and sociologists have commonly looked to extrasocial factors. In systemic terms, the sources of change are characteristically sought not in the system itself but in its parameters. To take a classic case that is relevant to the present study, Durkheim found the cause of increase in the division of social labor in the growth of moral density, which is in turn the product of increased population and population density (1964, pp. 256-82). But between increased population and social change come a number of people's decisions to act in different and unprecedented ways. Abstractions and statistics themselves neither act nor decide anything.

Classic functionalism, which appeared at one time to be moribund, regains some vitality when it is incorporated into the newer and broader ecological functionalism, for then at last it really does become a part of "a natural science of society." Social practices are explained by demonstrating their place in a functioning ecosystem rather than by reference to some mystical notion like "society" or some intuited condition like "social solidarity." Here again, even in as penetrating and sophisticated an analysis as Rappaport's study of the Tsembaga, we are instructed how various ritual practices serve "to maintain an undegraded environment . . . ," and so forth (1967, p. 199; see also Rappaport 1968, passim), but we do not learn *why* the Tsembaga act the way they do.

Similarly, in the present study, as I have indicated more than once, I have no quarrel with a functional interpretation of Vedda inheritance and residential norms and practice in terms of their effect in achieving a mutual adjustment of the man to land ratio in the several villages. But such an interpretation does not tell me why the Veddas go and live where they do.

Something is missing then, and that something is man; or rather, it is men and women acting severally and together, with all their peculiar bents and burdens. Most importantly, what men do means something to them. Social action is symbolically meaningful. This does not preclude the possibility of a functionalist study of symbolic structures, but functionalism in the analysis of collective representations moves either into psychology or towards structuralism, which differs from naturalistic functionalism in several important respects. It seeks to discover logical rather than material relations, and it rests upon the faith, which naturalistic or ecological functionalism does not require, that all men are sufficiently similarly constituted for one set of collective representations to be translatable and rationally intelligible to the practitioners of another. Most significantly, in the analysis of symbolic structures or cultures, the notion of function is stripped of any implication that it specifies material effects and is reduced to a more strictly logical or mathematical concept. This is welcome, but it does not directly help us account for social change, since it only emphasizes that structures are not agents.

I prefer to assert unequivocally that social structures and cultures are the products of human thought and action, and that therefore the causes of social change (and, for that matter, of social persistence) must be sought in human agency. The objective analyses of systemic functionalism can produce only descriptive findings. They can inform us only of the way things are and the direction they are tending. They can specify continuous social trends that may be statistically significant, but the probabilistic format in which their sociological truths are dressed carries the possibility that they may be inapplicable to any particular case in which we are interested. If we want to go beyond the continuity of trends in order to understand the events of history, we must abandon a scrupulous but possibly spurious objectivity and align ourselves with our subjects.

This is to advocate some version of the method of *verstehen* (see especially Weber 1968, pp. 3-22; cf. Evans-Pritchard 1964, pp. 80-85), which is not easy to justify before the bar of positivistic science. Indeed I will not attempt to do so, but will simply concede that, in my view, its success depends as much on the character of the practitioner as on any rules of scientific procedure. This is already a perilous position but the historical approach also confronts other, and perhaps more serious, difficulties.

The attempt to grasp and retain the particularity of events, which requires us to examine them in their full context, runs the risk of holding us in a theoretically sterile parochialism. It remains uncertain how successfully we can build a comparative sociology (i.e., a social anthropology) that is rich both in its general theory and in its respect for the particularities of local custom and history. There is no question of assessing the relative priority of these two concerns. Faced with the choice, anthropologists will continue to express different interests, and accordingly pitch their studies at different levels. The more challenging task, in the pursuit of which social anthropology has enjoyed some relative, if still modest, success, is to hold both interests in focus simultaneously. The goal is to evade assigning priorities by devising a synthetic method that allows full scope for both concerns.

In the tradition of social anthropology this requires, as a beginning, a synthesis of the more valuable contributions of Malinowski and Radcliffe-Brown. Malinowski's ethnographic studies display a vital appreciation of the Trobriand Islander as a social actor, but his later and more general theoretical formulations have failed to inspire. Radcliffe-Brown, by contrast, constructed a firmer framework for comparative analysis, but only by reducing men and women to automatons. Since World War II the problem has been broached by a number of scholars, the most decisively successful of whom, to my mind, are those who have absorbed the lessons of Leach's *Political Systems of Highland Burma* (1954), a work that combines a sophisticated application of a transformed concept of structure with a Malinowskian appreciation that the Kachins are the operators rather than the creatures of their culture.

One of Leach's crucial distinctions lies between the "technical" and the "ritual" aspects of social action, where "technique has economic material consequences which are measurable and predictable," while "ritual on the other hand is a symbolic statement which 'says' something about the individuals involved in the action" (1965, p. 13). This corresponds to my distinction between the naturalistic or systemic and the historical approaches. The technical aspects of social action can be examined and fitted together in terms of their mutual effects or functions ("material consequences that are measurable and predictable"), and the result presented as a social system seen as a natural system. The ritual aspects, by contrast, can only be interpreted from the inside. They are to be understood as constituting a structure of meaningful symbols whose integration is, in a broad sense, logical but not necessarily wholly consistent.

The final qualification is important, since it opens a way toward the structural analysis of social change. It can often be asserted within tolerable limits of distortion that the members of a particular society orient their actions to a shared set of symbols, but it does not follow that these symbols "mean" the same thing to all of them. On the contrary, they are frequently ambiguous and inconsistent and their meaning can never be definitely fixed. In other words, individuals and groups are free to reinterpret the significances of the actions both of themselves and others, and thereby to change the structure of their society.

In the present work I have identified a number of ecological, demographic, political, and economic conditions outside the Vedda community that are relevant to an understanding of Vedda history and society. From the systemic perspective these conditions, which include rainfall and other factors of the natural environment, government land policy, the presence of democratic institutions, and so forth, constitute the parameters of the Vedda social system. When they change, as for example when a new land policy is instituted, there are subsequent changes within the Vedda social system. They are therefore presented as factors that affect the determination of what the social system is at any particular time. Such factors are emphasized in my general discussion of paddy and chena cultivation (chapter 4), and of the over-all pattern of marriage, migration, and residence (chapters 5 and 7).

From the historical perspective, on the other hand, these factors are conditions of opportunity as much as a constraint, and when they change they alter the structure of opportunities that individuals and groups confront. Thus a change in official land policy forecloses or inhibits certain courses of action but makes others more feasible or attractive. Moreover, from this perspective, which is that of individuals and groups rather than roles and institutions, the social structure itself, considered as "a set of ideas about the distribution of power between persons and groups of persons" (Leach 1965, p. 4) or as "an idealized model which states the 'correct' status relations existing between groups within the total system and between the social persons who make up particular groups" (ibid., p. 9) is part of the milieu within which groups and individuals interact. Since this structure is neither totally consistent nor wholly unambiguous, groups and individuals are often free to act with propriety in more than one way. And, of course, they can always break the rules of propriety. But even leaving this last possibility aside, there remains an area of maneuverability that groups and individuals can quite properly exploit in pursuit of their private interests. My analyses of the development of household and occupational groups (chapters 3 and 4), and of the structural history of the Willachchiya Vedda villages (chapter 6), focus on the structures produced by the clash of interests within this arena of legitimate political and economic action.

My developmental models of the household, the productive group, and the village society are attempts to align these two perspectives. Only the general context within which social action takes place is determined, in the sense that it is already given by factors in the natural and cultural environments over which the Veddas have little or no control. To that extent the number of possible courses of action is finite. Beyond that there is a set of cultural norms that carry the moral force of tradition, such as the rules of bilateral inheritance, of ambilocal residence, of categorical cross-cousin marriage, and so on. I have shown that the application of these rules permits considerable freedom of action, but insofar as the Veddas do not challenge them in principle, their continued voluntary adherence to them further constrains their actions. Nevertheless the arena of legitimate social action remains large enough to forbid any rigid specification of developmental processes. The cycle of household formation follows a predictable course, but the timing and manner of the disjunction between parental and filial households can only profitably be understood with reference to the different ways in which particular individuals in particular circumstances perceive their interests and act to realize them. Similarly my model of the process of village development illuminates the general trend of Vedda social organization but in any particular case at any particular time it allows development to proceed in a variety of ways. The development that actually occurs, that is, the history that takes place and the structure that results is the product of political actions of which the decisive particularities are unpredictable.[6]

6. The position I am expressing was succinctly stated by Marx in a famous passage from *The Eighteenth Brumaire*: "Men make their own history, but they do not make it just as they please; they do not make it under circumstances chosen by themselves, but under circumstances directly encountered, given and transmitted from the past" (Marx 1963, p. 15). But compare the translation given in Marx (1913), which not only substitutes "man" for "men" but seems almost to anticipate Lévi-Strauss's famous metaphor of the *bricoleur* (1966): "Man makes his own history, but he does not make it out of whole cloth; he does not make it out of conditions chosen by himself, but out of such as he finds close at hand" (Marx 1913, p. 9).

The advantages of this approach may be summarily illustrated by some final observations on the problem of the relationship between cross-cousin marriage and the formation of "microcastes." I have sufficiently emphasized that "cross-cousin" marriage among the Anuradhapura Veddas is categorical and often ex post facto, and that it neither takes place within microcastes nor brings about their formation. Marriages among close "cross-cousins" and within a single village are certainly not uncommon, but there are no endogamous groups in Vedda society within the *variga* as a whole. Against the centripetal tendency to form small circles of endogamy ("microcastes") that are more narrowly circumscribed than the *variga* as a whole, we must therefore set the centrifugal tendencies that prevent fission. This phrasing poses the problems in terms of systemic pressures, but it is also a matter of strategy and choice. Given the evident advantages of close endogamy, such as the strengthening of existing alliances of marriage and kinship, personal familiarity, the consolidation of property or at least the prevention of its dispersal, and so on, what *other* considerations persuade many Veddas to marry spouses who are only very distantly related to them?

The external constraints—structural, demographic, and historical—are certainly real. In the first place, the obverse of cross-cousin marriage is the prohibition of marriage between those who cannot be presented as cross-cousins. The restriction of marital eligibility to a single category of kin already introduces structural constraints on the degree to which endogamy can be realized; that is, marriages between siblings or between first parallel cousins are not permissible.

Demographic factors, as I have shown, impose further restrictions, as does adherence to the cultural norm that the husband should be older than the wife. Many young men do not have female first or second cross-cousins who are both younger than themselves and not already married. The larger size of sibling groups in recent generations has, however, reduced the likelihood of this and, to say much the same thing rather differently, the greater population of present-day villages has increased the possibility of local endogamy. Against this must be set the impact of improved communications, and particularly the introduction of buses and bicycles, which have increased the opportunity for frequent interaction between members of different villages. Other external developments, such as the colonization schemes, seem to have raised the proportion of marriages that cross *variga* lines, although one must be careful not to assume a stable past when *variga* exclusiveness was rigorously maintained.

But all these considerations only define the circumstances with which individuals and groups, whether consciously or not, must deal.

There remains the arena within which maneuverability and choice are available, and Veddas decide how to act in this arena with reference to the material and ideal interests that they hope thereby to realize. Neighboring households in the village are related to one another, and may be units within some higher order grouping. Their members share certain common interests and values. But they are also, whether overtly or not, in competition with one another, particularly over access to land and over positions of authority and prestige. A marital alliance between two distinct groups may permit the consolidation of their respective fortunes, but while each retains the greater prospect of monopoly or dominance over the other, the shared advantages of alliance may be declined. The developmental process of the household is fissiparous. Siblings of the same sex are eventually separated, but a brother and sister can be reunited by the marriage of their children. Alliance is only possible between those who have previously been separated, and from this point of view cross-cousin marriage is seen, not as a driving compulsion to split the *variga* into ever smaller circles of endogamy, but as a countervailing strategy that mitigates the fissiparous tendency otherwise inherent in the rules of kinship, property, and inheritance. In brief, Leach's terse formula still stands: "Marriage unifies; inheritance separates; property endures" (1961a, p. 11). Veddas freely employ a variety of strategies to manipulate the far from automatic processes of marriage and inheritance, and thereby to acquire their share of enduring property, and it is their purposeful and meaningful actions that produce whatever "structure" the anthropologist attributes to the society as a whole.[7]

7. Because social action is purposeful and meaningful does not of course imply that the effects of social action are those that have been intended (Merton 1951).

Bibliography

The publications following are abbreviated in the bibliography.

Journal of the Royal Anthropological Institute	*JRAI*
American Anthropologist	*AA*
Journal of the Royal Asiatic Society	*JRAS*
Ceylon Journal of Historical and Social Studies	*CJHSS*
Administration Reports	*AR*

Abhayaratne, C. E. R., and Jayewardene, C. H. S.
   1967. *Fertility Trends in Ceylon.* Colombo: Colombo Apothecaries
      Co.
Amunugama, Sarath
   1964. "Rural Credit in Ceylon: Some Sociological Observations."
      CJHSS 7, no. 2: 135-43.
   1965. "Chandrikawewa: A Recent Attempt at Colonization in a
      Peasant Framework." *CJHSS* 8, nos. 1-2: 130-62.
Arasaratnam, J.
   1972. "The Ceylon Insurrection of April 1971: Some Causes and
      Consequences." *Pacific Affairs* 45, no. 3: 356-71.
Bailey, John
   1863. "An Account of the Wild Tribes of the Veddas of Ceylon:
      Their Habits, Customs and Superstitions." *Transactions of the
      Ethnological Society of London,* n.s., 2 (1863): 278-320.
Baker, Sir Samuel White
   1898. *The Rifle and the Hound in Ceylon.* 1854. London: Long-
      mans, Green.

Bastiampillai, Bertram E. St. J.
  1970. "The Revival of Irrigation Enterprise in Ceylon, 1870-1890."
    CJHSS 10, nos. 1-2: 1-26.
Bennett, John Whitchurch
  1843. *Ceylon and Its Capabilities.* London: William H. Allen.
Brodie, Alexander Oswald
  1856-58. "Topographical and Statistical Account of Nuwarakala-
    viya." *JRAS* (Ceylon) 3, no. 9: 136-61.
Brohier, Richard Leslie
  1934. *Ancient Irrigation Works in Ceylon.* Colombo: Central Bank
    of Ceylon.
Buchler, I. R., and Selby, H. A.
  1968. *Kinship and Social Organization.* New York: Macmillan.
Codrington, Humphrey William
  1938. *Ancient Land Tenure and Revenue in Ceylon.* Colombo:
    Ceylon Government Press.
Conklin, Harold C.
  1961. "The Study of Shifting Cultivation." *Current Anthropology* 2:
    27-61.
Davenport, W.
  1959. "Non-Unilinear Descent and Descent Groups." *AA* 61: 557-72.
Davy, John
  1821. *An Account of the Interior of Ceylon and of Its Inhabitants
    with Travels in That Island.* London: Longman, Hurst, Rees,
    Orme & Brown.
De Butts, Augustus
  1841. *Rambles in Ceylon.* London: William H. Allen.
Deschamps, Emile
  1892. *Au Pays des Veddas: Ceylon.* Paris: Société d'Editions Scien-
    tifiques.
De Zoysa, Louis
  1881. "Notes on the Origin of the Veddas, with a Few Specimens of
    their Songs and Charms." *JRAS* (Ceylon) 7, no. 24: 93-106.
Dickson, John Frederick
  1873. "Report on the North Central Province." *AR*, pp. 5-22.
D'Oyly, Sir John
  1929. *A Sketch of the Constitution of the Kandyan Kingdom.*
    Colombo: H. Ross Cottle, Government Printer.
Dumont, Louis
  1950. "Kinship and Alliance among the Pramalai Kallar." *Eastern
    Anthropologist* 4, no. 1: 3-26.
  1953a."The Dravidian Kinship Terminology as an Expression of
    Marriage." *Man* 54: 34-39.

1953b."Dravidian Kinship Terminology." *Man* 54: 143.

1957a. *Une Sous-caste de l'Inde du sud: Organization sociale et religion des Pramalai Kallar.* Paris: La Haye, Mouton & Co.

1957b. *Hierarchy and Marriage Alliance in South Indian Kinship.* London: Royal Anthropological Institute of Great Britain & Ireland.

1961. "Marriage in India: The Present State of the Question (1)." *Contributions to Indian Sociology* 5: 75-95.

1964. "Marriage in India: The Present State of the Question (2)." *Contributions to Indian Sociology* 7: 77-98.

1966. "Marriage in India: The Present State of the Question (3)." *Contributions to Indian Sociology* 9: 90-114.

Durkheim, Emile
1964. *The Division of Labor in Society.* French ed., 1893. New York: Free Press of Glencoe.

Dyson, Edward Trevor
1928. "Report on the North Central Province." *AR*, pp. G3-G16.

Emeneau, Murray Barnson
1937. "Toda Marriage Regulations and Taboos." *AA* 39: 103-12.
1941. "Language and Social Forms." In *Language, Culture and Personality,* edited by L. Spier, pp. 158-79. Menasha, Wisc.: Sapir Memorial Publication Fund.

Evans-Pritchard, Edward Evan
1964. *Social Anthropology and Other Essays.* New York: Free Press of Glencoe.

Farmer, Bertram Hughes
1956. "Rainfall and Water Supply in the Dry Zone of Ceylon." In *Essays on British Tropical Lands,* edited by R. W. Steel and C. A. Fisher, pp. 228-68. London: Phillips.
1957. *Pioneer Peasant Colonization in Ceylon.* London: Oxford University Press.

Fellowes, Robert [Philalethes]
1817. *The History of Ceylon from the Earliest Period to the Year 1815.* London: Printed for Joseph Mawman.

Firth, Raymond
1957. "A Note on Descent Groups in Polynesia." *Man* 57, no. 2: 4-8.
1963. "Bilateral Descent Groups: An Operational Viewpoint." In *Studies in Kinship and Marriage,* edited by I. Shapera, pp. 22-37. Occasional Papers, no. 16. London: Royal Anthropological Institute.

Fisher, F. C.
1885. "Report on the North Central Province." *AR*, pp. 7A-16A.

Forbes, Jonathan
1841. *Eleven Years in Ceylon.* London: Richard Bentley.
Fortes, Meyer
1969. *Kinship and the Social Order.* Chicago: Aldine.
Fortune, Reo Franklin
1932. *Sorcerers of Dobu.* New York: E. P. Dutton & Co.
Fox, Robin
1967. *Kinship and Marriage.* Harmondsworth: Penguin.
Freeman, H. R.
1915. "Report on the North Central Province." *AR*, pp. G1-G8.
1918. "Report on the North Central Province." *AR*, pp. G1-G8.
Furness, W. H., and Hiller, H. M.
1901. *Notes on a Trip to the Veddahs of Ceylon.* Bulletin of the Free Museum of Science and Art of the University of Pennsylvania, 3, no. 2: 68-87.
Goodenough, Ward Hunt
1955. "A Problem in Malayo-Polynesian Social Organization." *AA* 57: 71-83.
1968. "Componential Analysis." *International Encyclopedia of the Social Sciences,* 3: 186-92.
Goody, John Rankine, ed.
1958. *The Developmental Cycle in Domestic Groups.* Cambridge Papers in Social Anthropology, no. 1. Cambridge: At the University Press.
Gooneratne, B. M. W.
1970. "The Ceylon Elephant, *Elephas maximus Zeylanicus*: Its Decimation and Fight for Survival." *CJHSS* 10, nos. 1-2: 149-60.
Goonesekere, R. K. W.
1958. "The Eclipse of the Village Court." *CJHSS* 1, no. 2: 138-54.
Goonetileke, Henry Alfred Ian
1960. "A Bibliography of the Veddah: The Ceylon Aboriginal." *CJHSS* 3, no. 1: 96-106.
1970. *A Bibliography of Ceylon.* Zug and London: Inter Documentation Co.
Gough, E. Kathleen
1952. "Changing Kinship Usages in the Setting of Political and Economic Change among the Nayars of Malabar." *JRAI* 82, no. 2: 71-88.
1955. "Female Initiation Rites on the Malabar Coast." *JRAI* 85: nos. 1-2: 45-78.
1956. "Brahmin Kinship in a Tamil Village." *AA* 58, no. 5: 826-53.

1959. "The Nayars and the Definition of Marriage." *Journal of American Folklore* 71, no. 281: 240-72.

Gunawardana, R. A. L. H.
1971. "Irrigation and Hydraulic Society in Early Medieval Ceylon." *Past and Present* 53: 3-27.

Halliday, Fred
1972. "The Ceylonese Insurrection." *New Left Review* 69: 55-90.

Harris, Marvin
1971. *Culture, Man and Nature.* New York: Crowell.

Hartshorne, Bertram Fulke
1876. "The Weddas." *Fortnightly Review,* n. s., 19: 406-17.

Hayley, Frederick Austin
1923. *A Treatise on the Laws and Customs of the Sinhalese.* Colombo: H. W. Cave.

Herring, R. J.
1972. "The Forgotten 1953 Paddy Lands Act in Ceylon: Ideology, Capacity and Response." *Modern Ceylon Studies* 3, no. 2: 99-124.

Ievers, Robert Wilson
1887. "Report on the North Central Province." *AR,* pp. 196A-208A.
1899. *Manual of the North Central Province, Ceylon.* Colombo: G. J. A. Skeen, Government Printer.

Indrapala, K., ed.
1971. *The Collapse of the Rajarata Civilization in Ceylon and the Drift to the South-West.* Peradeniya: University of Ceylon.

Joachim, A. W. R., and Kandiah, S.
1948. "The Effect of Shifting (chena) Cultivation and Subsequent Regeneration of Soil Composition and Structure." *Tropical Agriculturalist* (Peradeniya) 104: 3-11.

Joinville, Joseph
1803. "Bedas or Vedas." In "On the Religion and Manners of the People of Ceylon." *Asiatic Researches* 7: 434-35.

Kay, Paul
1967. "On the Multiplicity of Cross/Parallel Distinctions." *AA* 69: 83-85.

Kearney, Robert N.
1973. *The Politics of Ceylon (Sri Lanka).* Ithaca: Cornell University Press.

Keesing, Roger M.
1975. *Kin Groups and Social Structure.* New York: Holt, Rinehart & Winston.

Kennedy, Kenneth, A. R.

1965. *Human Skeletal Material from Ceylon, with an Analysis of the Island's Prehistoric and Contemporary Populations.* Bulletin of the British Museum (Natural History) Geology, vol. 11, no. 4.

1967. "The Palaeo-Demography of the Veddas of Ceylon." Paper presented to the Conference on Ceylon at the University of Pennsylvania, August, 1967.

1972. "The Concept of the Vedda Phenotypic Pattern: A Critical Analysis of Research on the Osteological Collections of a Remnant Population." *Spolia Zeylanica* (Colombo) 32, no.: 1 25-60.

1974. "The Palaeo-Demography of Ceylon: A Study of the Biological Continuum of a Population from Prehistoric to Historic Times." In *Perspectives in Palaeoanthropology,* edited by A. K. Ghosh, pp. 95-112. Calcutta: K. L. Mukhopadhyay.

Knox, Robert

1911. *An Historical Relation of the Island Ceylon in the East Indies.* 1681. Glasgow: James MacLehose & Sons.

Kroeber, Alfred Louis

1909. "Classificatory Systems of Relationship." *JRAI* 39: 77-84.

1952. *The Nature of Culture.* Chicago: University of Chicago Press.

Leach, Edmund Ronald

1954. *Political Systems of Highland Burma.* London: London School of Economics & Political Science.

1959. "Hydraulic Society in Ceylon." *Past and Present* 15: 2-25.

1960. "The Sinhalese of the Dry Zone of Northern Ceylon." In *Social Structure in South East Asia,* edited by G. P. Murdock, pp. 116-26. Viking Fund Publications, no. 29. Chicago: Quadrangle Books.

1961a. *Pul Eliya: A Village in Ceylon.* Cambridge: At the University Press.

1961b. *Rethinking Anthropology.* London: Athlone Press.

1962. "On Certain Unconsidered Aspects of Double Descent Systems." *Man* 62, no. 214: 130-34.

1963. "Did the Wild Veddas Have Matrilineal Clans?" In *Studies in Kinship and Marriage,* edited by I. Shapera, pp. 68-78. Occasional Papers, no. 16. London: Royal Anthropological Institute.

1965. *Political Systems of Highland Burma.* Reprint. Boston: Beacon Press.

Lévi-Strauss, Claude

1949. *Les Structures élémentaires de la Parenté.* Paris: Presses Universitaires de France.

1953. "Social Structure." In *Anthropology Today,* edited by Alfred L. Kroeber, pp. 524-53. Chicago: University of Chicago Press.

1963. "The Bear and the Barber." *JRAI* 93, no 1: 1-11.

1966. *The Savage Mind.* London: Weidenfield & Nicolson.

Lewis, J. P.

1895. *Manual of the Vanni Districts.* Colombo: H. C. Cottle, Acting Government Printer.

Liesching, L. F.

1870. "Report on Nuvarakalaviya." *AR,* pp. 93-99.

Lounsbury, Floyd G.

1964. "The Structural Analysis of Kinship Semantics." In *Proceedings of the Ninth International Congress of Linguistics,* edited by H. G. Hunt, pp. 1073-93. The Hague: Mouton & Co.

The Mahavamsa or the Great Chronicle of Ceylon

1934. Translated by Wilhelm Geiger. London: H. Milford.

Maine, Sir Henry S.

1888. *Ancient Law.* 1861. New York: H. Holt & Co.

Marx, Karl

1913. *The Eighteenth Brumaire of Louis Bonaparte.* German ed., 1852. Translated by Daniel de Leon. Chicago: C. H. Kerr.

1963. *The Eighteenth Brumaire of Louis Bonaparte.* New York: International Publishers.

McLennan, John Ferguson

1876. *Studies in Ancient History.* London: B. Quaritch.

Merton, Robert King

1951. *Social Theory and Social Structure.* Glencoe, Ill.: Free Press.

Morgan, Lewis Henry

1871. *Systems of Consanguinity and Affinity of the Human Family.* Smithsonian Contributions to Knowledge, 17: 1-590.

1963. *Ancient Society.* 1877. New York: Cleveland, World Publishing Co.

Murdock, George Peter

1949. *Social Structure.* New York: Macmillan.

1967. "The Ethnographic Atlas: A Summary." *Ethnology* 6, no. 2: 109-233.

Murphey, Rhoads

1957. "The Ruin of Ancient Ceylon." *Journal of Asian Studies* 16, no. 2: 181-200.

Nagel, Thomas

1948. "Account of the Vanni, 1793." *JRAS* (Ceylon) 38, no. 106: 69-74.

Nevill, Hugh

1886-87. "The Vaeddahs of Ceylon." *The Taprobanian* 1, no. 6: 175-97; 2, no. 4: 121-27.

Obeyesekera, Jayasumana

1973. "Revolutionary Movements in Ceylon." In *Imperialism and Revolution in South Asia,* edited by E. Kathleen Gough and Hani P. Sharma, pp. 368-95. New York: Monthly Review Press.

Obeyesekere, Gananath

1966. "The Buddhist Pantheon in Ceylon and Its Extensions." In *Anthropological Studies in Theravada Buddhism,* edited by Manning Nash, pp. 1-26. Yale University Southeast Asia Studies Cultural Report Series, no. 13. New Haven: Yale University Press.

1967. *Land Tenure in Village Ceylon.* Cambridge: At the University Press.

1968. Review of Yalman (1967). *AA* 70, no. 4: 790-93.

1970. "Gajabahu and the Gajabahu Synchronism." *Ceylon Journal of the Humanities* 1, no. 1: 25-56.

1974. "Some Comments on the Social Backgrounds of the April 1971 Insurgency in Sri Lanka (Ceylon)." *Journal of Asian Studies* 33, no. 3: 367-84.

Parker, Henry

1887. "The Wanniyas." *The Taprobanian* 2, no. 1: 15-21.

1909. *Ancient Ceylon.* London: Luzac.

Percival, Robert

1805. *An Account of the Island of Ceylon.* London: C. & R. Baldwin.

Pieris, Ralph

1956. *Sinhalese Social Organization: The Kandyan Period.* Peradeniya: Ceylon University Press Board.

Pridham, Charles

1849. *An Historical Political and Statistical Account of Ceylon and Its Dependencies.* London: T. & W. Boone.

Queyroz, F.

1930. *The Temporal and Spiritual Conquest of Ceylon.* Translated by Fr. S. G. Perera. Colombo: A. C. Richards, Acting Government Printer.

Raghavan, M. D.

1953. "The Veddah Today." *New Lanka* (Colombo) 4, no. 3: 50-59.

Rajendra, M.

1952. "Report on the North Central Province." *AR,* pp. A163-A171.

Rappaport, Roy A.

1967. "Ritual Regulation of Environmental Relations among a New Guinea People." *Ethnology* 6, no. 1: 17-30.

1968. *Pigs for the Ancestors.* New Haven and London: Yale University Press.

Rhys Davids, Thomas William

1871. "Report on Nuvarakalaviya." *AR*, pp. 82-105.

Rivers, William Halse Rivers

1906. *The Todas.* London, New York: Macmillan & Co.

1907. "The Marriage of Cousins in India." *JRAS* (Great Britain and Ireland), pp. 611-40.

1914. *Kinship and Social Organization.* London: Constable & Co.

1924. *Social Organization.* London: K. Paul, Trench, Trübner & Co.

Roberts, Michael

1967. "The Paddy Lands Irrigation Ordinances and the Revival of Traditional Irrigation Customs, 1856-1871." *CJHSS* 10, nos. 1-2: 114-30.

1973. "Land Problems and Policies, c. 1832 to c. 1900." In *History of Ceylon,* vol. 3: *From the Beginning of the Nineteenth Century to 1948,* edited by K. M. de Silva, pp. 119-45. Peradeniya: University of Ceylon.

Robinson, Marguerite S.

1968. "Some Observations on the Kandyan Sinhalese Kinship System." *Man* 3, no. 3: 402-23.

1975. *Political Structure in a Changing Sinhalese Village.* Cambridge: At the University Press.

Sarasin, F., and Sarasin, P.

1892-93. *Ergebuisse Naturwissenschaftlicher Forschungen auf Ceylon.* Vol. 3. Weisbaden: C. W. Kriedel.

Sarkar, N. K., and Tambiah, Stanley Jeyaraj

1957. *The Disintegrating Village.* Peradeniya: Ceylon University Press.

Scheffler, Harold W.

1971. "Dravidian-Iroquois: The Melanesian Evidence." In *Anthropology in Oceania,* edited by L. Hiatt and C. Jayawardena Scranton: Chandler Publishing.

Schneider, David M.

1965. "Some Muddles in the Model: Or, How the System Really Works." In *The Relevance of Models in Social Anthropology,* edited by M. Banton. ASA Monographs, no. 1. London: Tavistock Publications.

Seligmann, Charles Gabriel, and Seligmann, Brenda Z.

1911. *The Veddas.* Cambridge: At the University Press.

Selkirk, James
  1844. *Recollections of Ceylon after a Residence of Nearly Thirteen Years.* London: J. Hatchard.
Selvaratnam, S.
  1961. "Some Implications of Population Growth in Ceylon." *CJHSS* 4: 33-49.
Seymour, A. W.
  1921. "Report on the North Central Province." *AR,* pp. G1-G12.
Singer, Marshall R.
  1964. *The Emerging Elite.* Cambridge, Mass.: M. I. T. Press.
Spencer, Herbert
  1897-1906. *The Principles of Sociology.* 3 vols. London, Oxford: Williams & Northgate.
Spittel, Richard Lionel
  1951. *Wild Ceylon.* 1924. 4th ed. Colombo: Colombo Book Centre.
  1957. *Far-Off Things.* 1933. 2nd ed. Colombo: Colombo Book Centre.
Srinivas, M. N.
  1952. *Religion and Society among the Coorgs in South India.* Oxford: Clarendon Press.
Stevenson, M. N. C.
  1954. "Status Evaluation in the Hindu Caste System." *JRAI* 84, nos. 1-2: 45-65.
Stirrat, R. L.
  n.d. "Catholicism in Sri Lanka: Some Preliminary Remarks on Ethnic and Religious Identity." Unpublished manuscript.
  1975. "Compadrazgo in Catholic Sri Lanka." *Man,* n. s., 10: 589-606.
Tambiah, S. J.
  1958. "The Structure of Kinship and Its Relationship to Land Possession and Residence in Pata Dumbara, Central Ceylon." *JRAI* 88, no. 1: 21-44.
  1963. "Ceylon." In *The Role of Savings and Wealth in Southern Asia and the West,* edited by R. D. Lambert and Bert Hoselitz, pp. 44-125. Paris: UNESCO.
  1965. "Kinship Fact and Fiction in Relation to the Kandyan Sinhalese." *JRAI* 95, no. 2: 131-73.
  1973. "Dowry and Bridewealth and the Property Rights of Women in South Asia." In *Bridewealth and Dowry,* edited by J.Goody and S. J. Tambiah, pp. 59-169. Cambridge Papers in Social Anthropology, no. 7. Cambridge: At the University Press.
Tamil, a native of Ceylon
  1865. "On the Weddas." *Transactions of the Ethnological Society of London,* n.s., 3: 70-71.

Teixeira, Pedro
   1902. *Relation of the Kings of Persia; Travels of Pedro Teixeira with his "Kings of Harmuz" and Extracts from his "Kings of Persia,"* Translated by W. F. Sinclair. London: Hakluyt Society.
Tennent, Sir James Emerson
   1859. *Ceylon: An Account of the Island, Physical, Historical and Topographical.* 2 vols. 4th ed. London: Longman, Green, Longman & Roberts.
Tylor, Sir Edward Burnett
   1920. *Primitive Culture.* 1871. London: J. Murray.
Valentyn, François
   1726. *Ond en nieww Oost-Indian.* . . . . Amsterdam: Johannes van Braam.
Van Goens, Ryckloff
   1932. *Memoirs of Ryckloff Van Goens.* Colombo: Ceylon Government Press.
Virchow, Rudolf
   1888. *The Veddas of Ceylon, and Their Relation to the Neighbouring Tribes.* Translated from the German. Colombo: Ceylon Asiatic Society.
Walker, E. O.
   1898. "The Veddahs of Ceylon." *Gentlemen's Magazine* 284: 10-18.
Warnapala, W. A. W. [Politicus]
   1972. "The April Revolt in Ceylon." Asian Survey 12, no. 3: 259-74.
Weber, Max
   1947. *The Theory of Social and Economic Organization.* Glencoe, Ill.: Free Press.
   1968. *Economy and Society.* German ed., 1925. Translated by Ephraim Fischoff. New York: Bedminster Press.
Wickremasinghe, R. L., E. W. Ikin, A. E. Mourant, and H. Lehmann
   1963. "The Blood Groups and Haemoglobins of the Veddahs of Ceylon." *JRAI* 93, no. 1: 117-25.
Wijesekera, N. D.
   1949. *The People of Ceylon.* Colombo: M. D. Gunasena.
   1964. *Veddas In Transition.* Colombo: M. D. Gunasena.
Wittfogel, Karl August
   1957. *Oriental Despotism.* New Haven: Yale University Press.
Wriggins, William Howard
   1960. *Ceylon: Dilemmas of a New Nation.* Princeton: Princeton University Press.
Yalman, Nur
   1960. "The Flexibility of Caste Principles in a Kandyan Community."

In *Aspects of Caste in South India, Ceylon and North-West Pakistan,* edited by E. R. Leach, pp. 78-112. Cambridge Papers in Social Anthropology, no. 2. Cambridge: At the University Press.

1962. "The Structure of the Sinhalese Kindred: A Re-examination of the Dravidian Terminology." *AA* 64: 548-75.

1963. "On the Purity of Women in the Castes of Ceylon and Malabar." *JRAI* 93, no. 1: 25-58.

1967. *Under the Bo Tree.* Berkeley and Los Angeles: University of California Press.

1969. "The Semantics of Kinship in South Asia and Ceylon." In *Linguistics in South Asia,* edited by T. A. Sebeok, pp. 607-26. Current Trends in Linguistics, vol. 5. Paris: Mouton.

Index

PUBLICATIONS ON ASIA OF THE SCHOOL OF
INTERNATIONAL STUDIES (formerly the Institute
for Comparative and Foreign Area Studies)

1. Boyd, Compton, trans. and ed. *Mao's China: Party Reform Documents, 1942-44.* 1952. Reissued 1966. Washington Paperback-4, 1966. 330 pp., map.
2. Siang-tseh Chiang. *The Nien Rebellion.* 1954. 177 pp., bibliog., index, maps.
3. Chung-li Chang. *The Chinese Gentry: Studies on Their Role in Nineteenth-Century Chinese Society.* Introduction by Franz Michael. 1955. Reissued 1967. Washington Paperback on Russia and Asia-4. 277 pp., bibliog., index, tables.
4. *Guide to the Memorials of Seven Leading Officials of Nineteenth-Century China.* Summaries and indexes of memorials to Hu Lin-i, Tseng Kuo-fan, Tso Tsung-tang, Kuo Sung-tao, Tseng Kuo-ch'üan, Li Hung-chang, Chang Chih-tung. 1955. 457 pp., mimeographed. Out of print.
5. Marc Raeff. *Siberia and the Reforms of 1822.* 1956. 228 pp., maps, bibliog., index. Out of print.
6. Li Chi. *The Beginnings of Chinese Civilization: Three Lectures Illustrated with Finds at Anyang.* 1957. Reissued 1968. Washington Paperback on Russia and Asia-6. 141 pp., illus., bibliog., index.
7. Pedro Carrasco. *Land and Polity in Tibet.* 1959. 318 pp., maps, bibliog., index.
8. Kung-chuan Hsiao. *Rural China: Imperial Control in the Nineteenth Century.* 1960. Reissued 1967. Washington Paperback on Russia and Asia-3. 797 pp., tables, bibliog., index.
9. Tso-liang Hsiao. *Power Relations within the Chinese Communist Movement, 1930-34.* Vol. 1: *A Study of Documents.* 1961. 416 pp., bibliog., index, glossary. Vol. 2: *The Chinese Documents.* 1967. 856 pp.
10. Chung-li Chang. *The Income of the Chinese Gentry.* Introduction by Franz Michael. 1962. 387 pp., tables, bibliog., index.
11. John M. Maki. *Court and Constitution in Japan: Selected Supreme Court Decisions, 1948-60.* 1964. 491 pp., bibliog., index.
12. Nicholas Poppe, Leon Hurvitz, and Hidehiro Okada. *Catalogue of the Manchu-Mongol Section of the Toyo Bunko.* 1964. 391 pp., index.
13. Stanley Spector. *Li Hung-chang and the Huai Army: A Study in Nineteenth-Century Chinese Regionalism.* Introduction by Franz Michael. 1964. 399 pp., maps, tables, bibliog., glossary, index.
14. Franz Michael and Chung-li Chang. *The Taiping Rebellion: History*

and Documents. Vol. 1: *History.* 1966. 256 pp., maps, index. Vols. 2 and 3: *Documents and Comments.* 1971. 756, 1,107 pp.

15. Vincent Y. C. Shih. *The Taiping Ideology: Its Sources, Interpretations, and Influences.* 1967. 576 pp., bibliog., index.

16. Nicholas Poppe. *The Twelve Deeds of Buddha: A Mongolian Version of the Lalitavistara.* 1967. 241 pp., illus. Paper.

17. Tsi-an Hsia. *The Gate of Darkness: Studies on the Leftist Literary Movement in China.* Preface by Franz Michael. Introduction by C. T. Hsia. 1968. 298 pp., index.

18. Tso-liang Hsiao. *The Land Revolution in China, 1930-34: A Study of Documents.* 1969. 374 pp., tables, glossary, bibliog., index.

19. Michael Gasster. *Chinese Intellectuals and the Revolution of 1911: The Birth of Modern Chinese Radicalism.* 1969. 320 pp., glossary, bibliog., index.

20. Richard C. Thornton. *The Comintern and the Chinese Communists, 1928-31.* 1969. 266 pp., bibliog., index.

21. Julia C. Lin. *Modern Chinese Poetry: An Introduction.* 1972. 278 pp., bibliog., index.

22. Philip C. Huang, *Liang Ch'i-ch'ao and Modern Chinese Liberalism.* 1972. 200 pp., illus., glossary, bibliog., index.

23. Edwin Gerow and Margery Lang, eds. *Studies in the Language and Culture of South Asia.* 1974. 174 pp.

24. Barrie M. Morrison. *Lalmai, A Cultural Center of Early Bengal.* 1974. 190 pp., maps, drawings, tables.

25. Kung-chuan Hsiao. *A Modern China and a New World: K'ang Yu-Wei, Reformer and Utopian, 1858-1927.* 1975. 669 pp., transliteration table, bibliog., index.

26. Marleigh Grayer Ryan. *The Development of Realism in the Fiction of Tsubouchi Shōyō.* 1975. 133 pp., index.

27. Dae-Sook Suh and Chae-Jin Lee, eds. *Political Leadership in Korea.* 1976. 272 pp., tables, figures, index.

28. Hellmut Wilhelm. *Heaven, Earth, and Man in the Book of Changes: Seven Eranos Lectures.* 1976. 230 pp., index.

29. Jing-shen Tao. *The Jurchen in Twelfth-Century China: A Study of Sinicization.* 1976. 217 pp., map, illus., appendix, glossary, bibliog., index.

30. Byung-joon Ahn. *Chinese Politics and the Cultural Revolution: Dynamics of Policy Processes.* 1976. 392 pp., appendixes, bibliog., index.

31. Margaret Nowak and Stephen Durrant. *The Tale of the Nišan Shamaness: A Manchu Folk Epic.* 1977. 182 pp., bibliog., index.

32. Jerry Norman. *A Manchu-English Lexicon.* 1978. 318 pp., appendix, bibliog.
33. James Brow. *Vedda Villages of Anuradhupura: The Historical Anthropology of a Community in Sri Lanka.* 1978. 268 pp., tables, figures, bibliog., index.